Choosing Web 2.0 Tools
for Learning and Teaching in a Digital World

Choosing Web 2.0 Tools for Learning and Teaching in a Digital World

Pam Berger and Sally Trexler

Foreword by Joyce Valenza

LIBRARIES UNLIMITED

AN IMPRINT OF ABC-CLIO, LLC
Santa Barbara, California • Denver, Colorado • Oxford, England

Library of Congress Cataloging-in-Publication Data

Berger, Pam.
   Choosing Web 2.0 tools for learning and teaching in a digital world / Pam Berger and Sally Trexler ;
foreword by Joyce Valenza.
      p. cm.
   Includes bibliographical references and index.
   ISBN 978–1–59158–706–4 (pbk. : acid-free paper) 1. Internet in school libraries. 2. Internet in education. 3. Inquiry-based learning. 4. Web 2.0—Study and teaching. 5. Electronic information resource
literacy—Study and teaching. 6. Internet searching—Study and teaching. 7. School librarian participation in curriculum planning. I. Trexler, Sally. II. Title.
Z675.S3B454   2010
025.042—dc22   2009054069

ISBN: 978–1–59158–706–4

14 13 12 11 10   2 3 4 5

This book is also available on the World Wide Web as an eBook.
Visit www.abc-clio.com for details.

Libraries Unlimited
An Imprint of ABC-CLIO, LLC

ABC-CLIO, LLC
130 Cremona Drive, P.O. Box 1911
Santa Barbara, California 93116-1911

This book is printed on acid-free paper ∞

Manufactured in the United States of America

Contents

Foreword

The game has changed—totally.

School library practice and teaching in general, must adapt to complete shifts in the information and communication landscapes. Folks who believe that Web 2.0, or whatever we next call the read/write Web, will go away, are hopelessly mistaken.

These shifts are not bandwagons. They represent profound changes in the way we do business, the way we do libraries, the way we must educate. Teacher librarians, as information and communication specialists, must lead change in their buildings or face irrelevancy.

Pam Berger and I launched our own professional friendship at around the same time Web 1.0 was born. Let's just say it was in the 1990s. Our friendship began in an ASCII text, pre-gui (graphic user interface) world. We met at an American Association of School Librarians' (AASL) meeting when Pam was chairing the ground-breaking KidsConnect and ICONnect projects. Through these projects, teacher-librarians made sense of the early Web for teachers and learners. Over 20 years our friendship continued to evolve. The Web grew too, in ways we could not have predicted. We spoke and wrote about searching as searching evolved. We shared what we learned. And when it became possible to share in more scalable ways, we both blogged, we created wikis, and worked on collaborative projects. Our avatars met and shared in Second Life. When Pam shares, she shares with a keen eye, identifying not just what may be new and shiny, but what is important and why it is important in terms of the learner. I've been an admirer of Sally Trexler's as well, following her work in AASL and at Allentown Public Schools.

So what does twenty-first-century practice look like? We have no textbook, no explicit guide for modern practice. With *Choosing Web 2.0 Tools for Learning and Teaching in a Digital World*, Pam and Sally break that ground and give us is a starting point for change and growth within an inquiry framework. They present new strategies for learning in a digital world, strategies that illuminate and clearly interpret both the AASL's "Standards for the 21st-Century Learner" and the well-respected Stripling Inquiry Process. They present a guidebook for exploring new practice: listing perfect entry points; posing essential questions; identifying the best possible examples; presenting realistic case studies; sharing rationale and practical steps for implementation. And they position the teacher-librarian and the school library program in the middle of the learning community with an emphasis on discovery, collaboration, and communication. Though their book is grounded on research and theory, it is also packed with years of solid experience. Filled with "Action Steps," it helps to answer the most critical and practical of questions, "What do I do now?"

Being an information (or media) specialist today means being an expert in how information and media flow TODAY! It is about knowing how information and media are created and communicated. It is about knowing and sharing how to evaluate, synthesize, and ethically use information and media in all their varied forms. It is about being able to communicate knowledge in new ways for new audiences using powerful new information and communication tools.

We have new rules for new practice. Teacher-librarians cannot opt out of this learning revolution. Learners everywhere need—no deserve—access to the information and communication tools of today's world. And they don't have it.

2.0 is an intellectual freedom issue.
2.0 is an equity issue.
2.0 is a librarians' issue.

I believe I speak for Pam and Sally when I say that I am thrilled by the new possibilities I see for teaching and learning. This is the best time in the history of time to be a librarian, and to be a teacher. This is an exciting moment in time to expand the notion of literacy to include richer experiences in reading and writing and communicating.

The game has changed. Shift is no longer optional. And Pam and Sally are great guides for us all.

Joyce Valenza

1

Learning, Literacy, and Web 2.0

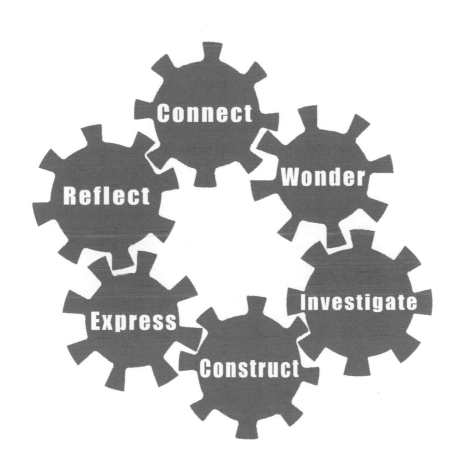

? ESSENTIAL QUESTIONS

What is Web 2.0 and why is it important to education?
What skills do our students need to be prepared for the twenty-first century?
What are Web 2.0 tools and how do they support inquiry learning?

Figure 1.1.   http://www.wordle.net

What Is Web 2.0?

The World Wide Web has changed since it was first introduced by Tim Berners-Lee in August 1991. Due to greater bandwidth, increased processing power and a new class of software applications that make it easy to accomplish sophisticated tasks with very little technical knowledge, the Web has moved closer to its designer's grand vision. "The original thing I wanted to do was make it a collaborative medium, a place where we can all meet and read and write. . . . Collaborative things are exciting" (Carvin 2005). During the first phase of the Web, which is now referred to as Web 1.0, users primarily surfed the Internet and downloaded information, but with the advent of Web 2.0, the Internet has become participatory and interactive: it is evolving into an interactive, rich multi-media driven space.

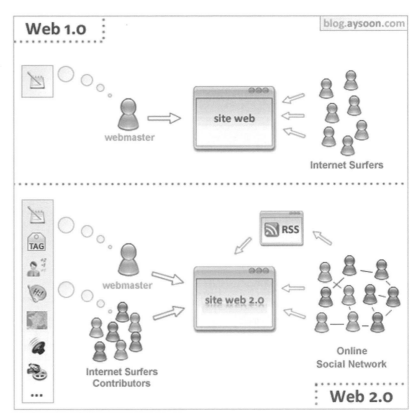

Figure 1.2.   Web 1.0 versus Web 2.0. http://www.sizlopedia.com/2007/08/18/web-10-vs-web-20-the-visual-difference/. Used with permission of Frédéric Cozic.

Web 2.0 is an umbrella term for the second wave of the World Wide Web that is loosely defined as the evolution to a more social, interactive Web that gives everyone a chance to create, share, publish, and collaborate. Tim O'Reilly, who is credited with coining the term, Web 2.0, wanted to denote the major changes in the Web that were taking shape after the dot.com bust (O'Reilly 2005). Before Web 2.0, Web masters or programmers posted Internet content and the exchange of information was mostly one way. Now, application such as wikis, blogs, photo and video sharing, and social networking sites allow ordinary users to post content online, making anyone with an Internet connection a participant and potential resource. Over 89 million Americans have posted content to the Internet (TechCrunchies 2009). Personal Web sites became blogs, text-based tutorials turned into streaming media, photos in desktop folders became organized collection being shared online, and taxonomy turned into folksonomy.

Web 2.0 Concepts

O'Reilly, a leader in Web 2.0 development, created a Web 2.0 meme (a phrase used to describe a catchphrase or concept that spreads quickly from person to person via the Web) (see Figure 1.4) to show the relationship of the principles and practices that

Although the Web was invented by Tim Berners-Lee, the concept of hypertext has been around for a while. Futurist Vannevar Bush first presented the concept in July 1945 issue of *The Atlantic Monthly* in "We May Think." In the 1960s Ted Nelson lead the charge into hypertext exploration using computers. He coined the actual term "hypertext" to describe a new type of document, a new literacy genre of branching, non-sequential writings on the computer screen.

Figure 1.3.   A Little History.

characterizes Web 2.0. The Web as a platform is a core concept meaning that the Web is the basic platform where everything is built; rather than packaged software programs loaded on individual computer hard drives, services are provided on the Web. This places the user in control of his or her data. It's a marked departure from Web 1.0 and provides for user-controlled data, scalability, user participation, and collective intelligence.

Although O'Reilly was thinking in a broader perspective, many of the concepts and ideas presented in his Web 2.0 meme clearly relate to technology use in the schools; Web 2.0 characteristics support the principles of good teaching and learning—active participation and collaboration.

- **User participation**. Web 2.0 applications encourage user to share their ideas, opinions, content, and more. "A core concept of Web 2.0 is that people are the content of the site. That is, a site is not populated with information for users to consume. Instead services are provided to individual users for them to build their network of friends and other groups (professional, recreational, etc.).

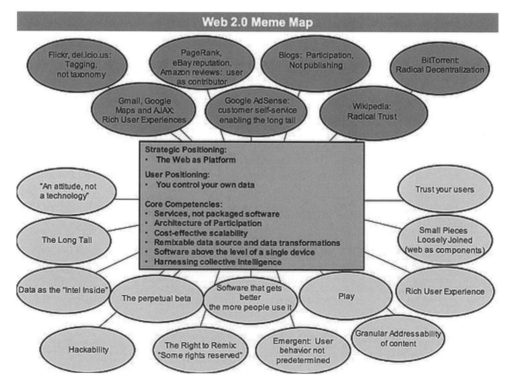

Figure 1.4.   What Is Web 2.0: Design Patterns and Business Models for the Next Generation of Software by Tim O'Reilly. © O'Reilly Media, Inc. 2005 (http://oreilly.com/web2/archive/what-is-web -20.html).

The content of a site then comprises user provided information that attracts new members of an ever-expanding network" (O'Reilly 2005). Social networking sites are probably most often associated with this concept since the primary purpose is to build networks. Facebook and MySpace are the most popular and well known with a combined membership of 380 million active accounts along with specialized sites such as Shelfari, goodreads, and LibraryThing for book lovers, attracting over 3 million Americans to network online. Steve Hargadon, on his blog, stevehargadon.com, on March 4, 2008, explains, "Amazon.com is for me the great example of how participation had become integral to an industry, and is a delicious irony, the book industry itself. The reviews by other readers are the most significant factor in my decision to purchase (and sometimes even read! a book now)."

- **Harnessing collective intelligence**. Collective intelligence is defined in Wikipedia as "a shared or group intelligence that emerges from the collaboration and competition of many individuals." It is based on the Web's original premise of shared information. "Hyperlinking is the foundation of the web. As users add new content, and new sites, it is bound in to the structure of the web by other users discovering the content and linking to it. Much as synapses form in the brain, with associations becoming stronger through repetition or intensity, the web of connections grows organically as an output of the collective activity of all web users" (O'Reilly 2005). New applications, services, and tools have been developed to allow users to more directly share. Wikipedia, an online encyclopedia that anyone can add to or edit an entry, along with del.icio.us, a social bookmarking site, and Flickr, a photo sharing tool, are a few of the pioneers of Web 2.0 services. Wikipedia, in addition to being user-content driven, personifies the Web 2.0 expression "radical trust," believing that if enough people contribute content, edit, and develop ownership it will contain relevant, usable information. Flickr and del.icio.us promote the use of "tagging," a type of collaborative classification called "folksonomy" that uses free flowing user-selected keywords as opposed to a taxonomy model that uses a prescribed classification system. When users "tag" a Web site in del.icio.us they can view other users' tags and add theirs to the mix. Users employ the multiple natural language "tags" to retrieve the desired Web sites (see Chapter 3, Social Bookmarking, for more explanation). A typical application of "harnessing the collective intelligence" in a school setting is a wiki, an easily created Web site that multiple users can add and edit content—a great resource for students to collaborate on research papers, team projects, study guides, etc.
- **Collaboration**. Free, flexible, and server-based programs are readily available to collaborate. Students can open their browsers and begin to edit word processing documents or spreadsheets in Google Docs or Zoho Notebook, create mindmaps in Bubbl.Us or MindMeister, or organize, share, and swap information in a Wikispaces and hold online meetings in Skype. Students no longer need to save a document and e-mail it to a classmate, edit it, and send it back. Today's electronic documents allow collaborators to work in a synchronous environment on a single document; groups of students can

Ten Reasons for Using Web 2.0 Tools in Education

Web 2.0 Tools

1. Motivate and involve students in learning, using tools that many are already using for personal purposes.
2. Align with the American Association of School Librarians' Standards for the 21st-Century Learner and International Society for Technology in Education's National Educational Technology Standards.
3. Prepare students with authentic skills for working in the real world.
4. Encourage collaborative learning strategies.
5. Support learning as a social process.
6. Allow for interactive learning.
7. Provide student with authentic audiences.
8. Are free and fun to use.
9. Provide an anytime, anywhere learning environment.
10. Connect students to a global community of learners.

create, share, and edit them online. Students can connect with each other and explore how their interests and abilities can be used to enhance class projects.

Web 2.0 applications are changing how we, including our students, interact with each other and the world. In our day-to-day lives, we are initiating exchanges of text and multimedia information through new Web tools that enable us to create, share, socialize, and collaborate with colleagues, family members, classmates, and newly developed network contacts. A few years ago students would search online to do research, type their papers in Word, print it out, and hand it into their teachers, perhaps sharing the key points with the classmates through a PowerPoint presentation.

Figure 1.5.   An Anthropological Introduction to YouTube (http://www.youtube.com/watch?v=TPAO-lZ4_hU). Used with permission of Michael Wesch (http://mediatedcultures.net).

Using Web 2.0 tools, these same students collaboratively locate, evaluate, and share relevant Web-based resources using a social bookmarking Web site; post, edit, and share their findings on a class wiki incorporating links to videos, photographs, podcasts, and other online resources for their teachers, classmates, and others to view and offer feedback. They are collaborating with peers, managing and organizing information, working in teams, and learning real-life skills. Typical Web 2.0 style services include blogging, user tagging, Really

Simple Syndication (RSS) feed, wikis, user ratings, user comments, video and photo sharing, community citation services, social bookmarking, and microblogging. Michael Wesch, a professor of cultural anthropology at Kansas State University, rather than using an ordinary PowerPoint for a presentation at the Library of Congress, created a 40-minute video entitled, "An Anthropological Introduction to YouTube" (video http://www.youtube.com/watch?v=TPAO-lZ4_hU). It's well worth your time to view it (see Figure 1.5).

Understanding Our Twenty-First-Century Learners

Our students are "digital natives," according to Marc Prensky, a speaker, writer, and educational software game designer. He believes the differences between today's teens' technology experiences and those of the adults in their lives, the digital immigrants, define the generation gap (Prensky 2001). Prensky believes today's students:

- Are no longer the people our educational system was designed to teach.
- Have changed not just incrementally from those of the past . . . but a big discontinuity has taken place.
- Represent the first generation to grow up with the new technology—and have spent their lives around it and using it.
- Think and process information fundamentally differently from their predecessors.

Educators in all different types of school and economic levels are increasingly dealing with a student population that is not only more wired than they are, but also the students grew up in a highly digital atmosphere that has trained them to absorb and process information in fundamentally different ways.

Research supports Prensky's beliefs. Youth are leading the transition to a fully wired and mobile nation. The majority of teens in the United States, 87 percent of those aged 12 to 17, use the Internet—that's 21 million youth. Specifically, 75 percent of on-line teens or about two-thirds of all teenagers use instant messaging and 54 percent know more instant messaging (IM) screen names than home telephone numbers. The Internet is their primary communication tool: 70 percent use IM to keep in touch and 56 percent of teens online prefer the Internet to the telephone. Teens are utilizing the interactive capabilities of the Internet as they create and share their own media creations. Fully half of the teens who use the Internet could be considered content creators (Lenhart and Madden 2005).

Researchers also found that college students feel the Internet has enriched their education. They use it for contacting professors, conducting research, working on projects with fellow students, and receiving messages from academic-oriented e-mail services (Jones 2002). The bottom line is that the changing nature of information and communications and how students are making sense of the world demands that we develop new strategies for teaching and learning. The Web offers new opportunities for learning. We no longer just search for information. We create it. We are active participants.

Today's students are immersed with new technologies; however, they report that their schools are not and they are text dominated and not effectively integrating digital technology and student learning. "Listening to Student Voices—Technology: Today's

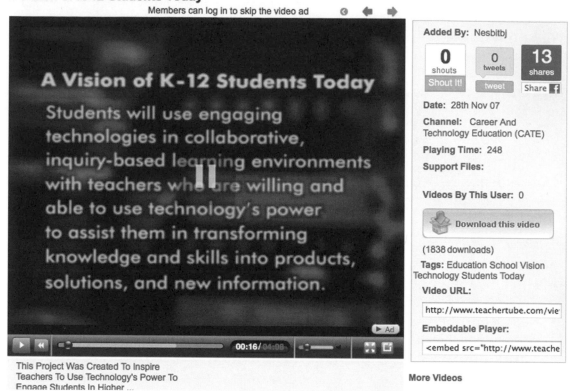

Figure 1.6.   A Vision of K-12 Students Today, YouTube (http://teachertube.com/viewVideo.php
?video_id=47293&title=A_Vision_of_K_12_Students_Today). Used with permission of Barbara
J. Nesbitt, instructional technology specialist, Easley, South Carolina.

Tech-Savvy Students Stuck in Text-Dominated Schools" (Education/Evolving 2005) sum-
marizes and report on students' attitudes and perceptions on using technology in school.

- **Technology is important to student education.** Students say that when they use
  the Internet, their motivation to learn and their academic performance improve.
  They complete their schoolwork more quickly; they are less likely to get stymied
  by material they don't understand; their papers and projects are more likely to
  draw upon up-to-date sources and state-of-the-art knowledge; and, they are
  better at juggling their school assignments and extracurricular activities.
- **Technology is not an "extra."** Students view textbooks as information relics;
  they want the most-up-to-date information at their fingertips, edited in real
  time. Students see technology as necessary, say, schools fall short.
- **Students desire increased in-school access.** Students say their schools and
  teachers have not yet recognized—much less responded—the fundamental
  shift occurring in the students they serve and in the learning communities
  they are charged with fostering. And, when teachers and schools react, often
  it is in ways that make it more difficult for students who have become accus-
  tomed to using the Internet to communicate and to access information. They
  feel that blocking and filtering software applications often raise barriers to
  students' legitimate use of the Internet.

- **Students want adults to focus more on "how to improve" than on "how to restrict" students' access to the Internet.** Students urge that there should be continued effort to ensure high-quality online information to complete school assignments be freely available, easily accessible, and age-appropriate, without undue limitations on students' freedom. It is common for schools to place social and technological restrictions on students' use of the Internet by, for instance, employing surveillance systems or requiring special teacher or administrative approvals.
- **Students want to use technology to learn, and in a variety of ways.** Many students are interested in learning from games, especially in math and science; many students want to witness and experience historic events or study foreign cultures, first-hand via some sort of virtual world, and many students express an interest in taking online or virtual classes.
- **Students want challenging, technologically-oriented instructional activities.** Students say the quality of their Internet-based assignments was poor and uninspiring. They want to be assigned more and more engaging Internet activities that are relevant to their lives. Many students assert that this would significantly improve their attitude toward school and learning.
- **Students want adults to move beyond using the "Internet for Internet's sake."** Students are uniformly more interested in—and see more value—in doing schoolwork that challenges and excites them than simply using the Internet for its own sake.

Understanding Learning in the Twenty-First Century

During the 1950s, Benjamin Bloom led a team of educational psychologist in the analysis of academic learning processes. The result is what we know today as Bloom's taxonomy that describes learning in six cognitive process dimensions: knowledge, comprehension, application, analysis, synthesis, and evaluation. In 2001 the taxonomy, which was one-dimensional, was updated by Lorin Anderson and David Krathwohl by combining both the cognitive and knowledge dimensions into a two-dimensional model to reflect relevance to twenty-first-century work (Anderson and Krathwohl 2001).

Anderson and Krathwohl explain the new terms as:

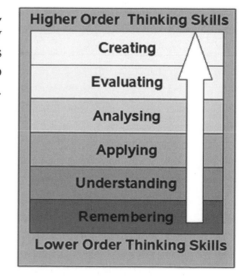

- **Remembering**—Retrieving, recognizing, and recalling relevant knowledge from long-term memory.
- **Understanding**—Determining the meaning of instructional messages, including oral, written, and graphic communication.
- **Applying**—Carrying out or using a procedure in a given situation.
- **Analyzing**—Breaking material into its constituent parts and detecting how the parts relate to one another and to an overall structure or purpose.

Figure 1.7.   2001 Revised Bloom's Taxonomy. Used with permission of Andrew Churches.

- **Evaluating**—Making judgments based on criteria and standards.
- **Creating**—Putting elements together to form a novel, coherent whole or make an original product.

In the revised taxonomy, the knowledge dimension represents the kind of knowledge to be learned and the cognitive dimension identifies the process dimension used to learn. Another important difference is that the new version uses verbs rather than nouns. Bloom's taxonomy's higher levels of thinking—analysis, evaluating, and creating—are the key to critical thinking and form a foundation for developing twenty-first-century skills. When educators have a solid understanding of learning theory such as Bloom's taxonomy and how students learn, they are better equipped to use technology to support student learning and the acquisition of higher order thinking skills.

Andrew Churches, in his article on Bloom's taxonomy on the TechLearning Web site, adds the processes and actions associated with the new Web 2.0 technologies to Bloom's revised model in an attempt to show how these technologies support the different levels of thinking.

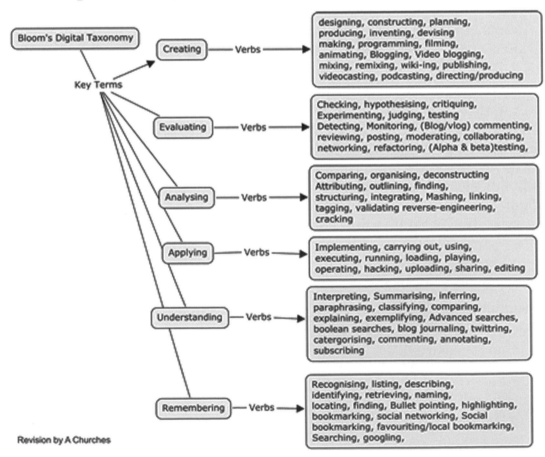

Figure 1.8.   Bloom's Taxonomy with Web 2.0. Used with permission of Andrew Churches.

Inquiry and Information and Communications Technology (ICT)

Most of the professional literature on pedagogy advises that to best prepare our students for the complex world in which they will live and work, we should develop interactive, inquiry-based, technology-rich curriculum. John Bransford and his colleagues in the book *How People Learn* argue that active, rather than passive, learners are better able to understand complex material and can more effectively transfer information and concepts learned in one setting to the process of solving problems encountered in another. In other words, when students are actively engaged in their learning and are required to apply what they have learned, they retain that knowledge. Not surprisingly, research shows that today's digital students learn more when engaged in meaningful, relevant, and intellectually stimulating schoolwork and that the use of technology can increase the frequency for this type of learning (North Central Regional Educational Laboratory [NCREL] and the Metiri Group 2003). The bottom line is that placing technology in schools and mandating its use is not enough to enable teachers and students to acquire the skills and proficiencies to use them effectively. We know that information and communication technology (ICT) can support more powerful knowledge-building experiences for learners "if we integrate well-designed technologies in the context of meaningful, mindful inquiry project, non-presentational pedagogies, access to resources and tools, and adequate support for technological maintenance and pedagogical renewal" (Breuleux 2001, 3).

Active, engaged learning is one of the major benefits of integrating technology into the curriculum; however, knowledge of pedagogy and how people learn must drive decisions on which technology is best suited for specific learning needs. "Pouring a solid foundation of good pedagogical design before adding on the layer of technology can become a critical factor in the success rate of technology integration" (Ziegenfuss 2005, 19–45). In developing the "Standards for the 21st-Century Learner," the American Association of School Librarians (AASL) identified nine common beliefs that support learning. The second belief listed, "Inquiry provides a framework for learning," focuses on students developing not only the skills, "but also the disposition to use the skills, along with an understanding of their own responsibilities and self-assessment strategies." The inquiry approach is focused on using and learning content as a means to develop information-processing and problem-solving skills. It's a student-centered approach, with the teacher as a facilitator of learning. Students are involved in the construction of knowledge through active involvement and, most important, asking questions; questions are at the heart of inquiry learning.

Stripling Inquiry Model

Barbara Stripling explains in *Curriculum Connections in the Library* that inquiry requires active engagement and that "inquiry places students at the heart of learning by empowering them to follow their sense of wonder into new discoveries and insights about the way the world works" (Stripling 2003, 4). Students identify what they already know, ask intriguing questions about what they do not know, investigate the answers, construct new understandings, and share those understandings

with others. The entire process is permeated with reflection and critical thinking, so that the result of inquiry is not only deep learning about the inquiry question but also the development of skills for independent learning.

The Stripling Inquiry Model has six phases; however, it's not a linear process but rather a recursive one in which the learner might revisit a previous stage to ask additional questions, organize information, etc., as the need arises. Each phase involves critical thinking skills that empower young people to learn on their own and develop the thinking skills to be an independent, lifelong learner.

Figure 1.9.   Stripling Inquiry Model.

The phases are:

Connect: observe, experience, connect a subject to self and previous knowledge
Wonder: predict, develop questions and hypotheses
Investigate: find and evaluate information to answer questions, test hypotheses
Construct: draw conclusions, arrive at new understandings
Express: apply understandings to a new context, share learning with others
Reflect: examine one's own learning and ask new questions (Stripling 2003, 8)

Technology and, in particular, Web 2.0 tools and services can be used throughout the inquiry process to support the appropriate thinking skills. The key is to focus on student learning, not the Web 2.0 technology. Focus on the phase(s) of inquiry that students are involved with and decide which technology tool can best support the thinking processes and instructional strategies associated with that inquiry phase to increase the effectiveness of both the learning experience and the use of technology. Figure 1.10 outlines the inquiry phases aligned with Web 2.0 technology tools and instructional strategies. The more specific alignment of Web 2.0 tools and inquiry learning will be explored and discussed in more detail in each chapter.

What Are the Essential Twenty-First-Century Skills?

As technology changes society and how we work, play, and conduct our daily lives, it also changes the skills kids need to thrive and compete in this new world. Thomas L. Friedman, in his book, *The World Is Flat*, when presenting the global challenges students

Phases of Inquiry	Teaching and Learning Strategies	Technology Tools/Resources
Connect Connect to self, previous knowledge Gain background knowledge to set context for new learning Observe, experience	Conversing Facilitated conversation Small group discussion and dialogue Research journals Learning logs Charting the inquiry/ information searching process Webbing Pre-reading aids (visual organizers, structures overviews, and semantic maps) Engagement and exploration activities	EduBlogs, Ning, Wikispaces, Skype GoogleDocs, Zoho Suite MindMeister, Bubbl.us, Mind42, and LooseStitch Google Earth, Teacher Tube, and Flickr
Wonder Develop questions Make predictions, hypotheses	Class brainstorming Peer questioning Question stems Anticipation guide	GoogleDocs templates, MindMeister and Bubbl.us
Investigate Find and evaluate information to answer questions, test hypotheses Think about the information to illuminate new questions and hypotheses	Find information Two column note taking • Notes/reflection • Main idea/details, examples Ideas from text/connections to prior knowledge Guided practice Organize sources; evaluate information	Google, Clusty, Ask, Kartoo, Exalead, and Intute Google Docs, Zoho Notebook, iOutliner, and SpringNote Wikispaces (pathfinders), Jing, and VoiceThread Google Reader, Diigo, Delicious, SimplyBox, Netvibes, Pageflakes, 30 Boxes, and TadaList
Construct Construct new understandings connected to previous knowledge Draw conclusions about questions and hypotheses	Charting, Mindmapping Composing Questioning: teacher-to-student, student-to-teacher, student-to-student	MindMeister and Bubbl.us Edublogs, Wikispaces, PBWorks, GoogleDocs, and Zoho Suite Polleverywhere, GoogleDocs, Zoho Suite Edublogs, e-mail, instant messenger, Skype, and Twitter

Phases of Inquiry	Teaching and Learning Strategies	Technology Tools/Resources

Express
  Express new ideas to share learning with others
  Apply understandings to a new context, new situation
	Use of rubric with specific criteria
	Select format based on needs of topic and audience
	Teacher and peer conferencing
		Google Docs and Zoho Suite
		VoiceThread, Glogster, Splashcast, Podcast, Animoto, Flickr, and SchoolTube
		Skype, Blogs

Reflect
  Reflect on own process of learning and on new understandings gained from inquiry
  Ask new questions
	Feedback from teacher and peers
	Reflection Log: I Used to Think/ Now I Know
		EduBlogs, Wikispaces, E-mail, and Ning GoogleDocs, VoiceThread, and podcast

Figure 1.10.   Inquiry and Web 2.0 Tools Integration Guide. Pam Berger and Barbara Stripling, 2009.

now face, points out that one in ten U.S. computer, software, and information technology industry jobs will move overseas in the next two years and one in four information technology jobs will be sent offshore by 2010. Global competition is increasing. "Soon technology will literally transform every aspect of business, every aspect of life, and every aspect of society." Friedman explains that the world is changing from a nexus of "command and control" to "connect and collaborate." "These digital, mobile, personal and virtual technologies; file changing and instant messaging; VoIP; videoconferencing; computer graphics; and new wireless technologies make all other changes happen faster, better and smarter" (Friedman 2005, 233–234). Our students need to be well prepared to meet these challenges. It's important to start asking ourselves: Who will be prepared for this new world? What skills will the twenty-first-century student need?

The Partnership for 21st Century Skills (http://www.21stcenturyskills.org), a group representing both education and business, has laid the groundwork with its 2007 publication "Framework for 21st Century Learning." These skills reflect changes in learner needs that have resulted from the changes in technology and society and also the changes needed in the method and delivery of learning. The document offers a broad framework with the traditional core subjects and three additional themes to address the changes we are experiencing.

1. Core Subjects and 21st-Century Themes
2. Learning and Innovation Skills
   - Creativity and Innovation Skills
   - Critical Thinking and Problem-Solving Skills
   - Communication and Collaboration Skills
3. Information, Media, and Technology Skills
   - Information Literacy
   - Media Literacy
   - ICT Literacy
4. Life and Career Skills
   - Flexibility and Adaptability
   - Initiative and Self-Direction

- Social and Cross-Cultural Skills
- Productivity and Accountability
- Leadership and Responsibility

The framework is designed to be supported by standards and assessments, curriculum and instruction, professional development, and learning environments.

AASL, in developing "Standards for 21st-Century Learner," began the document by defining nine foundational common beliefs:

- Reading is a window to the world.
- Inquiry provides a framework for learning.
- Ethical behavior in the use of information must be taught.

Visual Learners learn through seeing and retain information more effectively when it's presented in the form of pictures, diagrams, videos, and handouts.
Mapping, Charts and Diagrams: Bubbl.us, MindMeister, and Mind42.
Social Networking: Ning, FaceBook, and MySpace.
Videos and Photos: YouTube, TeacherTube, SchoolTube, Edublogs.tv, and Flickr.

Auditory Learners are most successful when they can listen to the information being presented.
Podcasts: Podserve, iTunes, and Educational Podcast Network.
Audio tools: Audacity and GarageBand.
Presentation tools: VoiceThread and SlideStory.
Text Readers: Acrobat Reader and ItCanSay.
Audio Books: LibriVox, FreeBooks.org, and History and Politics Outloud.

Kinesthetic Learners like to touch, manipulate, and work with what they are learning.
Surveys: SurveyMonkey.
Note taking: MyNoteIT and Google Docs and Spreadsheets.
Writing: Wikis, Google Docs and Google Spreadsheets.
Virtual Worlds: Teen Second Life, Whyville, and Habbo Hotel.
Mapping: Google Earth, also interactive models, simulations, and gaming.

Figure 1.11.   Differentiated Learning Chart.

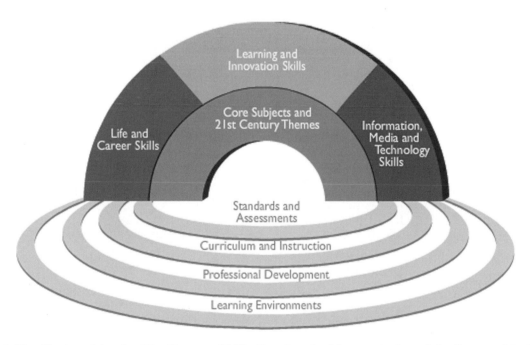

Figure 1.12.   Partnerships for 21st Century Skills. Reprinted with permission of the Partnership for 21st Century Skills.

- Technology skills are crucial for future employment needs.
- Equitable access is a key component for education.
- The definition of information literacy has become more complex as resources and technologies have changed.
- The continuing expansion of information demands that all individuals acquire the thinking skills that will enable them to learn on their own.
- Learning has a social context.
- School libraries are essential to the development of learning skills.

These beliefs are followed by four standards:

1. Inquire, think critically, and gain knowledge;
2. Draw conclusions, make informed decisions, apply knowledge to new situations, and create new knowledge;
3. Share knowledge and participate ethically and productively as members of our democratic society; and
4. Pursue personal and aesthetic growth.

Excerpted from "Standards for the 21st-Century Learner" by the AASL, a division of the American Library Association. © 2007, American Library Association. Available for download at www.ala.org/aasl/standards. Used with permission.

The International Society for Technology in Education Standards updated their 1998 NETS for students in 2007 identifying critical higher order thinking skills for students (http://www.iste.org/Content/NavigationMenu/NETS/ForStudents/2007Standards/NETS_for_Students_2007.htm).

1. **Creativity and innovation**. Students demonstrate creative thinking, construct knowledge, and develop innovative products and processes using technology. Students:
   - Apply existing knowledge to generate new ideas, products, or processes;
   - Create original works as a means of personal or group expression;
   - Use models and simulations to explore complex systems and issues; and
   - Identify trends and forecast possibilities.
2. **Communication and collaboration**. Students use digital media and environments to communicate and work collaboratively, including at a distance, to support individual learning and contribute to the learning of others. Students:
   - Interact, collaborate, and publish with peers, experts, or others employing a variety of digital environments and media.
   - Communicate information and ideas effectively to multiple audiences using a variety of media and formats.
   - Develop cultural understanding and global awareness by engaging with learners of other cultures.
   - Contribute to project teams to produce original works or solve problem.
3. **Research and information fluency**. Students apply digital tools to gather, evaluate, and use information. Students:
   - Plan strategies to guide inquiry.
   - Locate, organize, analyze, evaluate, synthesize, and ethically use information from a variety of sources and media.

- Evaluate and select information sources and digital tools based on the appropriateness to specific tasks.
- Process data and report results.

4. **Critical thinking, problem solving, and decision making**. Students use critical thinking skills to plan and conduct research, manage projects, solve problems, and make informed decisions using appropriate digital tools and resources. Students:
   - Identify and define authentic problems and significant questions for investigation.
   - Plan and manage activities to develop a solution or complete a project.
   - Collect and analyze data to identify solutions and/or make informed decisions.
   - Use multiple processes and diverse perspectives to explore alternative solutions.

5. **Digital citizenship**. Students understand human, cultural, and societal issues related to technology and practice legal and ethical behavior. Students:
   - Advocate and practice safe, legal, and responsible use of information and technology.
   - Exhibit a positive attitude toward using technology that supports collaboration, learning, and productivity.
   - Demonstrate personal responsibility for lifelong learning.
   - Exhibit leadership for digital citizenship.

6. **Technology operations and concepts**. Students demonstrate a sound understanding of technology concepts, systems, and operations. Students:
   - Understand and use technology systems.
   - Select and use applications effectively and productively.
   - Troubleshoot systems and applications.
   - Transfer current knowledge to learning of new technologies.

What Is the Role of School Library in Twenty-First-Century Learning and Teaching?

If we view teaching and learning as more than just delivery and consumption of information, then we see the library as a place that supports learning as a social process that focuses on the learner, interacting with other learners and resources, to create meaning. School librarians need to become leaders, advocates, and change agents willing to embrace the digital environment to ensure that students and staff are effective users of ideas and information. Competency begins with understanding and school librarians are in the ideal position as they collaborate with teachers to effectively model, integrate, and use Web 2.0 technologies in their teaching and learning. Action steps school librarians can use to take a leadership role include:

Action Step 1: Articulate a clear vision of technology, curriculum integration, and the use of Web 2.0 tools.
   - Create a wiki or a blog to share opinions and encourage discussion.
   - Hold a World Café (http://www.theworldcafe.com/worldcafe.html) to encourage dialogue and identify important questions.

Action Step 2: Revisit information literacy skills curriculum, especially in light of the new AASL "Standards for the 21st-Century Learner."

- Integrate new technologies into the information literacy skills. Identify which Web 2.0 tool(s) is best used to support the skills.
- Recruit a library advisory team to take an active role in integrating Web 2.0 into the curriculum and the library program by analyzing where and how the new technologies can be effectively integrated and taught.

Action Step 3: Keep teachers and administrators informed on the latest tools and best practices in the use and integration of Web 2.0 tools.

- Set up an RSS on your library Web site or wiki with links to relevant blogs, new sources, conferences, research, etc.
- Model the use of Web 2.0 tools. Don't expect faculty to collaborate and share if they don't see you doing it and talking about it. Join the Teacher-Librarian Ning, set up Google Reader, and open a Diigo account for bookmarking.

Action Step 4: Support professional development in twenty-first-century skills for teachers, administrators, and parents.

- Organize ongoing workshops for teachers and administrators to integrate digital literacy skills and Web 2.0 tools into the curriculum and their practice.
- Create your own Learning 2.0 professional development plan for faculty (http://plcmcl2-about.blogspot.com/).
- Recruit and train students to give one-on-one technology support to teachers and administrators.
- Host a "cybercafé" for parents. Demonstrate the benefits of Web 2.0 technologies to the teaching and learning process and share new resources and information.

Action Step 5: Increase personal Web 2.0 literacy—Embrace emerging technologies!

- Create a library blog to share books.
- Use a wiki with groups of student researchers.
- Hold a podcast forum on a current issue important to the school community.
- Set up an RSS Feed on the library Web site to highlight digital literacy issues.
- Use e-mail and instant messaging with students and faculty to support his or her information needs.
- Purchase e-books, MP3, and DVD players for student and faculty use.

In October 2006, The John D. and Catherine T. MacArthur Foundation launched its five-year, $50 million digital media and learning initiative to help determine how digital technologies are changing the way young people learn, play, socialize, and participate in civic life. *Confronting the Challenge of Participatory Culture: Media Education for the 21st Century* written by Henry Jenkins, director of the Comparative Media Studies Program at the Massachusetts Institute of Technology, the first white paper in a series to be published under the initiative, proposes "to shift the focus of the conversation about the digital divide from questions of technological access to those of opportunities to participate and to develop the cultural competencies and social skills needed for full involvement" (Jenkins 2006, 4). These skills build on the foundation of traditional literacy, research and information literary skills, technology skills, and critical thinking skills—the core skills of the school library program. "*Participatory Learning* includes the ways in which new technologies enable learners (of any age) to contribute in diverse ways to individual and shared learning goals. Through games, wikis, blogs, virtual environments, social network sites, cell phones, mobile devices, and other digital platforms, learners can participate in virtual communities where they share ideas, comment upon one another's projects, and plan, design, advance, implement, or simply discuss their goals and ideas together. Participatory learners come together to aggregate their ideas and experiences in a way that makes the whole ultimately greater than the sum of the parts" (HASTAC Initiative).

This initiative is indicative of the growing awareness of the need to understand the impact of emerging technologies on literacy and learning. "Digital media are helping to make the world smaller, spread ideas, and encourage collaboration across borders and among people who otherwise might not have an opportunity to work together" (MacArthur Foundation). The conversations will intensify as we wrestle with the questions: What skills do students need to fully participate in the twenty-first century? How can we ensure that they develop these skills? School librarians can be the catalyst to gain a deeper understanding of these issues by taking a leadership role in their schools, actively engaging students, teachers, administrators, and parents in the conversation.

Media Resources

A Portal to Media Literacy; Michael Wesch; July 10, 2008; 1:06:11; http://www.youtube.com/watch?v=J4yApagnr0s.

National Summit on 21st Century Skills: Intro Video; June 24, 2009; 4:43 min.; http://www.youtube.com/watch?v=xs_-77afyhk.

The Machine Is Using Us; Michael Wesch; March 8, 2008; 4:34 min.; http://www.youtube.com/watch?v=J4yApagnr0s.

The New Media Literacies; NML Staff, with Henry Jenkins; November 11, 2008; 2:51 min.; http://www.youtube.com/watch?v=pEHcGAsnBZE.

References and Additional Resources

Anderson, L. W. and D. R. Krathwohl, eds. 2001. *A Taxonomy for Learning, Teaching, and Assessing: A Revision of Bloom's Taxonomy of Educational Objectives*. New York: Longman.

Berger, Pam. 2010. Student Inquiry and Web 2.0. *School Library Monthly* 26 (5): 14–17.

Breuleux, Alain. 2001. Imagining the Present, Interpreting the Possible, Cultivating the Future: Technology and the Renewal of Teaching and Learning. *Education Canada* 41 (3). http://www.education.mcgill.ca/profs/breuleux/onlinepubs/BreuleuxEdCanFall2001.html.

Brown, Ann and Rodney R. Cocking. 1999. *How People Learn: Brain, Mind, Experience and School*. Washington, D.C.: National Academy Press.

Carvin, Andy. 2005. Tim Berners Lee: Weaving a Semantic Web. http://www.andycarvin.com/archives/2004/09/tim_bernerslee.html.

Churches, Andrew. 2008. Bloom's Taxonomy Blooms Digitally. http://www.techlearning.com/showArticle.php?articleID=196605124.

Education/Evolving. 2005. Listening to Student Voices—On Technology. http://www
    .educationevolving.org/pdf/tech_savy_students.pdf.

Friedman, Thomas L. 2005. *The World Is Flat*. New York: Farrar, Straus and Giroux.

HASTAC Initiative. 2009. Digital Media and Learning Competition. http://www.dml
    competition.net/theme.php.

Jenkins, H., K. Clinton, R. Purushotma, A. J. Robinson, and M. Weigel. 2006. Confronting
    the Challenges of Participatory Culture: Media Education for the 21st Century. The
    MacArthur Foundation. http://www.digitallearning.macfound.org.

Jones, Steve. 2002. The Internet Goes to College. Pew Internet and American Life Project.
    http://www.pewinternet.org/Reports/2002/The-Internet-Goes-to-College.aspx.

Lenhart, Amanda, et al. 2005. Teens and Technology. Pew Internet and American Life Project.
    http://www.pewinternet.org/Reports/2005/Teens-and-Technology.aspx.

MacArthur Foundation. 2008. MacArthur's $2 Million Digital Media & Learning Competition
    Focuses on Participatory Learning, Goes International. http://www.macfound.org/site/
    apps/nlnet/content3.aspx?c=lkLXJ8MQKrH&b=1139551&content_id=%7BE13B717D
    -138A-4037-8474-4D95A1C6A837%7D&notoc=1.

North Central Regional Educational Laboratory and the Metiri Group. 2003. *enGauge 21st Cen-
    tury Skills: Literacy in the Digital Age*. Naperville, IL: NCREL. www.grrec.ky.gov/
    SLC_grant/Engauge21st_Century_Skills.pdf.

O'Reilly, Tim. 2005. What Is Web 2.0? http://www.oreillynet.com/pub/a/oreilly/tim/news/
    2005/09/30/what-is-web-20.html.

Prensky, Marc. 2001. Digital Natives, Digital Immigrants. http://www.marcprensky.com/
    writing/Prensky/default.asp.

Stripling, Barbara. 2003. "Inquiry-Based Learning" in *Curriculum Connections through the
    Library*. Edited by Barbara Stripling and Sandra Hughes Hassell. Westport, CT: Libraries
    Unlimited.

TechCrunchies. 2009. Internet Statistics and Numbers in USA. http://techcrunchies.com/
    ?s=how+many+user+generated+creators.

Ziegenfuss, Donna. 2005. "By Instructional Design: Facilitating Effective Teaching and Learn-
    ing with Technology" in *Integrating Technology in Higher Educations*. Edited by
    M. O. Thirunarayanan and Aixa Perez-Prado. Lanham, MD: University Press of America.

2

Searching the Web

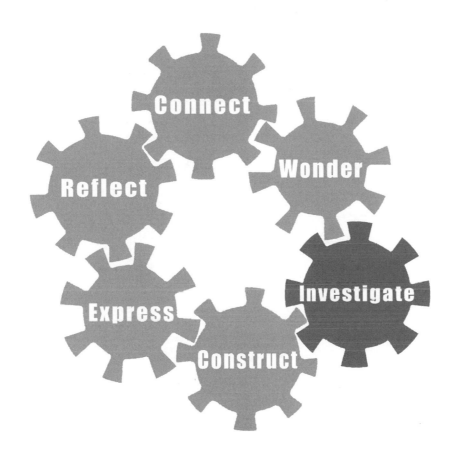

? **ESSENTIAL QUESTIONS**

How does the search process support inquiry learning?
What are the best instructional strategies to teach the search process?
Which search engines best support students' searching and exploration?

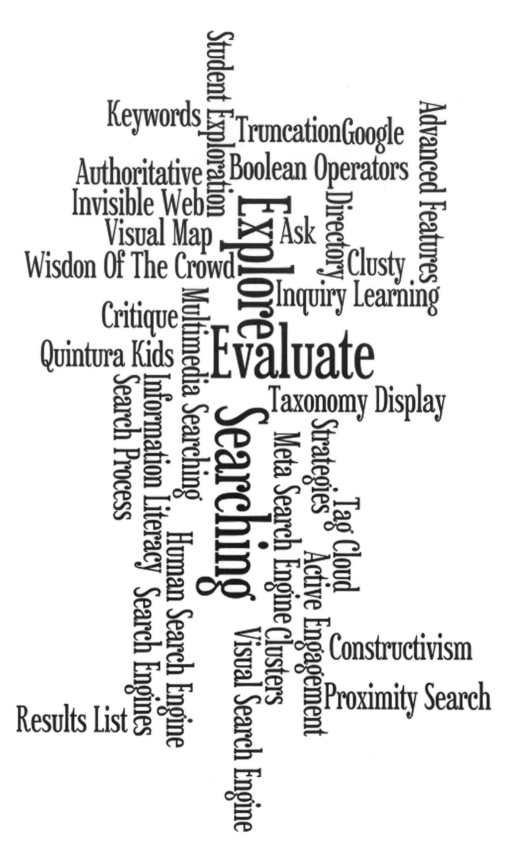

Figure 2.1.   http://www.wordle.net

Alisha slips off her iPod earbuds and sits down at the computer; she has about 15 minutes before she meets with her team. She's thinking about their last meeting when they brainstormed questions and discussed what they each knew about the topic. She pulls up the Research Wiki set up by Mr. Rodriquez, her teacher-librarian. He always uses a wiki so kids can work collaboratively in identifying the best search tools. A few of the search engines peak her interest as she scans the annotated list; she clicks on Quintura to see how the tag cloud is used. As she watches the screencast, she opens another window and follows along experimenting with different keywords.

Satisfied that she has mastered the new search engine, she returns to Google remembering a strategy Mr. Rodriquez recommended at the class research session—"type define: search term" to get definitions. She uses Google all the time but did not realize that it had advanced searching strategies. Cool, it worked! She scans the list of 20 or more definitions of global warming, looking at the URLs. She tags the Web page in her shared del.icio.us account to share with her teammates.

She moves to another search tool, Ask.com. When the class was comparing search engines, she noticed that Ask.com had a great results page—it gave listings of videos and up-to-date news on the search term and offered suggestions to narrow and broaden the search. She clicks on "Ways to Stop Global Warming" and "News" and gets an annotated list of world news stories. Her eyes go to the lower side of the screen where she sees a listing of RSS news feeds for "Top Stories," "World," "United States," "Science," etc. Great, she thinks to herself, "I'm going to suggest that the team set up some news feeds on our global warming wiki. Why spend time searching for the information when it can come to you?" She makes a mental note to add that to the research wiki to alert other students to this feature.

This will be a good start for her team. Before she leaves, she quickly reviews what she has gathered: definitions, videos, suggestions to narrow their search, related terms, and news feeds. Not bad for 20 minutes work, this will help her team focus their topic and decide on the essential questions they want to investigate. With two minutes to spare, she checks her e-mail.

How Has Searching Developed?

The first Web site, created on August 6, 1991, by Tim Berners-Lee, was also the first Web directory since he kept an ever-growing, categorized list of Web sites that other people created. It became the WWW Virtual Library (http://vlib.org).

In addition to being the most popular search engine, Google has a number of other great services that educators can use to support student learning:

Google Alert is an e-mail update service of the latest relevant Google results (Web, news, etc.) based on your choice of query or topic.

Google Docs is a free Web-based word processor, spreadsheet, and presentations that allow you share and collaborate online.

iGoogle is a start page tool where you can aggregate all the Google resources you use on your online desktop, e.g., Mail, Google Calendar. . . .

Google Reader constantly checks your favorite news sites and blogs for new content and posts them to one easy page.

GMail is a free e-mail service that integrates with Google's other services.

Google Apps is a free communication, collaboration, and publishing tools, including e-mail accounts on your school's domain (like student@your-school.edu).

Figure 2.2.   Google: Not Just a Search Engine.

If Only Search Engines Could Understand What We Want

Figure 2.3.   YouTube Video "If Only Search Engines Could Understand What We Want" (http://www.youtube.com/watch?v=q0Bfp4URgWQ). Show this brief video to students as a conversation starter. Are their experiences using search engines similar?

In 1994, there were fewer than 10,000 Web sites, but by 1998, it had grown to approximately 3.5 million Web sites. Google, the search engine with the goofy name and a new algorithm that produced results that were more useful, was launched and took the largest share of the search engine market very quickly. Google now commands 60 percent of all searches worldwide. Yahoo! is a distant second with 14 percent and MSM Live is third with 4 percent of the market. (You know a search engine is very popular when its name becomes a verb—Google it!)

The idea of Web searching has been around for as long as the Internet itself, but only in the past several years did it catch on with the mainstream. Now, it is the second most popular activity online, after e-mail (Pew Internet). But things change quickly on the Web and if you think Google will always be leader of the pack, think again; history shows how quickly search engines users become fickle. Alta Vista was the favorite home page in 1995 due to its index that offered lightning fasts results, but it was quickly replaced by Google, who not only indexed Web pages but ranked pages by who linked to it. Luckily, there is always pressure to create the latest and the best search engine to capture the highest revenue. Using the latest and most innovative technologies, search engine companies are continuously competing to develop the best search engine. It's not surprising that many of the search engines being developed have unique features based on Web 2.0 characteristics. We don't often think of search engines as being Web 2.0 tools since they are not new technologies but recent changes and updates have brought about customization, social search capabilities, and expanded content. This aligns with Web 2.0's characteristics that emphasize participation, publication, socialization, and sharing.

Student Information Seeking Behavior

Before we look at the search process, we need to look at our primary users, students. The ubiquitous nature of the Web and Google gives students an inflated sense of their abilities when it comes to conducting online research. Just ask any student if they need help and they will say, "No, I'm fine" or "I'll just Google." Kathleen Tyner in her book *Literacy in a Digital World* categorizes literacies into two groups—tool literacies which encompass computer, network, and technology; and literacies of representation that include information, visual, and media. Kids often fool their teachers and sometimes themselves into thinking they are digitally literate because they have strong "tool" or computer skills; however, they often lack "literacies of representation"—information literacy (Tyner 1998, 94). The two are very distinct and different skills.

Students expect a search engine to deliver accurate, analyzed answers, but it rarely, if ever, does. But even though students overrate their searching abilities and expect too much from the search engines, they are usually satisfied with their results; what they find is usually "good enough." Research shows that 93 percent of young people are satisfied or very satisfied with their overall experience of using a search engine. However, research also tells us 72.3 percent of search engines users experience "search engine fatigue" either "always," "usually," or "sometimes" when researching a topic on the Internet (Sterling 2007). The report discusses user frustration with clutter and the content of search results: "When asked to name their #1 complaint about the process, 25 percent cited a deluge of results, 24 percent cited a predominance of commercial (paid) listings, 18.8 percent blamed the search engine's inability to understand their keywords (forcing them to try again), and 18.6 percent were most frustrated by disorganized/random results." There was also a desire among many users that search engines be able to read their minds. "The survey respondents were asked whether they wished that search engines like Google could, in effect, read their minds, delivering the results they were actually looking for. . . . That capability is something that 78 percent of all survey-takers 'wished' for, including 86.2 percent of 18–34 year-olds and 85 percent of those under 18."

Although search engines can't read our minds, yet, innovation in the search industry is picking up. What we think of as "search" has expanded substantially in the last few years largely due to the new type of services offered and content that is available. Because of all the recent advancements in search engine development, it's difficult to categorize search engines into neat groups with specific features and capabilities since most overlap in different ways. Instead, what we have done in this chapter is to group them into strategies that highlight their capability to help students be successful searchers and to make sense of the information they are finding.

How Does the Search Process Support Inquiry Learning?

All of you, unfortunately, are faced with students doing *topic* research, such as a five-page paper on China or a PowerPoint presentation on the state bird.

Figure 2.4.   Stripling Inquiry Model.

The emphasis is on finding facts and cutting and pasting bits of information into some type of report with little real learning taking place. When faced with a topic research assignment, students immediately go to the first computer they see to open Google, type in their topic, and receive eleven million hits, and then they click on the print button—again, again, and again. With the amount of information available on the Web, students can easily cut and clip megabytes of information encouraging plagiarism.

The opposite of topic research is inquiry learning. "Inquiry is an approach to learning whereby students find and use a variety of sources of information and ideas to increase their understanding of a problem, topic or issue. It requires more of them than simply answering questions or getting the right answer, it espouses investigation, search, quest, research, and study. Inquiry does not stand alone; it engages interests and challenges students to connect their world with the curriculum" (Kuhlthau 2007, 2).

Effective searching skills fall into the investigative phase of inquiry; it focuses on students' ability to develop and use successful information and technology strategies for locating sources of information and seeking information from diverse genres, formats, and points of view. Educators implement a constructivist approach by placing the emphasis on teaching students to explore, critique, and evaluate search engines rather than on how to use a particular search engine. Students ask, "Which is the best search engine for my information need?" They choose which search engine is best for their particular information need: to predict, identify, organize, classify, describe, and be reflective, in both choosing the search engines they use and the results they find. School librarians in collaboration with classroom teachers decide which unit, curriculum topic, or grade level these strategies are best integrated and used. The student worksheet (see Figure 2.5) provides a template to compare search engines using authentic student search questions. Four search engines are identified (Ask, Kids Quintura, Clusty, and Google) based on their strengths and special features. Figure 2.6 is a summary sheet that outlines the special features of each search engine for librarians to use as they are teaching the comparison of search engines.

Search versus Discovery

It is helpful for students to be aware of the difference between search and discovery. Search is an on demand, focused activity; the user has a particular need to fulfill or a target in mind, whether it be a piece of information, a product, or a document. For best results, the user needs to construct a search with descriptive keywords to qualify as exactly as possible to the target. Discovery, related but less specific, is a browsing activity. It's exploratory in nature and is driven by a general goal to learn more about a particular topic(s). More often than not, students are engaging in exploration.

A benefit of the Web, when it comes to inquiry, lies in its hyperlinking capability, challenging and encouraging us as we link to new information, to both ask more questions and to expand and reflect on our questions. We pose a question to a search engine and the Web leads us to ask more questions and to become more aware of how much we do not know. The conception of searching the Web changes from finding a piece of information to one in which a search is embedded in how we think. Educators are challenged to make "search" become not only a "looking up" activity but also truly productive inquiry. As Joyce Valenza, points out, "young information seekers do not have the sophisticated skills or understandings needed to navigate complex

Comparison of Search Engines

My research questions are:

My keywords are:

	Ask.com www.ask.com	Kids.Quintura quinturakids.com	Clusty clusty.com	Google www.google.com
1. How many hits did I get when I executed my search?				
2. What types of information did I find?				
3. Was the information in the first three hits relevant to my research questions?				
4. What special features does this search engine have?				

Which search engine is best for my research questions and why?

Figure 2.5.   Student Handout: Comparison of Search Engines.

Special Features of Selected Search Engines

Ask www.ask.com	Kids Quintura kids.quintura.com	Clusty www.clusty.com	Google www.google.com
Strength: provides suggestions to narrow or broaden search	Strength: visual, interactive, and designed for kids	Strength: clusters concepts supporting organization	Strength: locates relevant information and more advanced features
*Can search: Web, images, news, videos, maps, answers, city, TV listings, events, recipes, and blogs.	*Adult filter can be engaged.	*Search tabs for Web, news, images, Wikipedia, blogs, etc.: Can also turn off undesired tabs. Four tabs can be customized.	*Can search Web, images, maps, news, video, and blogs.
*Skins—small gallery.	*Kid-friendly interface.		*Has advanced search features: search by language, file type, domain, and date.
*Six languages.	*Result list presented as a cloud (visual search engine).	*Search results are organized into "clusters" (not to be confused with "clouds").	*Can direct where keywords must show on the page—title, text, URL, links to the page, within a region of the world, and can indicate a desired numeric range.
*Can search by domain.	*Within the cloud, query words appear in red.	*Can also search by host, by file type, and in other languages.	
*Includes first sentence from site in "Results List."	*Can click on terms inside the cloud to refine results.	*Clusters appear in left panel, with sub-clusters and number of Web sites included in the cluster.	*Offers safe search filtering.
*Provides related searches in right side panel.	*Five browsing icons for: movies, music, sports and recreation, TV, and computers, games, and online.	*Sites in clusters can be opened in a new window and can be previewed without actually opening the site (quick peek).	*Can translate page to/from many languages, or can search in foreign language version of Google.
*Provides number of questions about topic in right side panel.	*Provides code to imbed cloud on Web site.	*Adult filter can be engaged.	*Offers shortcuts for searching, ex. Definition: pollution.
*Advanced search features.	*Search tabs include Web, images, and video.		
*Search by page modification, ranging from anytime—last week to two years ago.			

Figure 2.6. Special Features of Selected Search Engines.

From *Choosing Web 2.0 Tools for Learning and Teaching in a Digital World*
by Pam Berger and Sally Trexler. Santa Barbara, CA: Libraries Unlimited. Copyright © 2010.

information environments and to evaluate the information they find," and challenges school librarians to better prepare young people for more efficient and effective experiences on the Web (Valenza 2006, 18). The American Association of School Librarians' (AASL) "Standards for the 21st-Century Learner," encourage students to incorporate higher order thinking skills:

> 1.1.2 Develop and refine a range of questions to frame the search for new understanding.
>
> 1.1.3 Find, evaluate, and select appropriate sources to answer questions, refer to the searching process.
>
> 1.1.8 Demonstrate mastery of technology tools for accessing information and pursuing.

Excerpted from "Standards for the 21st-Century Learner" by the AASL, a division of the American Library Association. © 2007, American Library Association. Available for download at www.ala.org/aasl/standards. Used with permission.

Five Facts Students Need to Know about Search Engines

1. One search engine can't do it all. You can have a favorite search engine that you rely on most of the time; however, be aware of at least five or more additional search engines that you can use depending on your information need (i.e., narrow your topic, find a podcast, and easily compare results from three search engines). They all have unique features; know how to work them to your advantage.
2. There is an invisible Web that search engines can't penetrate.
3. Search engines can't read your mind.
4. Search engines do not evaluate the content on a Web site. When you locate information that appears to be relevant to your questions or topic, you still need to assess the credibility of the information.
5. One search engine can't search the entire Web. To do a through Web search of your topic, you'll need to use more than one.

Which Are the Best Search Engines?

There are over a thousand search engines on the Internet, although Google is the one used by a majority of people, students included. Listed below are 12 strategies incorporating over 17 different search engines that will help students to move away from total reliance on Google (see Table 2.1). As noted by Oren Etzioni, a computer scientist at the University of Washington, in an article in *The New York Times* on September 30, 2004, "The competition has shifted from crawling the Web and returning an answer quickly to adding value to the information that has been retrieved."

Most everyone agrees that Google is the best search engine to locate relevant information; however, it is not the best at presenting the results. For a long time, users have complained about the lack of prioritization and the need to place information within a context to better understand what they have retrieved. Students need to develop effective strategies to locate information and using one search engine all the time is not the most effective strategy, especially when alternative search engines with unique

Table 2.1. Search Engines Value to Students.

Search Engine	Added Value to Students
Google Advance Search Strategies (http://www.google.com)	Advanced search strategies encourages students to think more deeply about the topic
Ask.com (http://www.ask.com)	Great organization of info on results page—places information in a context
Clusty (http://clusty.com)	Clusters results to narrow down and refine generic search terms—helps students to find related topics
Browsys Finder (http://www.browsys.com/finder/)	Provides user access to multiple databases in relevant categories; many they would never know about—encourages comparison of results
Exalead (http://www.exalead.com)	Offers supports through phonetic spelling, truncation, etc.
Google Coop (http://www.google.com/coop/)	Creates a customized search engine for your students
Mahalo (http://www.mahalo.com)	Offers expert help
Quintura (http://www.quintura.com and http://kids.quintura.com)	Presents results as a dynamic tag cloud—encourages exploration of keywords and results
Google Scholar (http://scholar.google.com)	Offers quality academic results chosen by subject expert
Internet Public Library (http://ipl.org)	Offers evaluated, quality Web sites
Answers.com (http://www.answers.com)	Provides authoritative information
Intute (http://www.intute.ac.uk)	Provides annotated academic Web sites—helps students to understand the scope of their topic
50Matches (http://www.50matches.com)	Draws on the "collective intelligence" of the social group

features that target thinking process, unique content, and innovative display of results are available.

Alternative Search Engines

There are hundreds of new search engines being developed each year, far too many to cover in this chapter, so we have chosen a handful that we think are innovative, reliable, student friendly, and most important, meet students' needs. To see a full listing of the top 100 alternative search engines and which search engine to use for your specific information need, go to:

- Read/Write Web: http://www.readwriteweb.com/archives/top_100_alternative_search_engines.php

- Alt Search Engine blog: http://www.altsearchengines.com/
- Choose the Best Search Engine for Your Information Need: http://www
  .noodletools.com/debbie/literacies/information/5locate/adviceengine
  .html

The search engines in Table 2.1 are very different, but each one has unique features that are helpful to students in their searching, such as they cluster results by topics, (e.g., Clusty), limit searches to specific Web sites (e.g., Google Coop), arrange the results in unique ways (e.g., KoolTool), or compare results from major search engines (e.g., Intellways). Table 2.1 lists the search engines and the unique feature that supports learning; a full explanation and graphics follows.

What Are the Best Strategies to Teach the Search Process?

Go Beyond Basic Google

Okay. All of our students use Google and why not? It's considered the best so we all use it; however, don't stop there. Capitalize on students' natural tendency to use Google by teaching them some of Google's advanced features that will encourage them to search more effectively and to analyze the search results.

Synonym search: If you want to search not only for your search term but also for its synonyms, place the tilde sign ("~") immediately in front of your search term. For example, Figure 2.7 shows how to search for cheap, inexpensive, or discount travel.

Figure 2.7.   Google Synonym Search.

Word definition: The Google Define command will let you look up words online and find the meaning from different sources across the Web. Type "define:search term" such as "define:global warming" into the Google search box, without the quotes. Getting a quick definition is great, but also using this strategy helps to involve students in evaluation by comparing and contrasting results. Before the students click on any hits, have them break up into groups assigning each group to one result in which they need to evaluate the site and decide if they think the definition is accurate, lacking, biased, etc., and why (see Figure 2.5).

Google Alerts (http://www.google.com/alerts) are e-mail updates of the latest relevant Google results (Web, news, etc.) based on your choice of query or topic (see Figure 2.8). Students can monitor a topic for a research paper, stay current on a topic of interest to them, or even keep tabs on their favorite sports team. You can request an update once a as-it-happens, or once a week. To learn more about Google advanced features, go to http://www.google.com/intl/en/help/refinesearch.html or subscribe to Google's Librarians Newsletter at http://www.google.com/librariancenter/librarian _newsletter.html.

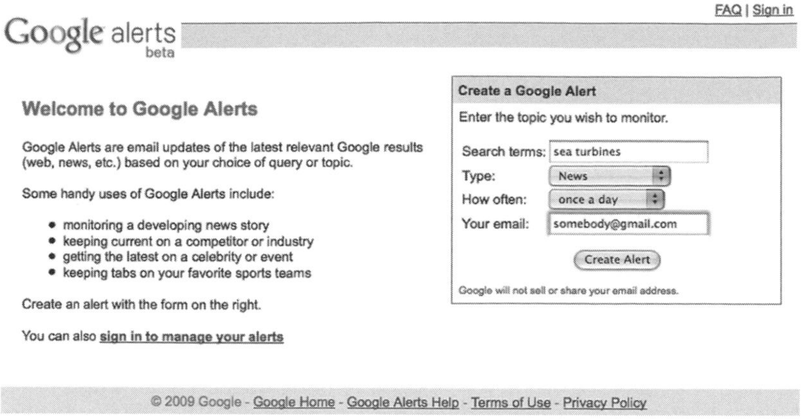

Figure 2.8.   Google Alert.

Use a Search Engine with a Good Results Page

Ask.com (http://www.ask.com), formerly known as Ask Jeeves, was redesigned and is better than ever; the results pages are richer and better organized than Google. Its opening search page is refreshingly simply with a clean design and a few choices to limit your search to the Web, images, news, etc. When doing a search on Michael Jackson's death in Ask.com, we received the latest news (from 25 minutes earlier) along with other relevant links in the center of the page; images and current news images, video, encyclopedia, and dictionary information on the right column and suggestions to narrow or expand the search with related terms on the left. Ask also allows you to save any entry in its search results to a special page called "MyStuff." You can save also save photos then organize everything into folders.

Clusty (http:/clusty.com) is a meta search engine which offers traditional search results along with clusters of results. Meta search engines are common but the great organizational way that Clusty presents its findings makes it stand out. A sidebar offers three tabs: "Clusters," "Sources," and "Sites." The data, grouped in "Clusters" on the left navigation pane according to logical groupings (headings and subheadings), helps students to narrow the focus if generic keywords are used. Searching Benazir Bhutto on Clusty (see Figure 2.10) provides results grouped by topics—her political life, the assassination, the

Figure 2.9.   Ask Search Engine.

current prime minister, biography, etc., as opposed to a Google search that just lists the results by relevance ranking, which does not add to the students' understanding of the topic. When researching, students can uncover buried sites by choosing a related cluster or related topics. The other two tabs are easily understood and helpful: narrow

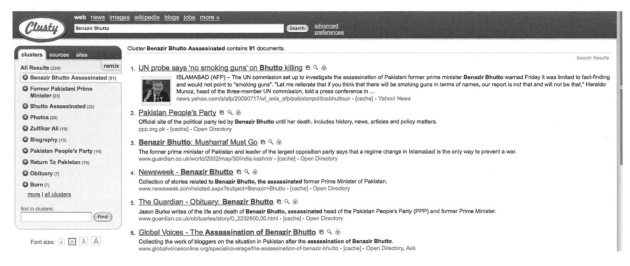

Figure 2.10.   Clusty Search. Used with permission of Vivisimo, Inc.

your search to a particular domain (com, org, net, edu, etc.) or limit your search to specific sources such as Ask.com or Live.com. Use the "Remix" button to view additional clusters that were not included in the first grouping.

Play the Field

If you think all search engines produce the same results, think again. Each one has its own algorithm to collect data so no two search engines will have exactly the same information in its databases. Browsys Advanced Finder (http://browsys.com),

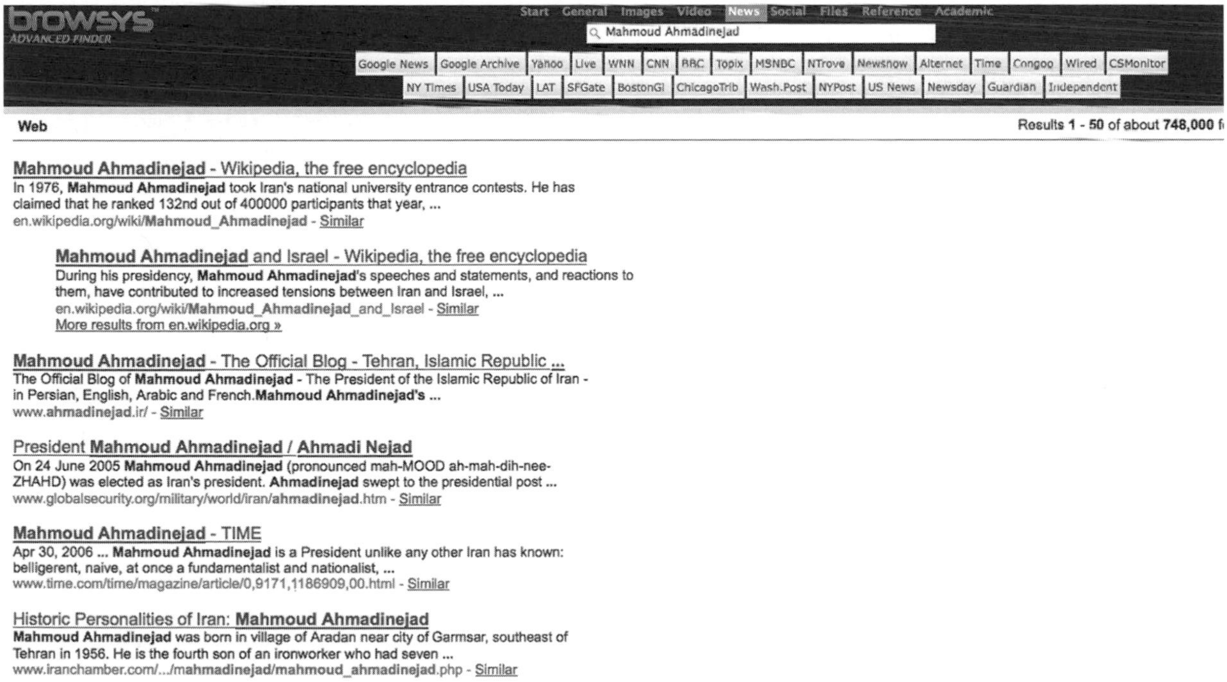

Figure 2.11.   Browsys Advanced Finder.

formerly known as Intelways and crossengine, is an interface to dozens of search engines enabling you to type in your search strategy once and click your way through the list of search tools one by one. It's also a great search tool if you don't know where to start; it has a particularly useful categorization of finding tools. Listed on the very top of the screen there are categories of tools for "General" searching, along with images, video, news, and social, then the option of searching by file type, academic, reference sources, etc. Click on any of these categories, and a new collection of search tools is displayed, specific to that type of search. The "Academic" tab includes Google Scholar, Academic Index, Factbites, Smithsonian, NASA and 15 science Web sites, Scirus, Science News, SciSearch, Science.gov, and more. The default, "Start," selection includes several Google search indexes (Web, images, news, and maps), other major search engines, Wikipedia, several multimedia search engines, and social bookmarking sites including del.icio.us and Digg. Students can easily compare search results from one site to another.

Another tool that compares search engines is Jux2 (http://www.jux2.com). It is designed to compare Google, Yahoo, and MSN. When you enter a keyword(s), it will display brief snippets that are common to all three search engines, as well as hits that are unique to one of the search engine for that search.

Use Advanced Search Features

Exalead (http://www.exalead.com; see Figure 2.12) search has results brimming with helpful information. Starting with the right column, users can narrow the search by choosing related terms or related categories; the middle column contains search results; and in the left hand column are thumbnail images of the Web pages. But, in addition, it's a powerful search engine that offers advanced features such as truncation, phonetic search, and proximity search.

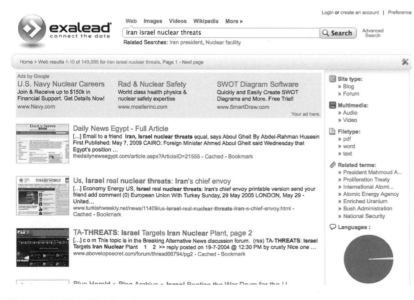

Figure 2.12.   Exalead.

Build Your Own Search Engine

One of the newest developments for search services that directly relates to the Web 2.0 concept is the option to "build your own" search engine. There are a number of tools for building customized filtered versions of leading search engines that are free and simple to set up. They offer features that allow you to limit the search to what you think is the most authoritative Web sites; accept recommendations for additional "best of breed" sites to add to your filter and make your customized search engine available on your Web site, wiki, or blog.

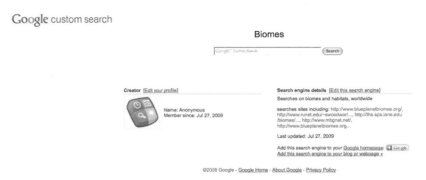

Figure 2.13.   Google Coop.

Google Custom Search Engine or Google Coop (http://www.google.com/coop/cse) can be used to create a search engine that includes a Web site or a collection of Web sites. Users can host the search box on the Web site and customize the colors on the page. View "How to Set Up a Google Search Engine" on YouTube to watch detailed instructions at http://www.youtube.com/watch?v=v5bi2H0YNEU. A similar tool is Rollyo (http://www.rollyo.com) and an example can be viewed that was created by the 21st Century Information Fluency's custom search, Inventors and Inventions Searchroll (http://rollyo.com/21cif/inventors_and_inventions).

Use Expert Help

Mahalo (http://www.mahalo.com) attempts to harness the intelligence of human powered search results. It's sometimes referred to as an "organic" or "human" search engine, since it combines computer algorithms and human researchers to look up a search query. Mahalo employs "guides" to handcraft results for the most popular search terms. If there is not one developed for your search, then you can request it. In a search on "climate change" results are grouped into categories: recent news stories, background articles, consequences, international developments, controversies, science and data, central figures, action on climate change, arguments against climate change, humor, related searches, etc. Other "human search engines" are ChaCha (http://chacha.com) and Stumpedia (http://stumpedia.com).

Safe Searches for Young Children

Ask Kids (http://www.askkids.com), a search engine designed for kids, ages 6 to 12, contains child appropriate Web sites chosen by the Ask Kids editorial staff as relevant and practical for learning or reference. The search results page is organized in a graphically-vivid three panel display that includes related images, currents events, videos, and encyclopedia results giving kids a handy "see also" section (see Figure 2.14). Yahoo

Figure 2.14.   Ask Kids Search Engine.

Kids! (http://kids.yahoo.com) is another good search engine for kids; all the Web sites in the directory are handpicked by an experienced educator. Similar to Ask Kids, it includes a number of fun features such as movies, sports, a cool page, activities, etc.

Use Visual Search Engines

We now have the opportunity to search and to view results graphically as well as a list of texts. Different views can lead us to new discoveries of information and support different learning styles. Search-Cube (http://www.search-cube.com) is a visual search engine that presents Web results in a unique, three-dimensional cube interface. It shows previews of up to 96 Web sites including text, video, and images. It's one of the latest search tools that switched from an ordered text list of results in favor of a 3D interface. The search results, which are pulled from Google, are displayed in a 3D cube that can rotate freely with your mouse or keyboard. The visual results are stunning and although you don't get the Google's relevance ranking, the visual display helps to organize the results for previewing (see Figure 2.15).

Another unique search engine is Viewzi (http://www.viewzi.com). It's extremely flexible, changing its appearance and function based on the search term. It presents the user with "views," each of which is essentially a customized search aggregator. Viewzi takes your search term, figures out what you are looking for, and presents the results in an appropriate view such as the "Albums," the "Weather," the "MP3," or 13 other view options.

Quintura (http://www.quintura.com) and Quintura for Kids (http://quintura kids.com) are tag cloud based search engines (see Figure 2.16). They present the results as a visual map (cloud) of tags related to your search query. When you enter your search term, you are presented with a visual map of related terms that you select and by doing so, you are continuously narrowing down the results that are updated and displayed in real time in the right hand column. It's very interactive: when you hover over a word in the cloud with the cursor, Quintura associates and highlights other words that are related to that word while changing the search results on the right to show you the articles it would come up with should you choose that keyword. Your primary search terms are displayed in red, so you can always return to them

Figure 2.15.   Search-Cube.

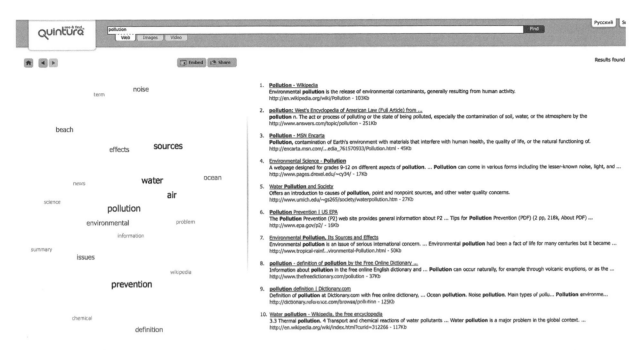

Figure 2.16.   Quintura.

while you are testing out new combinations of keywords. Quintura encourages exploration of a question or topic. Another visual search engine is Kartoo (http://www.kartoo.com).

Browse Scholarly Articles and Journals

Google Scholar (http://scholar.google.com) provides a simple way to search for scholarly literature (see Figure 2.17). It includes peer-reviewed papers, theses, books, abstracts, and articles, from academic publishers, professional societies, preprint repositories, universities, and other scholarly organizations. Another good site is Intute (http://www.intute.ac.uk), a free online service providing access to education and research resources. The service is created by a network of UK universities and partners. Subject specialists select and evaluate the Web sites in the database and write descriptions of the resources. For science, try Scirus (http://www.scirus.com/srsapp/).

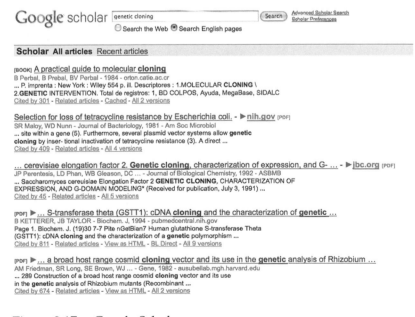

Figure 2.17.   Google Scholar.

Browse or Search Authoritative Subject Directories

Experts select, evaluate, and categorize Web sites and place them in subject directories for easy retrieval. These directories are especially helpful to students who are researching broad topics. The most well known are The Internet Public Library (http://ipl.org), Answers (http://answers.com), and Intute (http://www .intute.ac.uk/).

Use a Social Search Engine

Experiment using "wisdom of the crowd." The search engine 50 Matches (http:// www.50matches.com) is sort of a human-indexed Internet. It crawls through social book-marking sites such as del.icio.us and Diigo and indexes sites that users have tagged. The belief is that no search engine could either match the hours put into identifying sites than humans and no algorithm could calculate site quality better than humans. Another social search engines is Eurekster (http://www.eurekster.com).

Search the Invisible Web

There are parts of the Web that search engines can't access; they are typically non-html pages such as Adobe PDF files, multimedia, password protected pages, and PowerPoint files. This information is generally inaccessible to the software spiders and crawlers that create search engine databases. There are a few approaches to finding information in the invisible Web. A few resources are Direct Search (http://www.freepint.com/gary/direct.htm) and Infomine (http://infomine.ucr.edu) (see Figure 2.18).

Figure 2.18.   Direct Search.

Searching for Multimedia

Multimedia search engines have not yet evolved to the extent of their text-based counterparts. There are quite a few search engines that locate various file types (see Table 2.2), but overall, the ability to locate quality multimedia resources is lacking. Searching for text-based information and searching for multimedia information is very different. Text-based search engines match keywords or phrases to the search engine's index that is made of words from the Web sites' title, metadata, tags fields, and sometimes full-text, to identify appropriate resources. Unfortunately, search engines cannot search within a podcast or audio file or decipher an image to match a keyword; it has to rely on the limited descriptors of the content. The leading search engines have not yet stepped up to the plate to employ newer technologies to address the search gap for multimedia (Miller 2007, 37).

Searchers have two choices when using the general search engines to locate multimedia: they either select the tab reflecting the media type of interest (e.g., audio, images) and enter the search term(s) or they can enter the type of media and search term in the search box (e.g., podcast "space exploration"). Luckily, some new innovative strategies are coming. A few smaller search engine companies are developing new technologies to actually search and index the contents of the non-text media. Others are using voice recognition technology and natural language processing, as well as visual analysis of video to expose the contents; the result will be hits that are more precise.

In addition to the technical aspect of analyzing multimedia, other factor affecting its use in the classroom is user-generated content, production quality, and appropriateness of content for student use. When the big search engines enter the multimedia search engine business, text, video, and audio files will appear in the same result listing and greater advancement in this area will occur (Miller 2007, 37); however, as with the text files, the multimedia files will not be evaluated for quality, authority, or appropriateness for children. Web site evaluation will continue to be a vital student skill. Table 2.2 contains both general search engines and specialized search engines indicating which multimedia file type it searches.

What Are the Most Common Questions Asked about Search Engines?

What are the best search engines to use with visual learners?

Quintura (http://www.quintura.com) or Search-Cube (http://www.search -cube.com)

I want my students to use authoritative, high-quality resources. Which search engines are the best to recommend?

Google Scholar (http://scholar.google.com) and Intute (http://www .intute.ac.uk)

Which search engines will help students to find alternative or related topics?

Clusty (http://www.clusty.com) and Grokker (http://www.grokker.com)

I want my students to know that not all search engines are the same, especially when it comes to results. Which search engines are the best to compare results?

Browsys Advanced Finder (http://www.browsys.com/finder/) and Jux2 (http://www.jux2.com)

My students' research topics are usually too broad. Which search engine will help them to refine their topics?

Ask.com (http://www.ask.com) and Clusty (http://www.clusty.com)

I am working with young children and I want to keep them safe. Which search engines are best for this?

Ask Kids (http://www.askkids.com) or Quintura Kids (http://www.quintura kids.com)

Table 2.2.   Multimedia Search.

Search Engine Name	Audio	Video	Images	Podcasts
AllTheWeb (http://multimedia.alltheweb.com)	X	X	X	X/MP3
AltaVista (http://www.altavista.com)	X	X	X	X
AOL Search (http://search.aol.com)	X	X	X	
Ask.com (http://www.ask.com)		X	X	
Blinkx (http://www.blinkx.com)		X		
Creative Commons Search (http://creativecommons.org)	X	X	X	
Ditto.com (http://www.ditto.com)			X	
Dogpile Multimedia Search (http://www.dogpile.com)	X	X	X	
Education Podcast Network (http://www.epnweb.org)				X
Exalead (http://www.exalead.com)	X	X	X	
Find Sounds (http://www.findsounds.com)	X			
Flickr (http://flickr.com)			X	
Google Search (http://www.google.com)		X	X	
Internet Archive (http://archive.org)	X			
iTunes (http://www.itunes.com)	X			X
Live.com (http://www.live.com)		X	X	
Netvue.com (http://www.netvue.com)			X	
Open Video Project (http://open-video.org)		X		
Pics4learning.com (http://www.pics4learning.com)			X	
picsearch.com (http://www.picsearch.com)			X	
Podcast Alley (http://www.podcastalley.com)				X
Podcast Pickle (http://www.podcastpickle.com)				X
Podcastdirectory.com (http://www.podcastdirectory.com)				X
Podscope (http://www.podscope.com)				X
SkreemR.com (http://www.skreemr.com)				MP3
Teacher Tube (http://www.teachertube.com)		X		
Yahoo Search (http://www.yahoo.com)	X	X	X	
YouTube (http://www.youtube.com)		X		

How can I keep up with latest trends in search engines?

Below is a list of four resources to keep current with search engines:

Search Engine Land—http://searchengineland.com
Research Buzz—http://www.researchbuzz.com
Pandia—http://www.pandia.com
Google Newsletter for Librarians—http://groups.google.com/group/librarian
-newsletter

Action Steps

1. Explore three to five search engines; select the best ones to support student learning and introduce them to students. Have them compare search engines using the student handout in Figure 2.5 as a guide.
2. Present three innovative search engines to teachers at the next faculty meeting. When you demonstrate the search engines, use current curriculum topics.
3. Collaborate with teachers to review your school's curriculum maps. Together decide which unit or grade is best to teach searching skills.
4. Create a chart of five to seven new search engines; include the name, URL, and its unique features. Post the list on the library Web page, wiki, or blog.
5. Add a short cut to your preferred search engine on each library computer desktop.

Media Resources

Be CyberSmart: Researching the Internet Wisely; April 4, 2008; 4:35 min.; (with Joyce Valenza) http://www.youtube.com/watch?v=XuBwu33amnc.
Google Custom Search Engine; October 3, 2008; 5:14 min.; http://www.youtube.com/watch?v=iyTiVDpSAzY.
Google Tips: Some of the Lesser Known Functions; August 7, 2007; 7:12 min.; http://www.youtube.com/watch?v=Q9PFUKJsXfo.
Information Revolution; Michael Wesch; October 12, 2007; 5:29 min.; http://www.youtube.com/watch?v=-4CV05HyAbM.
Web Search Strategies in Plain English; September 23, 2008; 2:51 min.; http://www.youtube.com/watch?v=CWHPf00Jkqg.

References and Additional Resources

American Association of School Librarians. 2007. Standards for the 21st-Century Learner. http://www.ala.org/ala/mgrps/divs/aasl/guidelinesandstandards/learningstandards/AASL_Learning_Standards_2007.pdf.
Kuhlthau, Carol, et al. 2007. *Guided Inquiry: Learning in the 21st Century.* Westport, CT: Libraries Unlimited.
Miller, Ron. 2007. Multimedia Search Matures. *EContent* 32–37.
Pew Internet. 2009. Pew Internet Project Data Memo. http://www.pewinternet.org/~/media/Files/Reports/2009/PIP_Generations_2009.pdf.

Sterling, Greg. 2007. Report: 7 Out of 10 Americans Experience "Search Engine Fatigue." Search Engine Land. http://searchengineland.com/report-7-out-of-10-americans-experience-search-engine-fatigue-12509.

Tyner, Kathleen. 1998. *Literacy in a Digital World*. Hillsdale, NJ: Lawrence Erlbaum Associates.

Valenza, Joyce Kasman. 2006. They Might Be Gurus. *Teacher Librarian* 34 (1): 18–26.

3

Social Bookmarking

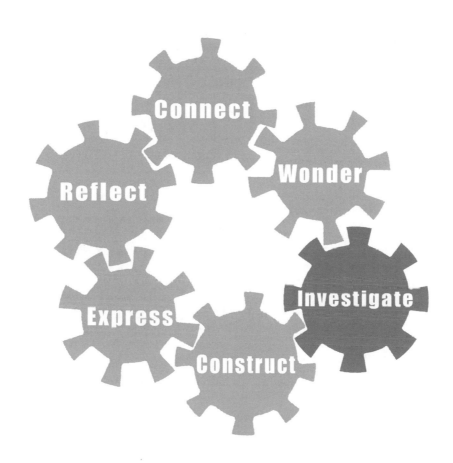

? ESSENTIAL QUESTIONS

What is social bookmarking and how does it engage students in the learning process?
How does social bookmarking support student exploration and discovery of information?
What are the best social bookmarking sites and how are educators and students using them?

Figure 3.1.   http://www.wordle.net

Carmen, an eighth grader at Frost Middle School, quickly sends a text message to her two teammates, Maya and Sam, as she leaves her science class, "MIRL in Lib 4P- diigo.com: biomes*." Carmen coasts along in most classes but when it comes to science, she revs up a notch; to her, science is real, undiscovered, exciting. Her class is studying biomes and they have formed into teams to research specific biomes.

Mr. Hutchinson, the science teacher, believes his students need to be scientists, to follow an inquiry framework and work collaboratively to solve problems and create new understandings. He carefully plans activities and chooses the best tools to support inquiry learning along with the school librarian, Ms. Cortez. Together they decide to introduce the students to Diigo so that the collaboration could be more seamless and transparent as they learn how to locate, critique, and share online science resources. They want the emphasis to be on developing appropriate collaboration, thinking, and information fluency skill.

Ms. Cortez, the school librarian, demonstrates a new social bookmarking tool. Carmen is psyched as she follows along on her computer as Ms. Cortez gives a brief tutorial to the class on how to tag Web sites, write evaluative annotations in the notes section, highlight important text, and critique each others' work by using sticky notes. She realizes immediately what a time saver this tool is; she doesn't need to e-mail URLs back and forth with her teammates, they are saved in one central online location with customized tags that made sense to them.

Students also learn that they can check out who else in Diigo has tagged Web sites on biomes. Carmen thinks this was a cool aspect of Diigo.com. Her teacher calls it tapping into the "collective intelligence." Carmen isn't sure she totally understands this concept but she does wish more teachers let them work like this—it makes learning more exciting. Mr. Hutchinson and Ms. Cortez smile as they watch the students enthusiastically interact, develop questions, and quickly master the new tool—the students are hooked!

*Translation: Meet me in the library at 4th period. We can set up accounts in Diigo.com to select and organize Web sites for our biome research.

What Is Social Bookmarking?

Social bookmarking opens the door to new ways of organizing, classifying, and sharing Web content while also encouraging student and faculty collaboration and higher order thinking. It's similar to Internet Explorer's *Favorites* and Netscape's *Bookmarks*, but with many more features and enhancements that allow users to share bookmarks with each other and to "tag" their Web sites, assigning keywords or terms that are relevant to them. Social bookmarking focuses primarily on creating connections rather than creating content (Richardson 2006, 90). Content is not actually being created through social bookmarking, but connections are being made within the tagging community membership and the content is being grouped through the use of tagging.

Tagging

At the heart of social bookmarking is tagging. It allows the user to not only bookmark the Web site, but apply a non-hierarchical descriptor or term called a "tag." Tags are user-added metadata about a site. It's a process in which the user assigns relevant keywords or tags (descriptors) to a Web site; it makes it a lot easier because controlled vocabulary is not involved and the user does not have to learn a classification system to participate. Usually several tags are assigned; however, if a compound word is needed, the user usually runs the terms together, such as socialbookmarking or uses the underscore, social_bookmarking. Since the user, not the content creator or a professional cataloguer, is the one who is tagging the Web site, the tags are based on the user needs and therefore are very relevant to the user.

The user can see what others have used as tags, and use those same general tags, but are free to create their own personal tag that will later help them remember why they valued the site. "Tagging is not about the right way or wrong way to categorize something and it is not about accuracy and authority, it's about remembering" (Kroski 2005). "The more search 'metadata' that we can apply to the content we create, the more easily it will be connected to other relevant artifacts, continuing the process of joining the many pieces of the web in flexible and dynamic ways and bringing us closer to the information we need and desire" (Richardson 2006, 93). And tagging is not just used to bookmark Web sites. It's commonly used in many Web 2.0 social tools that gather bits of digital data such as Flickr, 43 Friends, blog posts, etc. The site Technorati tracks tags for posts, blogs, videos, and photos. If you search Technorati using the tag "global warming," it produces lists of numerous blogs covering environmental issues, events, recent videos, photos, etc. Search with the tag "AASL" for the American Association of School Librarians; you'll see a list of school librarians who blog, photos of events related to the organization, videos of school libraries, etc.

Typically, tagging performs seven functions for bookmarks: the first four functions are intrinsic to the tagger and include: identifying what or who the Web site is about; identifying what it is (e.g., article, podcast, blog); identifying who owns it; and refining categories. The last three functions are relevant to the tagger only and include: identifying qualities or characteristics (e.g., funny, inspirational); self reference (e.g., mystuff, first name); and task organizing (e.g., to read, biomes paper). Personally-oriented tags can easily coexist with the more general tags that users apply to sites. Most users are tagging for personal use more than for public benefit, but that the public can benefit from the personal tagging anyway. And so even if the common user is tagging sites instead of trained professionals, "a stable tag pattern emerges after the first one hundred bookmarks are placed for a particular Web site . . . as a result, alternative views exist alongside popular ones without being disruptive to them" (Golder and Huberman, 2009).

Tag Clouds

Users can see their tagged Web sites either as a list or as a "tag cloud." A group of tags create a "tag cloud," a visual representation of the tags used for the site or resource that is weighted (see Figure 3.2). That means that the more a tag is used to describe a Web site, the larger it appears in the tag cloud. Students who are visual learners usually prefer the tag cloud to the tag list, but it's easy to switch between the two. School librarians who set up del.icio.us or Diigo accounts to recommend Web sites for students could create a tag cloud and post it on the library home page or wiki. Students who use del.icio.us can participate by tagging recommended Web sites to the library account.

Pamela Burke from the Marlboro School in Vermont (Burke, 2008) uses del.icio.us extensively with her students and faculty. "When students start a new unit, I plunk the feed for the appropriate tags on their classroom page." Her students then view the feed as a tag cloud.

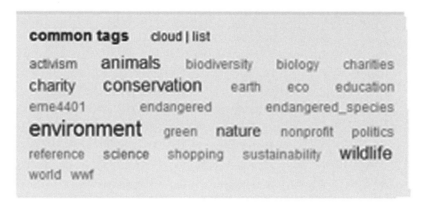

Figure 3.2.   Tag Cloud.

Folksonomy

Before the concept of tagging took hold, information was organized by expert cataloguers, librarians, subject specialists, etc., using a hierarchical system of classification or taxonomy. The idea behind tagging is that a community, working together has the capability of developing a new meaningful tagging system that allows for participation by all. The term, "Folksonomy," coined for the process of creating and assigning tags to Web sites reflects this belief. It's the combination of the term "taxonomy," the science of finding, describing, classifying with the word, "folks." Simply put, it's ordinary, everyday people, "folks," finding and describing Web sites. Folksonomies are created by users and taxonomies are created by professionals. Sometimes the tagging process is referred to as collaborative tagging, social classification, and social indexing. "Collaborative tagging is most useful when there is nobody in the librarian role or there is simply too much content for a single authority to classify; both of these traits are true of the Web, where collaborative tagging has grown popular" (Kroski).

Some libraries offer a combination of subject headings and tags in their online catalogs. The University of Pennsylvania has incorporated social bookmarking into their online catalog which they call Penn Tags; it represents what their educational community is saving and sharing. Members of the Penn community can collect and maintain URLs, links to journal articles and records in Franklin, their online catalog and their online video catalog. Users organize them by tagging and/or grouping them into projects. The Penn Tags home page (http://tags.library.upenn.edu) contains a "tag cloud" of the most popular tags (those that were used at least 107 times).

The larger tags, such as copyright, film, transportation, history, and Philadelphia represent topics or tags that are used the most; the larger the tag, the more times it was used. Figure 3.3 displays the tag cloud of the most recent items tagged. Click on any tag to see

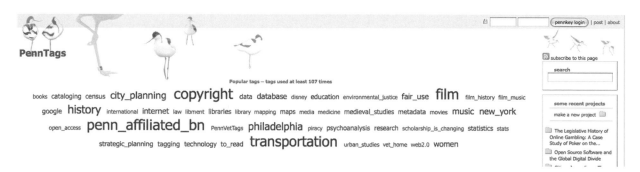

Figure 3.3.   Penn Tags Tag Cloud. Used with permission of University of Pennsylvania Libraries.

what items are included or search through groups of tags organized in the projects section. The site can be viewed and searched by tag owners or by tags. As with most social book-marking tools, you can subscribe via Real Simple Syndication (RSS) to an owner, a project (collection), or a tag, so as they are updated, you'll be notified as to the new content.

There are discussions focusing on the advantages and disadvantages of both folksonomies and taxonomies in the literature and the blogsphere. "Tagging doesn't provide a full body of related terms that might be relevant to the user's need, although they aid in the search for content, help in the discovery of new information and allow one to keep current on popular topics" (Kroski). Some librarians don't believe folksonomies will, should, or can replace traditional classification and taxonomy systems but still others believe it doesn't have to be an either/or situation. The two systems can harmoniously coexist (Etches-Johnson 2006, 58). The fact remains that folksonomic tagging is here and most believe that it "exists for the purpose of making a body of information easy to search, discover, and navigate over time" (http://en.wikipedia.org/wiki/Collaborative_tagging).

There are school librarians, such as Shayne Russell in Tabernacle, New Jersey, who has been using social bookmarking to encourage collaboration and organization. "I have had a couple of social studies project where one teacher teaches all 5 social studies classes for the grade level. We've used one Delicious account for the whole grade level because kids in different classes are researching the same topics. I start them out with a few links and they add more as they find them. For tags, they use whatever is meaningful to them AND their first name—that way it's easy for them to open up their own bookmarks without having to go through everyone else's. The teachers and I can see where they are getting their information, and they are able to find the sites again when they are citing information. Works great!"

Anything that is public and that exists on the Internet can and is being tagged, including Web sites, blogs, wikis, podcasts, screencasts, videos, articles, images, and other media. According to the Pew Internet Report, "28% of Internet users have reported tagging or categorizing content online. On a typical day, 7% of internet users say they tag or categorize online content" (Pew Foundation, 2008). Clay Shirky states that, "The significant benefit of these systems is that they don't recreate the structured, hierarchical categorization so often forced onto us by our physical systems. Instead, we are dealing with a significant break—by letting users tag URLs and then aggregating these tags, we're going to be able to build alternate organizational systems for one another, often without realizing it" (Shirky 2005). Students need to know about the strengths and weaknesses of tagging versus taxonomies as they learn to locate information in online catalogs, specialized databases, and the Web; they both serve the user in different ways and students can use both more effectively with a deeper understanding. Linda Braun (2006, 58) in her book, *Teens, Technology, and Literacy*, suggests we have students compare the two methods:

> The first step in reaching that balance is to help teens understand the global vs. personal nature of traditional and tag searching methods. A perfect example of that is a search for "me" in the library catalog (that integrates tags) and a site like Flickr. It's likely that in a library catalog a search for "me" within the traditional search fields—author, title, subject, description, and notes—will turn up items in which "me" is a part of a title of a specific item. However,

Table 3.1.   Folksonomies versus Taxonomies.

Folksonomies: Advantages	Folksonomies: Disadvantages
Informal, with no need to learn complex system	Quality
Open to the public	Not everyone a good tagger
Lower cost to create	No conceptual relationships among tags
Can respond quickly to change	Errors
Relevant-user's own terms	Inclusion of personal tags that others can't find
Easy to use	Use of single terms—not friendly to compound words, synonyms, homonyms, variant spellings, plurals, etc.
Supports discovery form of browsing	
Gets people involved in creating metadata	
Taxonomies: Advantages	**Taxonomies: Disadvantages**
Quality (created by experts)	Not open to the common man
Accuracy	Need to learn complex system
Standardization	Costly to create
Addresses plurals, compound words, synonyms, homonyms, variant spellings	Responds slowly to change
Hierarchical—shows parent/child relationships and related concepts	More difficult to use

if teens search for "me" as a tag in the library catalog, they will find lists of materials in which the tagger simply wanted to connect the material to his or her personal interest. In other words the results in the traditional form lead to material in which "me" is actually a part of the material—the title. But, the results using tags is all about the tagger and not about the content of the item.

For an interesting look at folksonomy, watch Michael Wesch's YouTube video, "Information R/evolution" (see Figure 3.4). "This video explores the changes in the way we find, store, create, critique, and share information. This video was created as a conversation starter, and works especially well when brainstorming with people about the near future and the skills needed in order to harness, evaluate, and create information effectively" (Wesch).

How Does Social Bookmarking Support Student Learning?

High School Students Collaborate Online in Journalism Class

Eleventh grade journalism students are learning how to evaluate editorial writing as they look at the content for biases, point of view, and use of stylistic techniques. They use a shared Diigo account, set up by their teacher, to bookmark three Web sites that contain editorials on the same

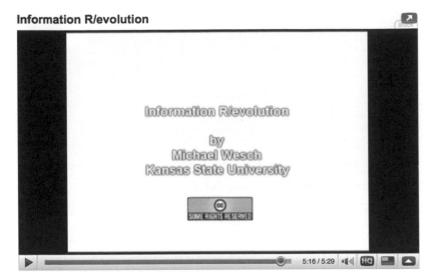

Information R/evolution

topic and add evaluative comments and tags based on their analysis. Once the task is complete, they must then look at two of their classmates' sites and comments and respond by using sticky notes. Each student is responsible for leading a class discussion on the merits of an editorial. Their teacher sees what sites they identify and leaves comments and notes to guide their investigation.

Figure 3.4.   "Information R/evolution" (http://www.youtube.com/ watch?v=-4CV05HyAbM). Used with permission of Michael Wesch (http://mediatedcultures.net).

Elementary Students' Showcase with Twenty-First-Century Tools

At the end of the school year, fourth grade students collect and organize the URLs of their Web-based learning projects to share them with classmates and parents at a year-end "Learning Fair." They use Diigo to bookmark their multimedia Web-based projects, such as a Civil War VoiceThread, the Weather Splashcast, and a podcast on Chihuly's Glass Art; they also shared what they had learned from the project in the comments section. Mrs. Coughlin, the school librarian teaches the students to use customized tags and create a Diigo list of their projects. In this way the students easily showcase their projects at the "Learning Fair" using Diigo's WebSlides and afterwards make them available on the Library's wiki using the Enhanced Linkrolls—her students are on the cutting edge and they are proud of it!

Social bookmarking tools are a natural to support twenty-first-century learning skills; they offer a structure that is intellectually engaging, encouraging students to not only locate but also to collaboratively tag, organize, and evaluate resources—thinking more deeply about the process. By tagging Web sites, students are identifying the content of Web site and organizing it to detect relationships among ideas which will lead to greater understanding. As indicated in the American Association of School Librarian's (AASL) "Standards for the 21st-Century Learner," learning how to effectively use technology to organize information collaboratively is a required twenty-first-century skill.

1.1.8 Demonstrate mastery of technology tools for accessing information and pursuing inquiry.
1.2.2 Demonstrate confidence and self-direction by making independent choices in the selection of resources and information.
2.1.2 Organize knowledge so that it is useful.
2.1.4 Use technology and other information tools to analyze and organize information.
3.1.2 Participate and collaborate as members of a social and intellectual network of learners.
4.1.7 Use social networks and information tools to gather and share information.

Ten Reasons to Use Social Bookmarking in Education

1. Provides a free, efficient, effective, and reliable way to save and organize Web sites, podcasts, wikis, blogs, articles, images, and other media.
2. Creates a collaborative environment. The process is so easy, it's almost transparent: students log on to the social bookmarking site with one click on the browser, form into groups, and share their work.
3. Supports a discovery/exploration process. It allows you to view others' tags and see what Web sites they are tagging.
4. Allows users to tap the "collective intelligence" of the Web. Allows you to see how many times a Web site is tagged by other people—the higher the number, the more likely the Web site has value.
5. Provides the opportunity for "sensemaking" through tagging, annotating, critiquing, or adding descriptions, highlighting, and adding sticky notes.
6. Provides an effective framework to collaboratively evaluate Web sites. Using the comments, highlighting, and sticky notes features students can effectively work independently, and then collaboratively share their findings and ideas and their classmates.
7. Encourages students to analyze the Web site content. Using tags, students gain practice assigning words or descriptors to Web site content.
8. Offers either public access or complete privacy for a class or group of students. Educators can choose what's best for their situation.
9. Supports anytime/anywhere learning—accessible 24/7 on the Internet. Students can login at a convenient time from any computer with Internet access.
10. Integrates with other newer technologies, such as RSS and

Figure 3.5.   Stripling Inquiry Model.

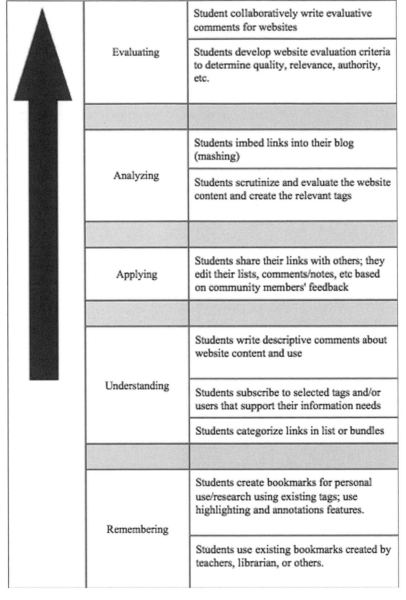

	Evaluating	Student collaboratively write evaluative comments for websites
		Students develop website evaluation criteria to determine quality, relevance, authority, etc.
	Analyzing	Students imbed links into their blog (mashing)
		Students scrutinize and evaluate the website content and create the relevant tags
	Applying	Students share their links with others; they edit their lists, comments/notes, etc based on community members' feedback
	Understanding	Students write descriptive comments about website content and use
		Students subscribe to selected tags and/or users that support their information needs
		Students categorize links in list or bundles
	Remembering	Students create bookmarks for personal use/research using existing tags; use highlighting and annotations features.
		Students use existing bookmarks created by teachers, librarian, or others.

Figure 3.6.   Social Bookmarking and Thinking Skills.

blogging. Students can set up an RSS for a specific tag and librarians can add tag clouds to their library home pages.

Inquiry Learning

Social bookmarking comes into play during the investigation phase of inquiry, when students locate resources, evaluate, and organize them (Stripling 2003). As students locate and organize all different types of information resources, they are applying order to chaos, organizing the resources so that it makes sense to them and so that the information can be retrieved later when needed. This often blends with the next phase, the constructive phase as they start to see patterns emerge, understand the information within a larger context, perhaps even develop new questions, and start to create new meaning. During the investigation phase of inquiry, we want students to carefully think about the information they are gathering and this is where social bookmarking can make a difference. Usually, students simply add new sites to their bookmarks or favorites without much thought to the content or its relationship to their questions, or even worse, just hit the print button—again and again. If you look at Lorin Anderson and David Krathwohl's article "Bloom's Revised Taxonomy" (Encyclopedia of Educational Technology, http:// coe.sdsu.edu/eet/Admin/TOC/index.htm), the bottom level is remembering, which focuses on listing, recognizing, and stating. We want to encourage students to have an increased depth of learning, so by using social bookmarking we can push their thinking to the higher levels, in which they apply, analyze, and evaluate. It all depends on how you structure the learning experience; Figure 3.6 outlines the tasks and thinking levels. Students collaborate as they tag, comment, and share resources within the

Figure 3.7.   Delicious Search Using Habitat Tag.

community of users; they develop evaluation skills as they add details and carefully ana-lyze Web sites and share their findings in the comments/notes field; and they give feed-back to their classmates as they write sticky notes commenting on each others' work. In addition, students can e-mail a copy of any page, marked up with their notes, to people who are not members of the social bookmarking Web site, to share and collaborate.

Exploration and Discovery

One of the real advantages of social bookmarking is the ability to share what you find with others and see what they have "tagged" perceiving additional uses. You might not agree or understand why someone tagged a site with certain words, it most likely has a personal meaning to them; however, it sometimes causes us to think about the topic in a new way. Mary Ellen Bates in her article on tagging agrees that tags often don't produce great results when searching for specific information, however, when we look at tags she suggests we question: Is that an aspect of the idea I missed? (Bates 2006, 64). This encour-ages students to think, reflect, and make meaning of the information they are collecting. Another strategy is to look at the tags for possible synonyms to use in keyword searching.

In the example below, a student could be searching del.icio.us under the tag "habitat." Figures 3.7 through 3.9 are reproduced with permission of Yahoo! Inc. © 2009 Yahoo! Inc. Delicious and the Delicious logo are registered trademarks of Yahoo! Inc.

The third link for the World Wildlife Organization (http://www.Worldwildlife.org) appears promising.

Figure 3.8.   Delicious Link Details.

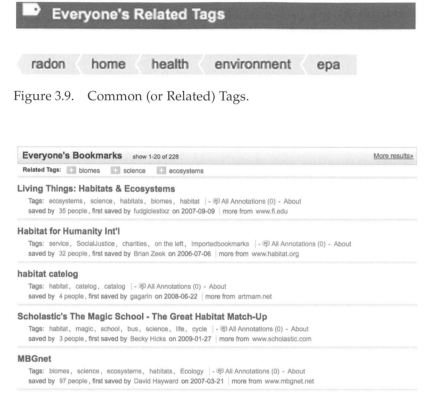

Figure 3.9.   Common (or Related) Tags.

Figure 3.10.   Web Site Tags in Diigo.

When the student clicks on the link to explore its content, a tag cloud appears to the right with related or common tags. The student would then be able to search under the related tags for further information. The student could use tags in the cloud as synonyms for the original tag, habitat. Related tags include environment, animals, conservation, wildlife, nature, biodiversity, and endangered species, as other possible searchable terms to locate more information on habitats.

In Diigo, the concept is the same. When you search under the tag "habitat," a group of four sites appear. If you select one of high interest, you can see tags that others used to describe the content of the site and you can then use some of those same tags to dig for additional sites dealing with habitats. Diigo figures 3.10 through 3.26 are used with permission.

Another way social bookmarking encourages discovery is the ability to have the Diigo toolbar indicate whenever a page you're on has notes left by you or other users, whichever you prefer. You can leave sticky notes and private pop-up annotations, attached to any highlighted text and those notes will remain available whenever you return to the page later. How often have you wished you could mark up a Web site with notes to help you remember something unique about it and share it with others? Kids do.

Teaching Evaluation

The collaborative aspect of social bookmarking adds to its effectiveness, "Research is more collaborative and students are more diligent about evaluating resources because they know their peers will be using them" (Des Roches 2007, 33). You can put Diigo to work for you in teaching Web site evaluation by using the annotations, highlight, and sticky notes features. Set up an account in Diigo and make the account public so students will have access to it without you forming them into groups. Choose a group of Web sites, some high quality and others with little redeeming value, focusing on a single curriculum topic so the Web sites can be compared and evaluated effectively. After developing appropriate evaluation question with students, have them log on to the Diigo page and evaluate each Web site. Instruct them to use the notes field to write their evaluative description guided by the questions the class developed; use the sticky notes to point out specific text, features, graphics, etc., that they think is important to support their evaluation. Ask students to revisit and critique each other's comments using sticky notes. At the end, have them delete the sites that do not receive a high rating and only keep the highly evaluated Web sites to use for their research (see the student handout, Figure 3.11).

Teaching Note Taking

Taking effective notes is crucial for students to understand and make meaning of the information they are locating and gathering. Traditionally, we have taught students to take notes on index cards, copying section of information found in books and print articles, and writing accompanying citations to give credit to the author. Using a social bookmarking Web site such as Diigo gives students the opportunity to take notes electronically, highlight relevant text on the Web site, save text to the bookmark, and use sticky notes to further mark important information. Using these Diigo features allows students to make connections among the different types of information they are collecting, and not just collecting strings of facts (see the student handout, Figure 3.11).

Six Social Bookmarking Strategies for Students OR Best Practices for Social Bookmarking

1. Go beyond just searching others' social bookmarking collections. Locate and tag Web sites that support your interests, assignments, projects, and hobbies.
2. Look at others' bookmarks and tags and use the "copy this" feature as you encounter great links in other peoples' collections. That way they are incorporated into your collection for easy access, including any annotations and sticky notes, if they are public.
3. Use the advanced features, such as highlighting and annotating to enhance your bookmark collection.
4. Share your insights by adding sticky notes to links that you find valuable and tell others how and why you would use them.
5. Subscribe to interesting tags and other users' collections. Let the information come to your desktop.
6. Be daring! Add your Diigo or del.icio.us links or tag cloud to your blog, wiki, or Web site. Share with an even wider audience than just the social bookmarking network.

What Are the Best Social Bookmarking Tools for Education?

There are quite a few social bookmarking Web sites; they all share similar features but a few have unique features. A few of the most popular social bookmarking tools are Diigo, del.icio.us, and Magnolia, among an ever-expanding group on the Web. Del.icio.us is hands down the most well known and most used; however, Diigo is the best social bookmarking Web site for research. We have chosen to highlight Diigo in

Social Bookmarking: How to Evaluate and Tag your Websites
http://www.diigo.com

It is extremely important to evaluate the credibility of the information you are locating and tagging. Follow the instructions below as you tag, describe and evaluate your information for later retrieval in Diigo.com

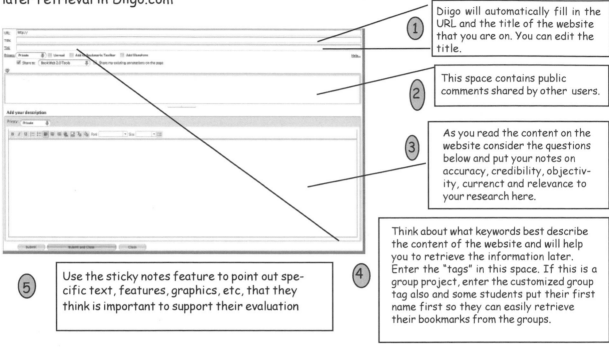

1 Diigo will automatically fill in the URL and the title of the website that you are on. You can edit the title.

2 This space contains public comments shared by other users.

3 As you read the content on the website consider the questions below and put your notes on accuracy, credibility, objectivity, current and relevance to your research here.

4 Think about what keywords best describe the content of the website and will help you to retrieve the information later. Enter the "tags" in this space. If this is a group project, enter the customized group tag also and some students put their first name first so they can easily retrieve their bookmarks from the groups.

5 Use the sticky notes feature to point out specific text, features, graphics, etc, that they think is important to support their evaluation

---

Is this site credible?

1. What is the domain: com, edu, gov?
2. Who created the site? Is there an "about us" link or an email link to contact the creator? Is the site creator associated with any particular organization?
3. Does any information contradict information you've found elsewhere?
4. Does the information appear biased?
5. When was the site created?

Does this site answer my inquiry question(s)?

6. Does the title indicate the content/purpose of the site?
7. Is the information easy to read and understand?
8. Do links support the content? Are they external or internal links?
9. Does the site contain a bibliography of other resources?
10. Does the site contain images, charts, pictures, videos, drawings, etc.? Do they support/ clarify the information on the page?

Advanced Task: Choose two other students' bookmarks in your group and using the Sticky Notes feature, react to their evaluative and descriptive comments.

Figure 3.11.   Student Handout—Social Bookmarking: How to Evaluate and Tag Your Web Sites.

this chapter because it has distinctive features that support active learning and sets it apart from the others. It not only organizes and tags bookmarks, it allows the student to mark up Web pages as they would a paperback book—with sticky notes, highlights, and comments—then share those notes with others. Diigo offers the opportunity to seamlessly collaborate (create a group), identify the key topics/concepts of the Web site (tagging), write brief evaluative or descriptive sentences (in description box), clip a section of text (highlight and save), and collaboratively discuss their work (using sticky notes). We have found that del.icio.us is the most popular, but it doesn't have the sticky note, highlighting, or clipping features that Diigo does. If students already use del.icio.us and they want to use Diigo, don't worry. Diigo allows them to save Web sites to multiple social bookmarking services simultaneously. Students can collaborate with classmates in Diigo but still be saving to their personal del.icio.us accounts.

Comparing Social Bookmarking Web Sites

Most social bookmarking sites share common features such as tagging, bundles, descriptions or annotations, ratings, auto suggested tags, popularly used tags, tag clouds, searching by tag or by user name, storage of collections privately or publicly, subscription by e-mail or RSS, importing and exporting of bookmarks, various browser compatibilities, ease of use, tutorials, and bookmarklets, to name some. Some features are more valuable than others in the educational setting. The chart in Table 3.2 lists the features of each tool.

Six Tips to Make Social Bookmarking Easier

1. **Check for age requirements**. Some social bookmarking tools have age requirements for the creation of a free account. All four Web sites listed in Table 3.2 require the user to be at least 13 years old. If your students are younger, you may want to use Diigo and create what's called a shared account. Set up the account then share the ID and password with the students in class; all use the same one. That way, even the younger children can help build the collection of resources as they search the Internet.

2. **Load a bookmarklet or a toolbar on your browser**. Toolbars are installed on the browser's toolbar and contain all the functions that the tool has to offer. Bookmarklets are little javascripts that allow you to save a Web site to your account without having to log in to it. They are usually less robust but do contain the most important functions of the tool. Bookmarklets are particularly handy if you are working at a shared computer. Click on the bookmarklet and after entering your account ID and password, your new resource is added to your account. Many social bookmarking tools offer both toolbars and bookmarklets to their users. Diigo's bookmarklet is called a "Diigolet" and will allow you to bookmark, highlight, and add sticky notes (see Figure 3.12).

3. **Do a live demonstration**. Do a hands-on demo with students as they fill out the Diigo dialog box. It's also a good idea to review social bookmarking terminology at this time. Don't take it for granted that all kids will know and understand the features of the tool. A few terms you might consider include: dialog box, URL, title, tag, comment, annotation, notes, subscribe, RSS,

Figure 3.12.   Diigo Bookmarklet.

highlight, sticky note, toolbar, bookmarklet (Diigolet), tag cloud, tag list, preferences, and lists.

4. **Add Diigo links to a library Web site or wiki**. To insert your Diigo links into your Web page, all you have to do is copy and paste the javascript. To locate the script, go to "My Tools" from inside your account. You will find a listing for "Enhanced Linkroll," which is used to add your Diigo links to your Web page. You can title the linkroll with a title of your choice and select your whole link collection or those links with a particular tag. You can also define your selection by indicating if you want all of the Web sites with a particular tag to appear, or only those with annotations. It's that easy! (see Figure 3.13).

5. **Add Diigo links to your blog**. Go to "My Tools" from within your account and select either blog this or daily blog post and follow the directions. Supported blogs include WordPress Blog, Blogger Blog, Live Journal Blog, Typepad Blog, Movable Type Blog, Windows Live Space, and Drupal Blog. Neither of these two options requires copying and pasting. You select your blog from a list and enter the URL, your user ID and password, and the Diigo links are automatically imported into your blog (see Figure 3.14).

6. Consider your browser when choosing a social bookmarking Web site; some browsers work better with bookmarking Web sites than others. Plan ahead and decide with the district technology staff what works best in your situation. Most school districts utilize Web-filtering software to block the unsavory and inappropriate on the Web. Your selected social bookmarking tool may have to be unblocked for staff and student use. Examine the tool's specifications to determine which would be best to use within the context of your network and operating system. Look at Table 3.2 for more detail.

Figure 3.13.   Display Options for Enhanced Linkroll.

Figure 3.14.   Diigo "Send to Blog" Dialog Box.

Focus on Diigo

As with other Web 2.0 tools, setting up an account with Diigo is easy. Go to the Diigo Web site (http://www.diigo.com) and click on "Join Diigo." Once you have an account, add the Diigo toolbar

Table 3.2.   Social Bookmarking Web Sites Comparative Chart.

Features	Diigo	Magnolia	Del.icio.us
Title	X	X	X
Tagging	X	X	X
Select tag from others' commonly used tag list	X	X	X
Category/bundles/topics creation	X		X
Bookmarklets	X	X	X
Import of bookmarks	X	X	X
Export of bookmarks	X	X	
Mark collection as public	X	X	X
Mark collection as private	X	X	X
How to tips	X	X	X
Browse by tags	X	X	X
Browse by user	X	X	X
Browse by category or topics	X		X
Search by tags	X	X	X
Search by user	X	X	X
Search in public	X	X	X
Search in my tags	X	X	X
Hot tags/new tags	X	X	X
Popular links	X		X
Subscribe to tags by RSS	X	X	X
Subscribe to user by RSS	X	X	X
Notification by email	X		X
Blogging tools	X	X	X
Tag Cloud	X	X	X
Shows site popularity in five other tools	X		
Advanced search options	X		
Browse by related tags	X	X	
Date added item	X		
Ratings	X	X	
Descriptions	X		X
Notes	X		X
Sticky notes	X		
Archive of page as of date viewed	X	X	
Highlight text on Web pages	X		
Save to other social bookmarking tools simultaneously	X		

Figure 3.15.   Diigo Teacher Console.

to your browser and you're ready to start bookmarking! You can also upgrade your general account to an educator account (http://www.diigo .com/education) that sets up a "Teacher Console" to easily create and manage student accounts and class groups (see Figure 3.15). Students don't need e-mail accounts; user IDs and passwords will automatically be generated for them, placing students in the same class into the same Diigo group, which gives them access to group features, such as group bookmarks and annotations and group forums. Diigo has established special student privacy settings: student accounts can only contact their teacher and classmates, student profiles are not indexed in the people search, nor are they made available in public search engines. Advertisements in the educator accounts only relate to education.

Bookmarking a Web Site

After you install the Diigo toolbar on your browser, click the "Bookmark" option to bookmark a page you want to save; a dialog box will open (see Figure 3.16). As you book-

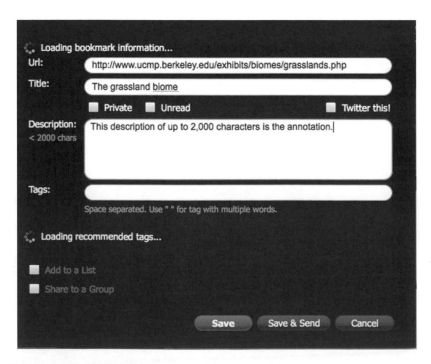

Figure 3.16.   Diigo Bookmark Dialog Box.

mark a Web site, the title, and URL will automatically be filled-in and saved along with the tags you assign to describe the Web site content. Write a description of the Web site (or have students identify how the Web site relates to their research questions), select your preference for keeping it public or private—if you want, add the bookmark to a group or a list or send out a Twitter—and click on "Save."

Understanding the Diigo Toolbar

The Diigo toolbar on your browser offers the same full range of features available as when you log in to

Figure 3.17.   Diigo Toolbar.

your Diigo account. The Diigo toolbar appearance may vary from browser to browser but features will be the same. Figure 3.17 shows the recommended toolbar settings for the beginner. If you want to add more buttons to your toolbar, such as comment, to add sticky notes to Web sites, click on options to add the wanted features.

- *Diigo Dropdown Menu* offers a quick way to see your bookmarks, groups, lists, home, friends; sign out, show or save annotations, import my bookmarks, invite my friends, or get help.
- *Bookmark* allows you, most importantly; to save a Web site, but it also permits you to remove a bookmark and assign default tags with one click.
- *Highlight* allows you to select pictures or text on the Web page containing up to 2,000 characters to save along with your bookmark, as well as how you want to handle annotations on the page: see all, see only private, etc.

Figure 3.18.   Diigo Dropdown Menu.

- *Send* allows you to send content to your e-mail and Diigo friends; to your Blog; to Twitter; to Facebook; and to Get Annotated links or Extract Annotations.
- *Options* relates to settings for the toolbar and menus such as setting highlight styles, keyboard short cuts, and saving to other bookmark services such as del.icio.us, Ma.gnolia, or Simpy.
- *Read Later* marks a page for later reading.
- *Unread* finds unread pages. Once you click a link, its unread status will automatically be converted to read.
- *Recent* provides a list of your recently saved Web sites.
- *Add a Filter* helps sort through saved Web sites by tags, by lists, by read, or by recent, among other options.

Top Features Not to Miss for Educators

Social bookmarking tools support organization and collaboration and in turn, through the interaction with other learners, encourage students to question and see connections. Some special features that support student learning are highlighted below.

Use Tag Clouds

The tag cloud supports the visual learner (see Figure 3.19). Students can toggle back and forth between the tag

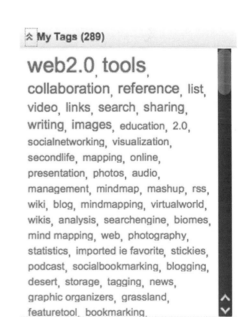

Figure 3.19.   Tag Cloud.

⋀ My Tags (289)	
web2.0	129
tools	64
collaboration	29
reference	23
list	15
video	14
links	13
search	11
sharing	11
writing	11
images	10
education	9
2.0	9
socialnetworking	8

Sort by: alpha | **freq**   Expand
View as: cloud | **list**

Figure 3.20.   Tag List.

cloud to the tag list, a visual and a text list. When looking at the tag list (see Figure 3.20), the number of Web sites using that tag is included in parenthesis while the tag clouds visually represent the tags in your account, the more frequently used, the larger the tag is represented.

Highlight and Annotate

Learners can highlight specific sections of text on Web sites that are relevant to their research questions, saving them time when returning to the page to gather notes for research (see Figure 3.21). The highlighted sections are easily identifiable and the student also has the option to annotate the section (add a description of up to 2,000 characters), which allows the highlighted area to be attached to the saved page. When looking at your saved Web sites, an "Expand This" button appears; clicking on it will show the highlighted annotation. Students can collect multiple highlights on a page and attach them to the Web site—a great feature if the Web site is large and contains a lot of pertinent information.

Post Sticky Notes

Sticky notes can be used in multiple ways to support learning: it allows members in the community to collaborate and discuss the Web sites by leaving descriptive and evaluative notes on shared Web sites offering new meanings from others' comments within the sticky note; it can be used by students to comment and offer criticism of others' comments; and it could be utilized to highlight specific text, sections, and special features of a Web site (see Figure 3.22).

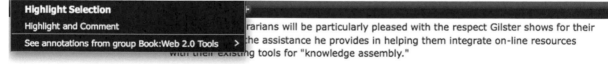

Highlight Selection
Highlight and Comment
See annotations from group Book:Web 2.0 Tools   >

rarians will be particularly pleased with the respect Gilster shows for their
he assistance he provides in helping them integrate on-line resources
with their existing tools for "knowledge assembly."

For more information about Paul Gilster, *Digital Literacy* and his other books, please visit the **Wiley Web site.**

Content Evaluation
When is a globe-spanning information network dangerous? When people make too many assumptions about what they find on it. For while the Internet offers myriad opportunities for learning, an unconsidered view of its contents can be misleading and deceptive. This is why critical thinking about content is the Internet competency upon which all others are founded. You cannot work comfortably within this medium until you have established methods for judging the reliability of Web pages, newsgroups postings, and mailing lists.

Any teacher who has used the Internet in a classroom setting can tell you how troubling it is to see children taking World Wide Web pages at face value, without the evaluative skills to place them in context. In that sense, the Internet can, in the wrong hands, become a tool of propaganda.

Figure 3.21.   Diigo Highlight and Annotate.

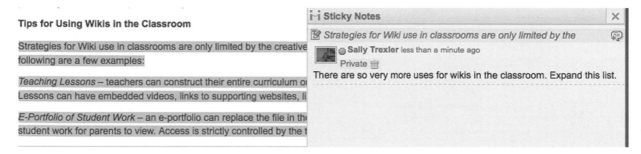

Figure 3.22.   Diigo Sticky Notes.

Extract Annotations

This feature allows learners to collect all the annotations and sticky notes from a particular Web site, or across multiple Web sites. You can print or copy and paste them into a Word document to use for your off-line research notes. If inserted into a word processing program, they can again be copied and pasted into any user-generated digital project (see Figure 3.23).

Subscribe via RSS

RSS brings the information to the learner. It continually updates and delivers the information rather than the user returning to the Web site to seek additional information. It saves time, is very efficient, and offers a more comprehensive approach to the researcher. Diigo offers RSS feed support for lists, groups, etc.

Create Lists

Lists allow learners to better manage their bookmarks by placing them in broad or narrow groups, regardless of tags. Learners can subscribe to a list rather than to all the bookmarks in the account. They can also create a WebSlide, which is like a slideshow of links in each list, to visually share their findings with their collaborative group or their teacher.

Send to Collaborate

Sending allows learners to share a section of a page, a

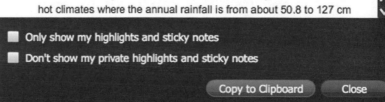

Figure 3.23.   Diigo Extract Annotations.

Figure 3.24.   Diigo Subscribe via RSS.

Send to: some of my friends ☐ Private? ☐ Important? ☑ Include quotes

Start typing a friend's name or email address.

Subject: Chaparral Biome

Message: Rich formatting »

The animals are all mainly grassland and desert types adapted to hot, dry weather. A few examples: coyotes, jack rabbits, mule deer, alligator lizards, horned toads, praying mantis, honey bee and ladybugs.

Quotes:

Chaparral Biome

• Chaparral is characterized as being very hot and dry. As for the temperature, the winter is very mild and is usually about 10 °C. Then there is the summer. It is so hot and dry at 40 °C that fires and droughts are very common.

(Send) (Cancel)

Figure 3.25.   Diigo Send to Collaborate.

collection of pages, or links contained in one of their lists to other teammates or to a colleague or another student to keep them up-to-date on important findings. The recipient does not have to have a Diigo account or a Diigo toolbar installed, and, all the highlights, annotations, and sticky notes are included. Don't overlook the other means of sharing—sending to your blog, to Twitter, or to Facebook.

Share with Enhanced Linkrolls

Adding linkrolls to a Web page, blog, or wiki allows learners to share bookmarks with a specific audience (e.g., classes, grades, or clubs) and a wider audience. The links will appear as a tag list or a tag cloud. Even if students are collaborating with others in your class or school, they can reach out to others not geographically close and get feedback.

Create a Group

Creating a group allows you to collaborate with various people with whom you share interests. You can create multiple groups for multiple purposes so that you do not have to share your entire collection with everyone, but rather share selected resources with others who share your interests. A student or teacher can create a group for a social studies project and just share Web sites appropriate to that project with others in the class. They can have a different group to share science class resources and yet another group for sharing links with the English class. The beauty of the group function is that as new Web sites are added, you can also indicate that you want to share with a particular group by using the drop-down box and selecting the group name when you are in the tagging process. The group members automatically receive an e-mail notifying them that new resources have been added and they just click on the links to explore them more closely.

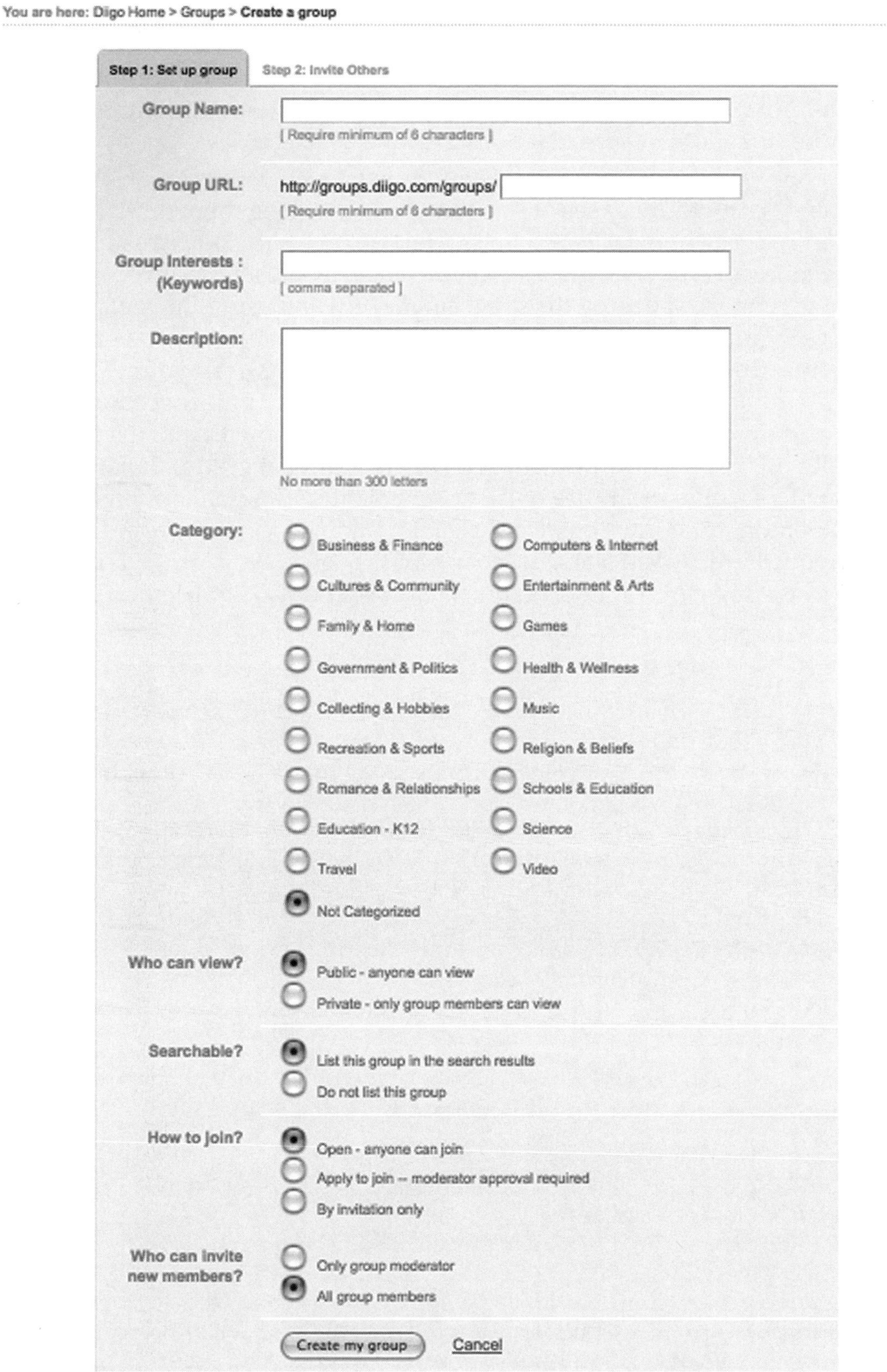

Step 1: Set up group	Step 2: Invite Others

Group Name:

[Require minimum of 6 characters]

Group URL: http://groups.diigo.com/groups/

[Require minimum of 6 characters]

Group Interests :
(Keywords)

[comma separated]

Description:

No more than 300 letters

Category:

○ Business & Finance   ○ Computers & Internet

○ Cultures & Community   ○ Entertainment & Arts

○ Family & Home   ○ Games

○ Government & Politics   ○ Health & Wellness

○ Collecting & Hobbies   ○ Music

○ Recreation & Sports   ○ Religion & Beliefs

○ Romance & Relationships   ○ Schools & Education

○ Education - K12   ○ Science

○ Travel   ○ Video

◉ Not Categorized

Who can view?

◉ Public - anyone can view

○ Private - only group members can view

Searchable?

◉ List this group in the search results

○ Do not list this group

How to join?

◉ Open - anyone can join

○ Apply to join -- moderator approval required

○ By invitation only

Who can invite
new members?

○ Only group moderator

◉ All group members

(Create my group)   Cancel

Figure 3.26.   Diigo Create a Group.

Action Steps

1. Open an account on a social bookmarking Web site; add bookmarks, tags, annotations, etc. Edit your browser's favorites or bookmarks and import the links into your social bookmarking Web site.
2. Look over your school's curriculum map, units of study, and information fluency curriculum to see where social bookmarking might best support learning.
3. Introduce your students to the social bookmarking tool by using the handout in Figure 3.11. Review the parts of the screen area using the proper terminology so everyone is speaking the same language when using the tool. Model how you use your own account so they begin to understand how it works.
4. Introduce your faculty to social bookmarking. Ask your administrator for 20 minutes at the next faculty meeting. Set up a public account ahead of time and demonstrate a few features focusing on how this tool supports' student learning. Follow it up with brief presentation at grade/department meetings with specific examples of other schools' use of social bookmarking.
5. Demonstrate how powerful social bookmarking can be. Add a tag cloud to your library Web site, a teacher's Web page, a blog, or a wiki. Put a link next to the tag cloud that explains what it is and how to use it.

Media Resources

Annotating With Diigo; February 2, 2009; 55 sec.; http://www.youtube.com/watch?v=vGgiyYKdCEQ.

Diigo Presents WebSlides (New Version); September 16, 2007; 2:41 min.; http://www.youtube.com/watch?v=o8ytul9YKH0.

Diigo V3: Highlight and Share the Web! Social Bookmarking 2.0; March 19, 2008; 3:59 min.; http://www.youtube.com/watch?v=0RvAkTuL02A.

Getting Started With Delicious; April 5, 2007; 7:43 min.; http://www.youtube.com/watch?v=NGXElviSRXM.

Social Bookmarking: Making the Web Work for You; April 8, 2008; 9:27 min.; http://www.youtube.com/watch?v=kcecBgRd3ig.

Social Bookmarking in Plain English; Lee Lefever; 3:25 min.; Commoncraft; http://www.youtube.com/watch?v=x66lV7GOcNU.

References and Additional Resources

Bates, Mary Ellen. 2006. Tag, You're It! *Online* 30:64.

Braun, Linda. 2006. *Teens, Technology, and Literacy; Or Why Bad Grammar Isn't Always Bad*. Westport, CT: Libraries Unlimited.

Burke, Pamela. Shared in an e-mail to the author on February 1, 2008.

Des Roches, Donna. 2007. All Together Now. *School Library Journal* 53 (1): 33.

Encyclopedia of Educational Technology. http://coe.sdsu.edu/eet/Articles/bloomrev/.

Etches-Johnson, Amanda. 2006. The Brave New World of Social Bookmarking: Everything You've Always Wanted to Know but Were Afraid to Ask. *Feliciter* 52:52–58.

Golder, Scott and Bernardo A. Huberman. 2005. The Structure of Collaborative Tagging Systems. HP Labs. http://www.hpl.hp.com/research/jdl/papers/tags/tags.pdf.

Kroski, Ellyssa. 2005. The Hive Mind: Folksonomies and User-Based Tagging. http://infotangle.blogsome.com/2005/12/07/the-hive-mind-folksonomies-and-user-based-tagging/.

Raine, Lee. 2006. Pew Internet and American Life Project. http://www.pewinternet.org/PPF/r/201/report_display.asp.

Richardson, Will. 2006. *Blogs, Wikis and Podcasts, and Other Powerful Web Tools for Classrooms*. Thousand Oaks, CA: Corwin Press.

Russell, Shayne. In an e-mail message to the author on February 2, 2008.

Shirky, Clay. 2005. Ontology Is Overrated: Categories, Links, and Tags. http://www.shirky.com/writings/ontology_overrated.html.

Stripling, Barbara and Sandra Hughes Hassell, eds. 2003. *Curriculum Connections through the Library*. Westport, CT: Libraries Unlimited.

Figure 4.1.   http://www.wordle.net

4

Managing and Organizing Information

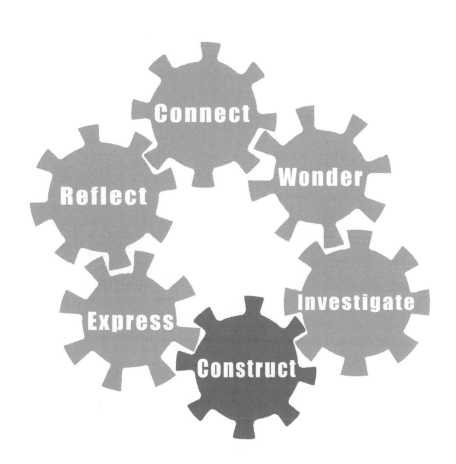

? ESSENTIAL QUESTIONS

What tools support student organization and management of information?
What organizational strategies help to reduce information overload?
How do personal information spaces support learning across the curriculum?

It's Friday morning and Terell arrives at school early. Knowing that the library will be open, he heads there first and makes himself comfortable at a computer near the window. He knows everything he needs this morning is on his "Personal Information Space" that the librarian and tech teacher had helped him to create at the beginning of the year. He leans back on his chair, grabs the keyboard and puts it on his lap, and starts typing in the URL—presto, his personal work/information space pops up. This really keeps him organized and saves so much time.

He first checks his to-do list for new tasks and then his calendar to see if any dates have been added by his teachers or classmates. The calendar is electronically shared so it's easy for one member to create a new entry or an update and send it out electronically to align with other members' calendars. Terell's eyes scan the screen as he quickly glances at the local weather report, The New York Times headlines, and the word-for-the-day. He clicks on his e-mail link and scans his inbox for the latest messages; he decides most messages can wait till later. He opens his Twitter account and "tweets" two friends to tell them he is in the library and then focuses his attention on the social studies project. He clicks on the second tab on the top of the screen, "My Collaborative Space," where he has organized collaborative tools and resources to work with his classmates and teachers: Google Docs, MindMeister, LooseStitch, class wikis, and a RSS feed on the his current social studies topic—World War II. Clicking on Goggle Docs, he opens up the shared document, reads the latest change made by his classmate, writes some additional notes, and saves it. Wow, it's getting late—five minutes until his meeting with the science team. His assignment is to find an article on global warming. Quickly he clicks on the third tab, research, on his information space. He scans the resources on the page and zooms in to find an article. With a few minutes to spare, he sets up a new feed on the topic using Google Alert. Satisfied that he has enough info for the meeting, he checks YouTube on his fun page to see how many hits his language arts classes' video project received—cool, over 100 so far! Eight o'clock—times up! He quickly stuffs his back pack and heads off to the team meeting while adjusting the volume on his iPod Shuffle.

How Can Web 2.0 Tools Be Used to Support Organization and Management of Information?

Organizing and managing information can be daunting for students. First, consider the amount of information that is being published every day, "A weekly edition of *The New York Times* contains more information than the average person was likely to come across in a lifetime in seventeenth-century England" (Wurman 1989, 32). And, the amount of information produced is increasing by 30 percent each year (Woods, The Information Explosion). Some of the increase is due to the new types and channels of information and the ease of duplication and transmission of data across the Internet. New types of media such as blogs, wikis, Nings, and podcasts are working their way into the mainstream on the tails of digital information channels such as Really Simple Syndication (RSS) feeds, e-mail, and text messages. According to the 2008 IDC report, The Diverse and Exploding Digital Universe, "by 2010 the digital universe will be 10 times greater than it was in 2006" (IDC, 2).

Add students' personal communications, scheduling demands, and academic deadlines (for research and group projects, team meetings, class assignments, readings, extracurricular events, etc.) to the mix, and the result is a student swimming in a sea of data, confused and frustrated. It's called information overload: when there is too much information to digest, a person is unable to locate and make use of the information that one needs. When one is unable to process the mass amounts of information, overload occurs. In her article, "The Information Overload: Causes," Kelly Woods gives five causes of information overload.

1. The sheer volume of information available.
2. The convenience of information access (due, in large part, to continuing developments in technology).
3. The diversity of information available.
4. The continuing trend of interdisciplinary research.
5. The fact that more searching is being done by end-users (not professionals).

Inquiry Learning

Librarians need to take a leadership role, in collaboration with classroom and technology teachers, to teach students the skills, strategies, and tools for organizing and managing digital information. To be information literate, a student should understand and develop an organizational support system that allows them to not only locate, evaluate, and apply information, but also do it effectively and transparently. These management/organization skills are embedded into the information literacy process continuum in the construct phase and are usually described as arranging, categorizing, extracting, grouping, and selecting (see Figure 4.2). Using Web 2.0 tools and applications, librarians can help students make sense of information, organize it into manageable pieces, and develop a broader understanding of the information world. It's through this organization process that they start to see patterns and relationships between pieces of information and how to make sense of the information.

The tools included fall into five categories— start pages, graphic organizers, calendars, outliners, and list makers. They assist the user in managing their work flow, in meeting their deadlines, and avoiding procrastination. The last item is so important when working within

Figure 4.2.   Stripling Inquiry Model.

a group where students rely upon their team members to accomplish their assigned tasks on time. If information is organized, users retain the information more efficiently, communicate more effectively, and more readily recognize if additional information is needed or if some information needs to be discarded. These tools are essential alongside the conventional productivity tools of word processor, database builder, or spreadsheet maker, offering substantial benefits to students learning. As with all Web 2.0 tools, they allow 24/7 access and are interactive.

What Are Personal Information Spaces?

Personal information spaces (or start pages), a home away from home online, are coming into their own. They differ from the old-style Web portals because they can be personalized by adding RSS feeds, widgets, and Web pages in multiple-tabbed pages. Although many people use them as well-organized RSS feed readers for blogs and other dynamic Web sites, that's only scratching the surface—start pages can help students get organized, motivated, and involved with their learning. Where users once had to check several different Web sites to locate desired information (news, weather, e-mail, research topics, blogs, class wikis, etc.) and tools (to-do lists, calendars, outliners, graphic organizers, etc.) now information is contained within the start pages, saving the searching, selecting, loading, and logging-on time that was previously spent on those tasks.

These start pages can be thought of as "Personal Information Spaces," a place where students have access to the tools and information to explore, create, and interact with classmates and teachers; it's a strategy for learning. The new American Association of School Librarians' (AASL) "Standards for 21st-Century Learners," encourages learners to develop organizational skills to support inquiry learning:

1.1.8 Demonstrate mastery of technology tools for accessing information and pursuing inquiry.
1.1.9 Collaborate with others to broaden and deepen understanding.
2.1.4 Use technology and other information tools to analyze and organize information.
3.1.4 Use technology and other information tools to organize and display knowledge and understanding in ways that others can view, use, and assess.
4.1.6 Organize personal knowledge in a way that can be called upon easily.

Excerpted from "Standards for the 21st-Century Learner" by the AASL, a division of the American Library Association. © 2007, American Library Association. Available for download at www.ala.org/aasl/standards. Used with permission.

Web 2.0 principles of user participation and collective intelligence come into play as students plan, organize, and manage their personal information spaces and collaborate with classmates and others.

In designing and using personal information spaces, students learn to:

• Organize multiple types and channels of information effectively.
• Use creativity to design appealing and effective spaces.
• Practice authentic information literacy skills.

- Evaluate Web-based tools and incorporate them into a well organized information spaces.
- Be motivated and engaged in their own learning.

There are quite a few start page services/Web sites available on the Web, but after evaluating them on customization, appearance, ease of use, content, and social features, only three passed muster. The top ones, Netvibes (http://www.netvibes.com), Pageflakes (http://www.pageflakes.com), and Protopage (http://www.protopage.com), are heavily used in K-12 because pages can be shared and made public. Another popular one is iGoogle (http://www.google.com/ig), however, it is intended for personal use rather than group use since it contains the user's e-mail and therefore not ideal for sharing with others. The start pages share common features such as: tabs, themes, and color customizing when designing your space; Web feed capability, widgets, Web search capability, toolbar bookmarklets, and e-mail on the content side; and mobile phone versions and browser compatibility on the accessibility side.

Key information elements, such as news, weather, stock reports, sport scores, videos, music, photos, blogs, and podcasts; tools such as calendars, to-do lists, and search engines; and communications such as e-mail and Skype can be added by using RSS feed technology or widgets which are third party micro-application that can be embedded into a Web site and automatically updated. Widgets, supposedly short for "window gadget," are available on free widget libraries found on the Web, as well as from the start page Web sites. Feeds are also available on the start page site and the choices seem endless; they are grouped into categories such as news, business, sports, technology, shopping, travel, and entertainment.

Figure 4.3.   Netvibes Widgets.

Creating Personal Information Spaces

Creating a personal information space is a good process for students to go through: it helps them to think through what information resources and tools they need and what the best way to organize them is. The process is deeply embedded into the information skills continuum and aligns with "Standards for 21st-Century Learners." Teachers and media specialists should provide suggestions of resources and tools for students to see and models to learn from, but be sure to give them the support and time to organize their personal information spaces themselves.

There are primarily two steps—select content and arrange the content on the page(s). The first step involves students thinking about what tools and resources they need. What types of projects are they working on? What tools are generally used—word processing, graphic organizer, and/or social bookmarking? What applications or Web pages do students check every day—news, sports, YouTube, and/or school Web site? Providing students with potential tools and resources will help guide their thinking and offer new possibilities (see Figure 4.4).

The second step is to arrange the items in a logical way. For middle and high school students, use four pages, each with a tab for easy access: a personal page, a research/library page, a collaboration page, and a fun page; for elementary students, use one

Student's Personal Information Space

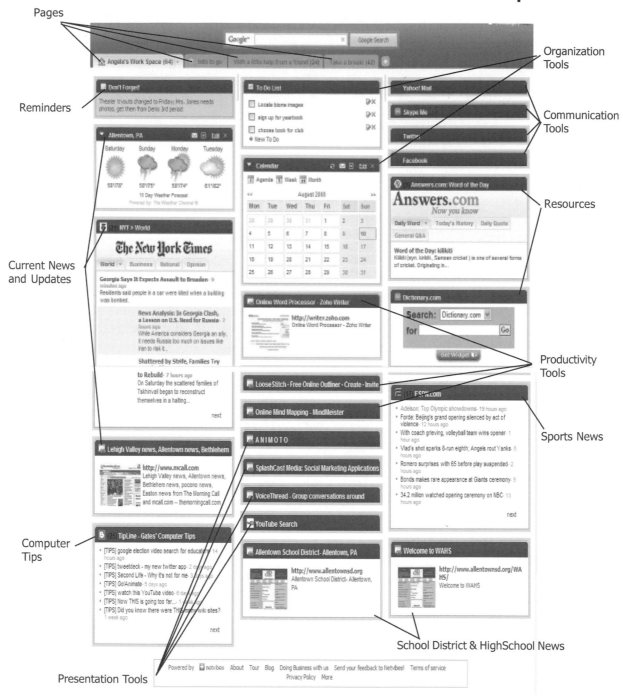

Figure 4.4.   Student's Personal Information Space.

Identifying Your Information Needs:
Planning a Personal Information Space

Welcome to your online home away from home; when you login this is the first webpage you'll see - a place where you have access to the tools and information resources to explore, create and interact with classmates and teachers; it's a strategy for effective learning.

Student Information Space - Personal Page

This planning sheet is to help guide you to choose the best tools and resources to support your learning and communications needs.

There are primarily two steps — select content and arrange the content on the pages. The first step involves thinking about what tools and resources you need. The second step is to organize the information on four separate pages with tabs: Your Personal Space, that includes current news, email, organization tools, reminders, etc; Your Research Page, that includes links to online databases, school library online catalog, search engines, etc.; Your Collaborative Space, that includes links to your class wikis, blogs, and tools that support collaboration and Your Fun Page, that includes comics, YouTube, puzzles, etc. There are a few services that offer free Information Spaces (start pages): NetVibes (http://netvibes.com; Protopage (http://portopage.com) PageFlakes (http://pageflakes.com)

Instructions: Read over the list of potential tools and resources that you might want to inlcude in your Information Space; everyone's space will be different. Choose what you need to stay organized, complete tasks, stay connected to classmates and teachers, locate information, etc. Your Information Space can be changed and edited as your information and communication needs change. Ask your teachers and school librarian for additional recommendations. As you design your SIS ask yourself some questions: What types of projects are you working on? What tools do you generally use? What applications or web pages do you check every day? What are the most authorizative resources online?

Figure 4.4.   continued

Let's Get Started

1. *Personal Information Space* focuses on tools and resources that support your information and organization needs. Check below which type of information you want to include on your personal page:

KEEP UP TO DATE ON THE NEWS

School district website ☐
Local newspaper site ☐
State and/or natioanal
    news websites ☐
Sports news ☐

BE ORGANIZED
Reminder notes ☐
To Do List ☐
Calendar ☐

OUTLINE, BRAINSTORM, WRITE...
LooseStitch Outliner ☐
ZohoWriter/Google Docs ☐
Mindmeister/Bubbl.us ☐

COMMUICATE
Email ☐
Skype ☐
Twitter ☐
Facebook ☐

Share Media
Animoto ☐
VoiceThread ☐
YouTube ☐
SplashCast ☐
Podcasts ☐

2. *Collaborative Work Space* is an area to gather common work spaces and resources from classmates and teachers Check below which type you want to include:

COLLABORATIVE CONTENT DEVELOPMENT
my teachers' blogs ☐
class wiki pages ☐
classmates' blogs ☐
RSS feeds on specific
    group topics ☐

COLLABORATIVE TOOLS
Google Docs pages ☐
MindMeister ☐
Loose Stitch ☐

3. *Library/Research Information Space* targets information resources that you will need for school assignemnts, research and projects. Check below which information sources you want to add to your research page:

RESOURCES
School library online databases ☐
School and public library catalogs ☐
Diigo bookmarks ☐
Google Scholar ☐
Wikipedia ☐
Google Earth ☐
Thesaurus ☐
Search widgets ☐
Video ☐
Podcasts ☐
Blogs ☐

---

4. *Fun Page*

☐ Flickr
☐ Wordle
☐ Comics
☐ MTV news
☐ Sudoku
☐ Movie times
☐ Good Reads website
☐ How Stuff Works

or two pages: a subject-specific page, such as one for reading or science, and the second page should be a fun page. Examples of these are in figures 4.5–4.8. Of course, there are so many great variations of information spaces: A student could have a start page with tabs for language arts, math, and science, and place content appropriate for those topics on them. A teacher could have tabs for class sections or for the various disciplines that he or she teaches. The class information space could contain a dictionary, an encyclo-

An important feature of creating and using information spaces (start pages) is the ability to bring desired Web pages onto your start page (rather than just linking to them), placing such items as the school's online catalog or online subscription database right next to Google, Wikipedia, etc. Face it. Kids go to Google first; however, if online subscription databases and other authoritative resources are sharing the same space, it increases the chances of students using them. Just select the "Web Page Widget," available on all three top start page tools (Netvibes, PageFlakes, and Protopage). Edit the widget by entering the URL and name of the resource and clicking on the "Add This Widget" to my page. Presto! Equal billing!

Figure 4.5. Information Spaces: Top Feature Not to Miss—For Educators!

pedia, a calculator, the teacher's wiki or blog, to-do list for class activities, a calendar with assignment/project due dates, podcasts pertinent to the topic of study, and links to valuable Web sites. And it would all be centralized for easier student access. A large part of the learning process is for students to analyze their information needs and create personal information spaces that support their learning and information needs.

A typical high school student's personal information space is shown in figures 4.6 and 4.7. Each page contains boxes into which feeds or widgets are placed. You can have multiple pages, each with its own tab. Students choose themes and move the boxes around to customizable layouts. Content is organized by pages and accessed by clicking the page tab, making it easy to locate items. Content has the appearance of being integrated and can be moved from one section to another seamlessly. The example in figures 4.6 and 4.7 shows the two pages in a high school information space (for a fictitious student named Angela), first in outline form and then in graphic form. Please note: these pages were created by the authors and are not "default" pages within Netvibes.

1. Personal Information Space
    a. Productivity Tools
        i. To-do list
        ii. Calendar
        iii. Zoho Writer
        iv. Graphic organizer
        v. Outliner
    b. Important News
        i. Weather
        ii. News headlines (national)
        iii. News headlines (local)
        iv. School home page
        v. Sports news (national)
    c. Communications
        i. E-mail link
        ii. Skype link

             iii. Twitter
             iv. Facebook
        d. Resources
             i. Dictionary
             ii. Word of the day
        e. Presentation Tools
             i. VoiceThread
             ii. Animoto
             iii. SlideStory
             iv. YouTube

2. Collaborative Work Spaces (see Figure 4.6)
    a. Collaborative Content Development
        i. Teachers' blogs
        ii. Class wiki pages
        iii. Classmates' blogs
        iv. RSS feeds on specific group topics
    b. Collaborative tools
        i. Google Docs pages
        ii. MindMeister
        iii. LooseStitch

3. Library/Research Page (see Figure 4.7)
    a. Resources
        i. School library online databases
        ii. School and public library catalogs
        iii. Diigo bookmarks
        iv. Google Scholar
        v. Wikipedia
        vi. Google Earth
        vii. Thesaurus
    b. Search Widgets
        i. Video
        ii. Podcasts
        iii. Blogs
    c. Tools
        i. Zoho Notebook
        ii. Noodle Bib Express

4. Fun Page
    a. Comics
    b. Flickr
    c. Goodreads
    d. Sudoku
    e. Movie times
    f. How Stuff Works
    g. People.com
    h. MTV news
    i. Wordle

Figure 4.6. Netvibes Personal Information Space—Angela's Collaborative Page.

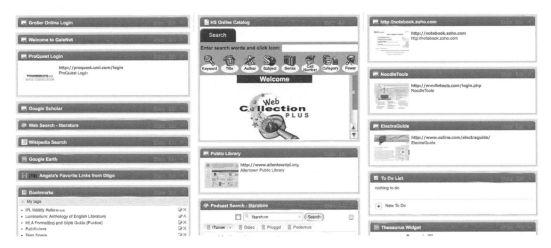

Figure 4.7. Netvibes Personal Information Space—Angela's Research/Library Page.

Figure 4.8. Protopage Elementary Reading Information Space.

Personal information spaces can be created on specific subjects and are especially valuable for elementary and middle school students. The example in Figure 4.8 demonstrates an elementary space focusing on reading using Protopage.

How Can I Use Web 2.0 Tools to Support Specific Organization and Management Tasks?

If users are interested in having students use a few organizational tools, separate from the student information space, there are stand-alone tools that can be used for specific organizational tasks. The most popular are calendars, graphic organizers, outliners, and to-do lists.

Online Calendars

For students, organizing time, setting task priorities, and keeping track of events and important due dates can be daunting. If students work in groups, keeping track of who has responsibility for what is an added responsibility that begs for clear organization and calendaring. The new breed of Web 2.0 online calendars, that allow for collaboration and 24/7 access, prioritize and manage tasks, effortlessly note division of labor and task responsibilities, and help improve the work process, could be the answer. These tools help manage projects, tasks, meetings, and appointments. There are a myriad of calendaring tools available online. Some are standalones, such as 30 Boxes (http://30boxes.com/welcome.php), AirSet (http://www.airset.com/AirSet.jsp #app.Home), and Cozi (http://www.cozi.com). Even among those titles, additional features expand the intent beyond the idea of just calendaring such as file sharing, messaging, and contact lists. Other online calendar tools such as Google Calendar (http://www.google.com/calendar/), Yahoo! Calendar (http://calendar.yahoo.com/), and Zoho Planner (http://planner.zoho.com/) are stand-alone modules but are a subset of larger office suite tools that also include other modules such as spreadsheet, presentation, word processing applications, document sharing and collaboration, searching, and note taking. Those tools will be addressed in Chapter Five, which deals more closely with content collaboration.

The stand-alone online calendars look like their print counterparts, but can be manipulated to show a daily, weekly, monthly, or yearly view of tasks and, of course, can be shared, so that when one member of a team adds or updates a date or event, it can be sent electronically to other team members' calendars.

Features include items such as:

- Event begins and end dates, times, repeatability option, and details.
- Reminders sent by e-mail or Short Message Service (SMS)—and 30 Boxes even offers Twitter.
- To-do list that is printable, can be e-mailed, reordered by dragging and dropping.
- Subscription by RSS.
- Sharing via e-mail (30 Boxes allows for buddy list, blog posting, My Space posting, and by tags).

- Privacy features.
- Code to imbed into Web sites or blogs.
- Searches within the calendars for specific events.
- Support of subscriptions to other calendar tools.
- Mobile phone component.

A good stand-alone calendar is 30 Boxes, which includes a variety of great features.

Twelve Things to Know about 30 Boxes

1. Event entering or editing includes places for notes, reminders, and tags.
2. Tags can be color coded.
3. Events can be searched by tags.
4. Personal Web settings include spaces for the following programs so that people can contact users a variety of ways.
   AIM
   Yahoo
   MSN Messenger
   Skype
   Personal avatar
5. Sharing can be done by allowing others to see the total schedule, the total schedule *except* private events, or through a custom view that specifies particular tags, i.e., just share a science group schedule with team (with tag "science"), or just share an English project schedule (with tag "eng project") with classmates.
6. Contains a to-do list that can be printed or e-mailed.
7. Uses e-mail or SMS to send reminders.
8. Can post 30 Boxes schedule or events on MySpace, Facebook, Blogger, Flickr, Webshots, Word Press, Vox, LiveJournal, Twitter, or other RSS Feeds by entering ID information for those tools in the Web settings section of a 30 Boxes account. Users only have to update your schedule in one place.
9. Includes a location for your event and the ability to add a Google map for the address
10. Add an event by e-mail.
11. Import contacts from Yahoo! Mail, Gmail, Outlook, Hotmail, and Plaxo.
12. Outlook, iCal, or a Yahoo! Calendar users can add events in those tools to a 30 Boxes calendar.

Using any type of calendar is a boost to organization, but Web 2.0 calendars have the added advantage of sharing and updating events and meetings electronically. Sharing by invitation is a *safe* way for students to collaborate with other students in their project groups. For example, a student can share by tag and rather than have everyone in his or her group see everything on his or her calendar, just show the pertinent details to group members under the tag "Science" or "English."

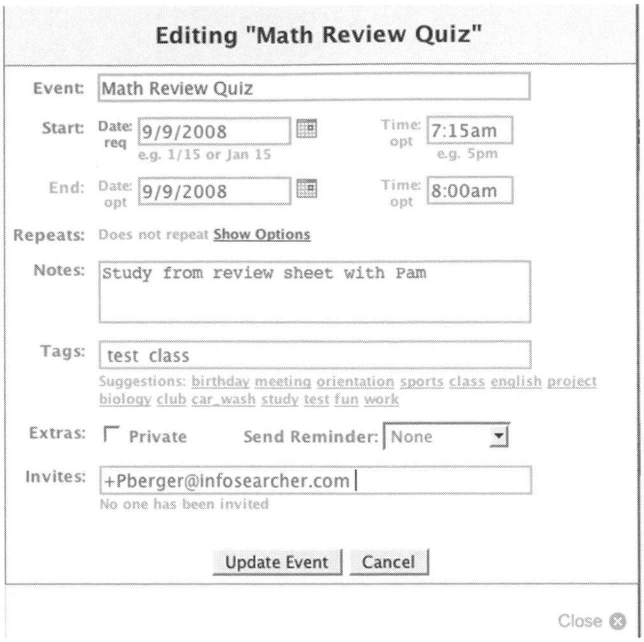

Editing "Math Review Quiz"

Event: Math Review Quiz

Start: Date: 9/9/2008 req e.g. 1/15 or Jan 15   Time: 7:15am opt e.g. 5pm

End: Date: 9/9/2008 opt   Time: 8:00am opt

Repeats: Does not repeat **Show Options**

Notes: Study from review sheet with Pam

Tags: test class

Suggestions: birthday meeting orientation sports class english project biology club car_wash study test fun work

Extras: ☐ Private   Send Reminder: None ▾

Invites: +Pberger@infosearcher.com
No one has been invited

Update Event | **Cancel**

Close ⊗

Figure 4.9.   30 Boxes Editing Event Entry.

Benefits of Using Online Calendars

Online calendars help keep students' lives in order, both academically and personally. Any calendar will allow the user to plan ahead and avoid scheduling conflicts but online calendars make group scheduling and collaboration easier. They allow for sharing so members can add, delete, and edit events. Task responsibilities can be noted along with the task and due date, and multiple calendars can be created and maintained for various groups and projects across the curriculum. For those worried about privacy, settings can be set to allow public viewing or invite viewing which is by invitation only. Many of the online calendars even provide notifications, reminders, and alerts so team members can receive an electronic invitation to attend a meeting.

Let's take a closer look at 30 Boxes. You can quickly enter the event and then click the add button. From there, edit the event to add more details.

Students can set the start and end date and time, make it a repeatable event, enter notes and tags (which are searchable and sharable), set the privacy level, set a reminder (by e-mail or SMS), and invite others to the event (see Figure 4.9).

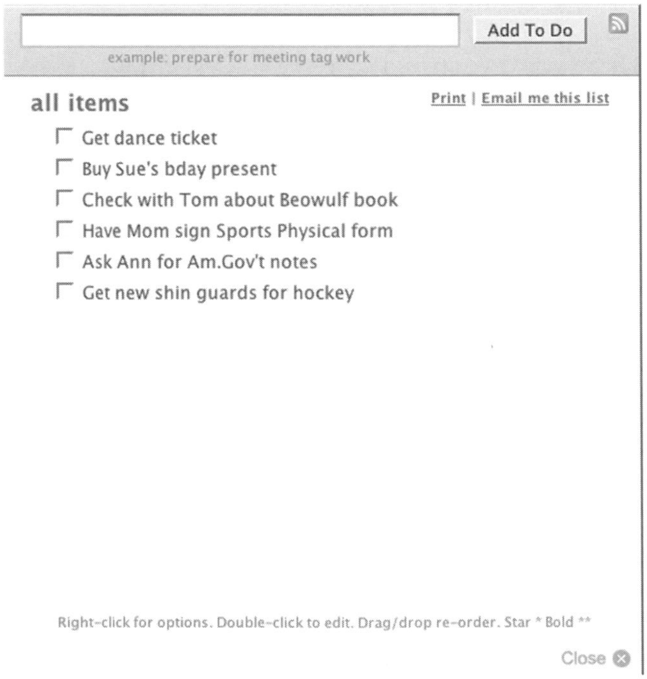

They can quickly add items to the to-do list and either print it out or e-mail it to themselves or their classmates. Click on any item and edit it or delete it. It is an easy way to itemize tasks to be accomplished and names could be included to assign the task (see Figure 4.10).

By entering their own user identification into the boxes for the various applications, users can update their calendar or events into those programs and requires that they only have to update their calendar in one place (see Figure 4.11). If a student has a Twitter account and enters their Twitter account username, they can be sent reminders of events using Twitter. If a student wants to receive text messages on their cell phone, they just enter their phone number, phone carrier, and time zone into the SMS reminders dialog box.

[   ] **Add To Do**
example: prepare for meeting tag work

all items   Print | Email me this list

☐ Get dance ticket
☐ Buy Sue's bday present
☐ Check with Tom about Beowulf book
☐ Have Mom sign Sports Physical form
☐ Ask Ann for Am.Gov't notes
☐ Get new shin guards for hockey

Right-click for options. Double-click to edit. Drag/drop re-order. Star * Bold **

Close ⊗

Figure 4.10.   30 Boxes To-Do List.

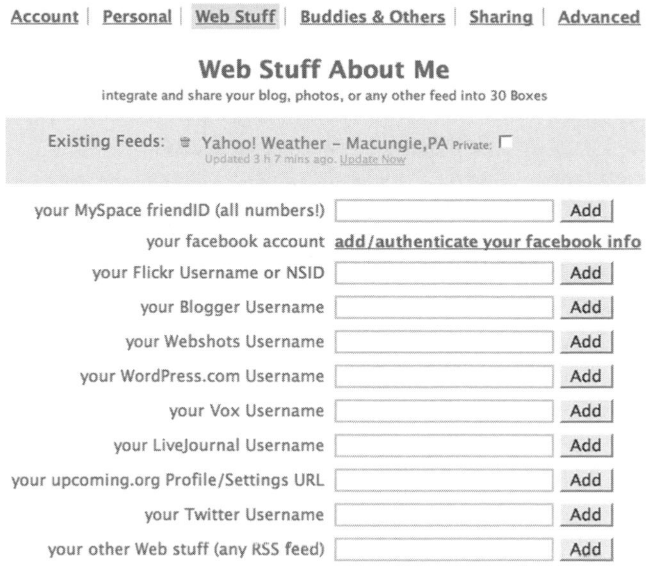

Use the shared view default (where private events are not shown), share the entire view (including private events), or create a custom view to share. The custom view shows how users can select a particular tag or several tags to share.

Graphic Organizers

Graphic organizers are not new to education: elementary students use Venn diagrams to compare and contrast frogs and toads, middle school students use a herringbone graphic to identify the main idea and supporting details of a short story, and high school students use a concept map to brainstorm key questions regarding the disappearance

Figure 4.11.   30 Boxes Web Settings.

of the rain forest. Graphic organizers, mindmaps, and concept maps have been used for many years as a visual tool for gathering, sifting, sorting, and sharing information in many disciplines. They visually represent concepts, information, or knowledge that allows the mind to see meaningful visual patterns and relationships and construct new insights and understandings.

Newly developed electronic organizers have removed some of the barriers of previous print-bound organizers and allow for the free collaborative flow of creativity and information among students. They are used in all types of learning: brainstorming, memory development, visual thinking, problem solving, classifying, and communicating. Because it's digital, students can easily edit, revise, and quickly add to an organizer or map, encouraging students to think in new ways, see connections and patterns, and clarify their thinking. They allow the user to represent, by text, symbol, or images, existing knowledge on a topic, making it easier to identify the gaps in understanding, and what needs to be further researched for a fuller understanding of the topic.

There are free graphic organizer templates available on the Web for various applications across the K-12 curriculum: compare or contrast ideas, sequence events, hypothesize, analyze ideas, predict, and evaluate. These are good examples of the how graphic organizing can be used to organize thinking, such as the fishbone model. They can be found at teAchnology (http://www.teachnology.com), Eduscapes (http://www.eduscapes.com), and Write Design Online (http://www.writedesignonline.com).

There are quite a few good Web-based online organizer/mapping tools including Bubbl.Us (http://bubbl.us/), Mind42 (http://www.mind42.com), MindMeister (http://www.mindmeister.com), and WiseMapping (http://www.wisemapping.com/c/home.htm). They all share some common features as shown in Table 4.1.

As can be seen from the comparison chart in Table 4.1, Bubbl.Us is the simplest of the tools with the least features. It is a simple graphic organizing tool—making it a good choice for elementary school. It's a great brainstorming and outlining tool that allows students to add rectangular shapes and connect them in a meaningful manner.

Table 4.1.   Comparison Chart of Graphic Organizers/Mapping.

Feature	Bubbl.Us	WiseMapping	Mind42	MindMeister
Unlimited maps	X	X	X	six for free
Drag and Drop	X	X	X	X
Zooming	X	X	X	X
Create siblings and children	X	X	X	X
Shapes can be colored	X	X	X	X
Collapse/expand branches	X	X	X	X
Invite other to view only or to collaborate	X	X	X	X
Real-time collaboration	X	X	X	X
Maps can be imbedded into other tools	X	X	X	X
Print maps	X	X	X	X
Export map as PDF	X	X	X	X
Auto save		X	X	X
Concept boxes use text	X	X	X	X
Publish maps to blogs or Web sites. URL or code provided		X	X	X
Concept boxes use links		X	X	X
Concept boxes use icons		X	X	X
Concept boxes use images			X	X
Add notes			X	X
Simultaneous editing/changes seen after refreshing screen	X			
Simultaneous editing/changes seen immediately		X	X	X
Revision history		X	X	X
Export maps as images/PNG, JPEG, GIF		PNG, JPEG	PNG	GIF, JPG, PNG
Add/search by tags		X		X
Skype conference call imbedded			X	X
Add Widgets			X	X
Track changes by collaborator—color coded			X	X
Export map as RTF			X	X
Notification of changes sent by e-mail				X
Notification of changes sent via SMS (Twitter)				X
Assign tasks (with priorities)				X
Add attachments				X

They can change the color of the "bubble" and the text as they "drag and drop" the bubbles around the screen; share with friends (full editing access or read-only); embed their maps into blogs or Web sites; print or save as image files (.jpg or .png file); and create unlimited maps or "sheets" (see Figure 4.12).

Of the other three most popular organizers, Mind42, MindMeister, and WiseMapping, MindMeister is the only one that includes all the desired features listed; however, users are limited to six free maps at one time (you can delete a map to make room for a new one or pay a membership fee). In comparing graphic organizers, look carefully at their features, some are more important than others. A top-priority feature for students is the ability to enhance the concept box with visuals.

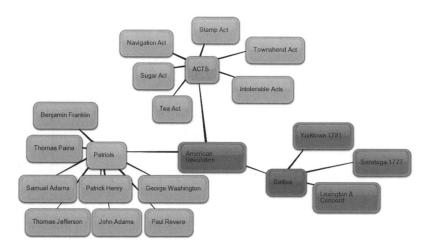

Figure 4.12.   Bubbl.Us Map on American Revolution.

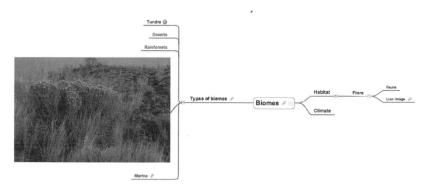

Figure 4.13.   Mind42 Map Showing Graphic.

Mind42 and MindMeister use links, images, and notes in the concept boxes. Figure 4.13 demonstrates the similar Mind42 map with an added graphic of the grasslands. Mind42 images used with permission of IRIAN Solutions GmbH.

The Benefits of Using Graphic Organizers

Graphic organizer tools are useful across the curriculum whenever students need to brainstorm, visualize ideas, discern main ideas, organize ideas, show relationships among ideas, and refine creative thinking. Research has found the graphic organizers are most effective for students when educators, "provide instruction to students and model their use; students are given the opportunity to practice using them; and teachers provide feedback to students" (http://writedesignonline.com). With the new Web 2.0 tools,

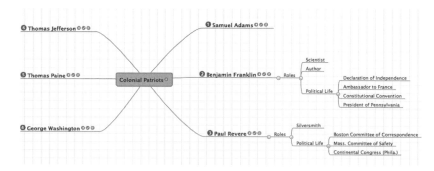

Figure 4.14.   MindMeister Map on the Colonial Patriots Showing Expanded Nodes.

Colonial Patriots

I. Benjamin Franklin (link)

  A. Roles

    a). Scientist
    b). Inventor

    c). Author
      1. Poor Richard's Alamanck

    d). Political Life

      1. Declaration of Independence

      2. Ambassador to France

      3. Constitutional Convention

      4. President of Pennsylvania

Figure 4.15. MindMeister Map on American Patriots in Outline Form. *Note: Further editing was done in Microsoft Word to add indentations and numerations.*

students can now do all of these thinking activities collaboratively with classmates, pushing the envelope a little further by being in a social learning context. Also, graphic organizers present information visually and in small pieces (keywords, phrases, and/or graphic icons or photos) and are therefore very supportive of visual learners as well as English language learners. They support the following AASL's "Standards for 21st-Century Learners":

1.1.7 Make sense of information.
2.1.2 Organize information so that it is useful.
2.1.4 Use technology to analyze and organize information.
3.1.4 Use technology . . . to organize, display knowledge and understandings in ways others can view, use, and access.
4.1.6 Organize personal knowledge in a way that can be called upon easily

Excerpted from "Standards for the 21st-Century Learner" by the American Association of School Librarians, a division of the American Library Association. © 2007, American Library Association. Available for download at www.ala.org/aasl/standards. Used with permission.

Outliners

A very similar tool to graphic organizers is online outliners. Like the traditional outlines and graphic organizers, they serve as a step in the thinking/writing process as they support students to organize their ideas in a logical manner. An outline presents a picture of the main ideas and the subsidiary ideas of any subject; it graphically displays the hierarchy of ideas and their relationship to each other. Students use outlines for a variety of tasks to write an essay, a term paper, a book review, or a speech, or close reading of any topic. For any of these, an outline will show an overview and important details.

Using an outlining tool is helpful to student collaborative groups as they design projects together. The members can contribute ideas and concepts within a natural flow of give and take. As the work progresses, the headings' or subheadings' content can be assigned to the different group members so each member has some accountability for the project. One of the most useful outliners for students is LooseStitch (http://www.loosestitch.com).

The toolbar on the top of the screen provides users with

An important feature of graphic organizers is the ability to add notes and links to items in maps. Graphic representation of information enhances learning for all students but is especially helpful for the English language learner and visual learner.

Figure 4.16. Graphic Organizers: Top Feature Not to Miss—For Educators!

the tools to begin immediately: to add/delete a row, indent, move up/down, expand all/collapse all, print, and import Outline Processor Markup Language (OPML) files from other outlining tools. Click on the text and easily change the color, add, delete, indent, outdent, move up/down, and save (see Figure 4.17).

Figure 4.17.   LooseStitch Outline and Create Space.

To make it more collaborative, students can invite others to view their outline or share it by sending an e-mail invitation or send it as a text file (and later open in Microsoft Word), as OPML file (compatible with other outline tools), and/or as HTML. Using the code provided, publish it to your Web site or blog and LooseStitch will automatically update any changes users make or make it public on the LooseStitch server by entering a description of the outline contents and adding tags in the section called "Get Ideas." Users can create as many outlines as needed and invite as many friends as wanted—it's all free.

Some online outliners are targeted to specific purposes.

Thesis Statements

The Ozline Thesis Builder & Outliner (http://www.ozline.com/elcctraguide/thesis.html) and an Online Outliner @www.2Learn.ca (http://www.2learn.ca/senior/compass/senoutline.html) have a dialog box for either a thesis statement or a topic idea with guiding questions. The main screen of this type of online outliners is very minimal offering the user a series of input boxes where text can be entered and then manipulated to show a hierarchical relationship between main idea and supporting ideas. The outline generated is based on user input and can be saved as a page link, sent as a link to a friend or teacher. If using 2Learn.ca, print and use the outline as a guide for your writing; or in Ozline.com, copy and paste your outline into a Word document.

Cambridge Rindge and Latin School (http://www.crlsresearchguide.org/New OutlineMaker/NewOutlineMakerInput.aspx) offers guiding tips as users enter concepts and numeration and indentation is built into this outliner. Outlines can be printed or saved as a text file for further work in Word. The more advanced students will find it useful, as a basic understanding of outlining rules would prove helpful in manipulating this particular outlining tool.

An important feature of online outliners is the ability to convert the outline to a text file, using the Export as .txt or .rtf feature. This allows students to bring the outline into a word processor to flesh out the major concepts and begin writing.

Figure 4.18.   Outliners: Top Feature Not to Miss—For Educators!

I. Parts of a plant
 A. Roots
   1. Carry water and nutrients
 B. Stems
   1. Carry water and nutrients to leaves
     a). xylem cells move water
     b). phloem cells move food
   2. Provide support for the plant
     a). nodes are where leaces join the stem
     b). internodes are between the nodes
 C. Leaves
   1. Catch light
     a). cuticles
     b). veins
   2. Create food by photosynthesis
 D. Flowers
 E. Fruit
 F. Seeds

Figure 4.19. LooseStitch Outline in RTF Format.

Quick and Easy

Sproutliner (http://sproutliner.com) is an easy tool to use to quickly get ideas down with easy editing, drag and drop to rearrange content (an advantage over using paper and pencil), and a help box with brief directions on using the tool. To begin, enter the name of your outline, add concepts by entering text and then clicking the Enter or return key. To make concepts indent below a heading, enter your text and then use the Shift+Enter keys. When finished, print out the outline. Another tool to explore is Checkvist (http://checkvist.com)—it is new and show great promise.

Read*Write*Think (http://www.read writethink.org/) has a barebones little outliner, called a NoteTaker for grades 3–12 in the interactive area. Users can opt to include bullets, Roman numerals, or letters in the outline.

Thirteen Reasons to Use Online Outliners

1. Provide a sense of purpose and direction for the written piece.
2. Indicate what will be written about in each paragraph.
3. Help to organize ideas.
4. Help avoid repetition.
5. Help keep from forgetting to include anything.
6. Save time.
7. Help with the flow of the written piece.
8. Help with the transition from idea to idea.
9. Lend themselves to group collaboration (those that can be shared) and design for a project.
10. Provide a visible structure of a written piece.
11. Show relationships between ideas.
12. Provide an ordered overview of what is written.
13. Make it easier to see major and minor points.

Online To-Do Lists

In Arnold Lobel's much loved children's book, *Frog and Toad Together*, one of the chapters, *A List*, tells the story of how Toad, after making his to-do list, becomes inconsolable when it is captured by the wind and flies away. Toad stood frozen as Frog ran after it. Sadly, he was unable to retrieve it; however, the story ends happily as Toad writes the list on the ground with a stick as best as he can remember it, crosses out the each item completed, and then lays his head down to fall asleep. Although most of us, including our students, don't take to-do lists quite as seriously, they do serve an important function. To-do lists capture tasks so they are not forgotten and therefore give everyone peace of mind—just what Toad needed to fall asleep. It's the "benefits that come from getting task commitments out of your brain and into a consistent location—namely, a list, something by which users can concretely follow your progress towards some defined goal" (McNamee, http://www .britannica.com/blogs/2007/01/on-lists-and -listmaking/).

Popular online list makers include Ta-da List (http://www.tadalist.com/), Remember the Milk (http://www.rememberthemilk.com/), Bla-bla List (http://blablalist.com/), Todoist (http://todoist.com/), TaskTHIS (http://taskthis.darthapo.com/), tasktoy (http:// www.tasktoy.com/), and gubb (http://www.gubb.net/). They share some common features such as:

- Ability to create multiple lists
- Editing
- Sorting/reordering (using drag and drop)
- Sharing
- RSS syndication
- Printing

Some list makers, such as Ta-da List, are very simple and easy to use. Students can create a free account and log in. First, begin a list by typing the items one by one and clicking on "+Add this item." Each time users add an item, it will immediately appear on the list, along with the box to add more items.

Resort items, if needed, by dragging and dropping the item to its new location in the list (see Figure 4.20).

Share with others by sending an e-mail invitation; these individuals can then edit your list.

Remember the Milk is a more feature packed to-do list (see Figure 4.22). It allows students to organize their tasks into tabs and tags, set priorities, make time specific tasks with automatic reminders and repeat intervals, take notes, and collaborate among users.

Most list making tools require an e-mail account to register and some require students to be 13 years of age to use. Check requirements for the particular list maker that appeals.

Figure 4.20.   Ta-da List Showing Re-sort Mode.

Seventeen Reasons to Use Online List Makers

- Organize tasks.
- Create a loose plan to reach goals.
- Help set prioritiesTrack progress.
- Allow for collaboration.

If you plan to have students work in collaborative groups, teaching them to break down the project and assign tasks to each member helps a lot in the overall planning stages. An added benefit of Web 2.0 to-do lists is the ability to assign tasks to individuals and to search the various tasks by tags. Group member names could be entered along with the task or the group member's name could be used as a tag. Clear accountability helps sustain and support collaboration.

Figure 4.21.   Lists: Top Feature Not to Miss—For Educators!

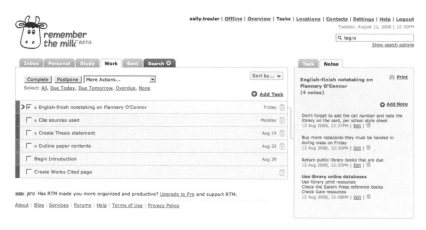

Figure 4.22.   Remember the Milk—Task List with Four Notes.

- Make tasks easy to read.
- Help de-clutter the mind.
- Help motivate the user to complete task (as tasks are checked off).
- Encourage better time management.
- Are accessible 24/7.
- Are shareable.
- Help defeat procrastination.
- Don't require complete sentences—words or short phrases suffice.

- Help get things accomplished.
- Keep tasks from getting lost or forgotten.
- Offer a measure of control over your life.
- Help de-stress your life.
- Provides a central storage space for tasks.

Action Steps

1. Explore the three recommended start pages (Netvibes, Protopage, and Pageflakes) to determine which one best suits the needs of your students. Work with a collaborative teacher to develop a curriculum information space to use with his or her students.
2. Ask administrator to share this tool at the next faculty meeting. Develop a few information spaces in different curriculum areas and demonstrate how easy it is to add widgets and feeds, including online subscription databases. Be sure to explain the advantages to students. Offer to meet with teachers in grade levels, departments, and individually, to create information pages for his or her classes.
3. Model the start page for students. Use the "Planning the Personal Information Space" (see Figure 4.4). Have students contribute ideas for inclusion, or if old enough, have them create their own start page, then model and guide the activity.
4. Review the curriculum and see where outlining, calendars, to-do lists, and graphic organizers can best support the inquiry/information literacy process.
5. Create a screencast using Jingproject.com to help students and faculty use the organizational tools in this chapter. Post the videos on the library Web site, blog, or wiki. Ask students to help design and create them.

Media Resources

Bubbl.us Basics: Brainstorming and Mind-Mapping Online; May 31, 2007; 9:20 min.; http://www.youtube.com/watch?v=AllXU_3nktU.

Free Brainstorm/Mind Mapping Software (Bubbl.us); March 25, 2009; 6:37 min.; http://www.youtube.com/watch?v=I2nrVVqikjE.

Mindmeister; April 29, 2008; 4:28 min.; http://www.youtube.com/watch?v=Ca58W1Q-oLw.

Mindmeister—Mindmaps with Team Spirit; September 20, 2007; 9:34 min.; http://www .youtube.com/watch?v=FChJkOch0Fw.

Pageflakes; November 15, 2007; 6:10 min.; http://www.youtube.com/watch?v=UAq4tanY0ao.

Ta-da Lists: Get Your To-Do's Done!; June 22, 2007; 8:18 min.; http://www.youtube.com/watch ?v=Q3ZVwQDt6X8.

Using Google Calendar for a Class Calendar; July 17, 2008; 6:00 min.; http://www.youtube.com/ watch?v=SrqH74JuzK0.

References and Additional Resources

Adam, Anna and Helen Mowers. 2007. Get Inside Their Heads with Mind Mapping. *School Library Journal* 53:24.

Anderson, Mary Alice. 2007. E-Scheduling. *MultiMedia & Internet* 14:29–31.

Boller, Barbara. 2008. Teaching Organizational Skills in Middle School: Moving toward Independence. *The Clearing House* 81:169–70.

Buzan, Tony and Barry Buzan. 1994. *The Mind Map Book: How to Use Radiant Thinking to Maximize Your Brain's Untapped Potential*. New York: Dutton.

International Data Corporation. The Diverse and Exploding Digital Universe: Executive Summary 2008. http://www.emc.com/digital_universe/.

Loertscher, David. 2007. Children, Teens, and the Construction of Information Spaces. *Teacher Librarian* 35:14–17.

McNamee, Gregory. On Lists and Listmaking. *Britannica Blog*. http://www.britannica.com/ blogs/2007/01/on-lists-and-listmaking/.

Morton, Ella. 2008. Start-Page Smackdown: Netvibes, Pageflakes, iGoogle and Live.com. http://www.cnet.com.au/start-page-smackdown-netvibes-pageflakes-igoogle-and-live -com-339286371.htm.

Muchmore, Michael. 2008. It's Snowing Web Content. *PC Magazine* 27:45.

Padilla, Cynthia. 2007. Research 2.0: Useful Web Applications for Researchers. *Online* 31:30–35.

Woods, Kelly. Causes. *The Information Overload*. http://www.slais.ubc.ca/COURSES/libr500/ 03-wt1.2/www/K_Woods/vol3.htm (accessed September 5, 2008).

———. The Information Explosion. *The Information Overload*. http://www.slais.ubc.ca/ COURSES/libr500/03-wt2/www/K_Woods/vol1.htm (accessed September 5, 2008).

Wurman, Richard. 1989. *Information Anxiety*. New York: Doubleday.

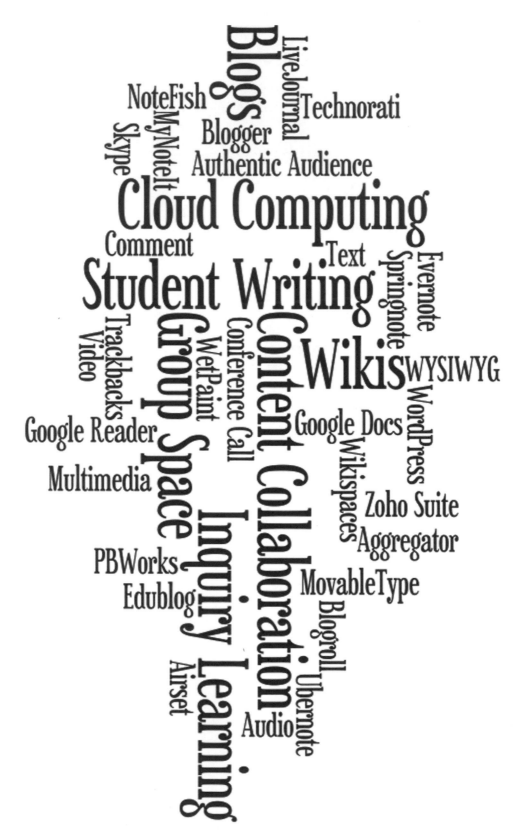

Figure 5.1. http://www.wordle.net

5

Content Collaboration

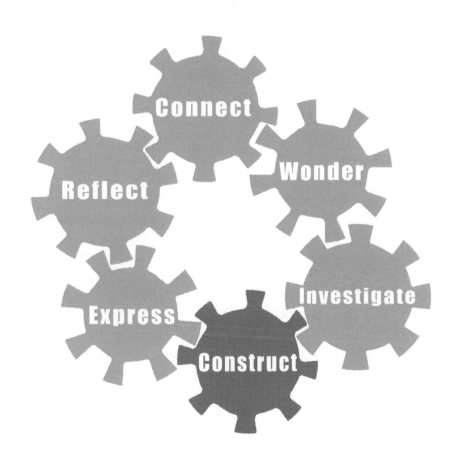

ESSENTIAL QUESTIONS

What are the best Web 2.0 tools to support collaborative content development?
How are educators using these tools to support inquiry learning?
How do these tools enhance student writing?

As a senior, José is excited to begin work on his thesis paper; he gets to focus his energies on researching a subject of his choice. In these last few months of high school, he's become restless and looks forward to the doing this project. He listened to last year's seniors' thesis presentations and was impressed by how different each one was and how enthusiastic the students were about their focus of study, but he also knows how much work and time it took to complete. He's glad that one of his classmates, Zack, has a similar focus and their language arts teacher, Mr. Horn, has agreed that they could work together as a research team.

The first thing they do is to set up a wiki. It's here that they share documents, links to important Web sites, video podcasts, post questions, and personal journaling. As they progress through their research and start to write, they agree to use Google Docs; they love the simultaneous editing feature. They keep both of these tools private, just giving rights to their teacher and Mrs. De Silva, their librarian, who give them suggestions on both resources and search strategies. Using these tools gives them freedom to collaborate 24/7 and also helps to organize and structure their work. Mr. Horn and Mrs. De Silva periodically check in with them via their wiki to leave suggestions questions and notes.

As Jose and Zack continue to do research, they come across one author who seemed to be the expert on their topic. They read almost everything they can get their hands on that she published but they still have questions; they need to talk to her. They decide to e-mail her and ask if she will Skype with them. She agrees. Jose and Zack "call" the content expert through Skype. They ask permission to record the call to capture the details. For an hour, the two high school researchers discuss their mutual passion and knowledge on the topic with an expert in the field. As they speak, Zack and Jose add the suggested Web sites and resources she mentioned to their wiki, share their thesis and research outline that's on Google Docs, and get immediate feedback. By the time the Skype call is over, they have a clearer direction to pursue, are able to fine tune their essential questions, and feel they are ready to post their first "expert" podcast on the class wiki to share with their classmates. They know they still have a lot of work to do, but they are feeling it's all worth it as they high-five each other at the end of their Skype call.

What Are Content Collaboration Tools?

Content collaboration tools, such as wikis, blogs, Google Docs, and Zoho Suite, provide students with appealing, collaborative, online environments that support questioning, engagement, and sharing of ideas. As students share information, exchange ideas, and question each other, it provokes them to examine their existing knowledge and devise a plan to pursue their unanswered questions. These tools encourage collaborative learning: a blogger finds his or her "voice" through sustained reflection (writing and feedback); a team of students collaboratively add content to the class wiki, and student partners collaboratively research and write using Google Docs. Learning has a social context and these tools provide a collaborative environment to question, share, analyze, and synthesize. The American Association of School Librarians' (AASL) "Standards for the 21st-Century Learner," encourage the use of technology to collaboratively contribute as a member of a social and intellectual network of learners:

1.1.9 Collaborate with others to broaden and deepen understanding.
1.3.4 Contribute to the exchange of ideas with the learning community.

1.4.2 Use interaction with and feedback from teachers and peers to guide own inquiry process.

2.1.5 Collaborate with others to exchange ideas, develop new understandings, make decisions, and solve problems.

3.1.2 Participate and collaborate as members of a social and intellectual network of learners.

4.3.1 Participate in the social exchange of ideas.

Excerpted from "Standards for the 21st-Century Learner" by the AASL, a division of the American Library Association. © 2007, American Library Association. Available for download at www.ala.org/aasl/standards. Used with permission.

How Do These Tools Support Inquiry?

A distinguishing characteristic of Web 2.0 tools is the ability to "harness the collective intelligence," thus allowing users to share and collaborate. Each type of Web 2.0 tool accomplishes this task in a different way: the tools in this chapter create a space for collaboration, content development, and interaction and in doing so, encourage analysis and synthesis of information. In the inquiry process, learners start with questions, they think about what they know about the subject, where they will find relevant information and, how they will organize, manage, and evaluate the information. Then, the really hard part comes, the need to do something with the information, other than copying and pasting it—the need to analyze and synthesize the information so that it makes sense, and so that they understand the relevance of the information to their questions and create new meaning. As students move through these inquiry phases of connect, wonder, investigate, construct, express, and reflect, they prefer to dash through the investigate phase to the express phase—ignore the important thinking and "sense making" that takes place in the construct phase—and typically, copy the information and paste it into a PowerPoint with lots of bullets, color, and wiz bang but very little understanding of the subject. Learners need to examine the evidence and resources they have found to draw conclusions and arrive at new understandings.

What Are the Best Content Collaboration Tools for Education?

The Partnership for 21st Century Skills (P21) has identified collaboration as one of the key skills necessary for survival in the twenty-first-century workplace. In the P21 "Framework for 21st Century Learning," they define collaboration as the ability of students to demonstrate the ability to work

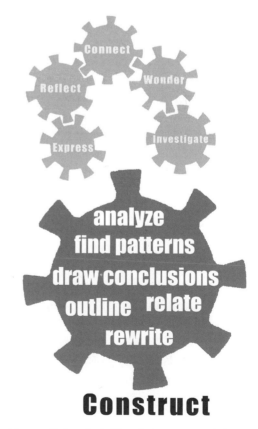

Figure 5.2.   Stripling Inquiry Model.

effectively and respectively with diverse teams, exercise flexibility, and willingness to be helpful in making necessary compromises to accomplish a common goal and assume shared responsibility for collaborative work and value the individual contributions made by each team member (http://www.21stcenturyskills.org/). "Easily accessible and user-friendly, collaboration tools allow students to explore, share, engage, and connect with people and content in meaningful ways that help them learn" (Lomas 2008, 4). For the purposes of this book, collaboration tools are defined as those that enable remote collaboration, encourage document construction, and are designed so that there is an expectation of active participation.

Wikis

Wikis are the quintessential collaborative tool. Users can easily incorporate a wide variety of information formats: text, photos, graphics, videos, animation, links, and feeds, without knowledge of HTML coding. Students can work online, synchronously or asynchronously, eliminating the hassle of scheduling onsite meetings. Wikis offer educators a variety of viewing and editing options that are sure to meet any districts' policies; the editing and viewing settings can be designed as public, private or semi-private, open to the world, or for members only.

What sets them apart from other Web-based tools is the potential they provide for collaboration. Content is usually created by a number of authors, providing a variety of perspectives on the topic addressed. Wikis focus on *authoring* content, rather than just *downloading* existing content on the Web. Student authors select, evaluate, write, revise, edit, and publish information and ideas to their collaborative wiki Web site. The term "wiki" comes from the Hawaiian word for "quick" or "fast" meaning that users can quickly create and share information on a Web site. It's also quick and easy to set up a wiki. Three basic steps are required: name the site, add the creator or administrator's name and password, and set the level of privacy desired—who can read and edit the wiki. After that, the what you see is what you get (WYSIWYG) editing mode allows for fast content input.

Wikis and Student Learning

Wikis are versatile but they are most powerful when used to support a collaborative thinking process:

- Collaborative research, enabling student researchers to share their data online
- Collaborative problem solving, for groups to share their understanding and come to consensus
- Dynamic journals or notebooks, for organizing notes, ideas, and brainstorming
- Electronic portfolios, for collecting and organizing electronic resources
- Portals, designed to be the starting point for a specific topic or subject
- Resource aggregators, such as a bibliography or pathfinder, to guide students to good resources (Lamb and Johnson 2008).

Additional suggestions for using wikis include: presentation space, personal start page, lesson summaries, course syllabus, course links, resource notes or class handouts, school or class newspaper, showcase for student projects, course evaluations,

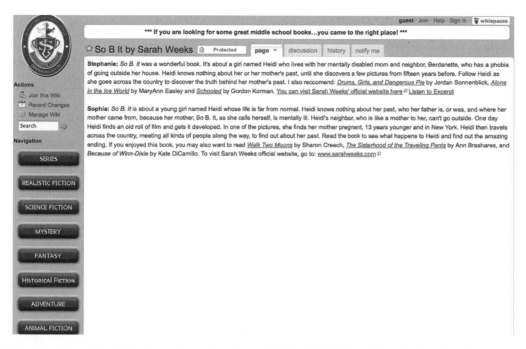

Figure 5.3.   Student Book Review from Southern Lehigh Middle School. Used with permission of Corry Robbins.

venue for posting surveys and forms, school, class or library calendar, and student-created classroom vocabulary list.

To see a glimpse of how wikis are being used in schools, let's take a mini tour. Start at the Southern Lehigh Middle School wiki created by librarian Corry Robbins, entitled SLMS Book Exchange (http://slmsbookexchange.wikispaces.com). At this first stop, browse over 485 student book reviews listed by eight genres and a section for series books. After receiving training, students at Southern Lehigh post a brief book synopsis and recommendation for any book in the library collection. The review criteria and process pushes the kids to think and write carefully. Some reviewers compare books to similar works, include links to author sites and create podcasts (see Figure 5.3).

Second Stop is the Internet Public Library wiki for teens—IPL's Teen Poetry Wiki (http://www4.ipl.org:8080/index.php/Main_Page). Step right up: this wiki allows teens to post their own poetry, and in a space called "Open Mic," as a member comment and offer feedback to the teen poets. To promote a safe environment, IPL.org requires teens to become members of the wiki, while encouraging teen poets to keep themselves anonymous by using a screen name. They also post a disclaimer regarding appropriateness (no stereotyping, swearing, violence, sex, etc.). Other areas of the wiki that users will want to check out are: exquisite corpse (a game), word play experiments, poet of the week (with links), recommendations and inspirations (things that inspire the teen poets), and teen space poetry links. Next stop is a social studies classroom (see Figure 5.4).

Mr. Bruce's U.S. History wiki was created by eighth graders in Union City, Michigan (http://mrbruceshistory.wikispaces.com/). "Created for students by

Figure 5.4.   IPL Teen Poetry Wiki.

students, the pages here offer valuable information that can be referenced by anybody looking for help with topics such as the branches of government, checks and balances, the Articles of Confederation, the Constitution, Lewis and Clark, the War of 1812, Manifest Destiny, and so many more!" Also included are map quiz study guides, a syllabus, online assignments and tools, and additional examples of student work. Mr. Bruce shares an inside view of his history classes through his classes' working wiki.

Wikis are used with all curriculum areas. A high school science class wiki, "Impact of Climate Change" (http://primaryextension.wikispaces.com/), outlines requirements for a project on the first page and provides links to related resources, student multimedia projects, and slideshows. A mathematics wiki at Lower Merion High School (http://lmmath.wikispaces.com/) combines the use of a wiki with student blogs. The wiki home page highlights unit summaries which link to student blogs. Explore the variety of content on Mr. Bariexca's Honors English class wiki in Flemington, New Jersey on British Romanticism (http://britishromanticism.wikispaces.com/). The focus is on art, music, and poetry but one of main purposes is to introduce authentic learning. Mr. Bariexca explains, "In the spirit of service learning, I wanted my Honors English students to not only research and present information, but to create a document that can be used as a resource by other students, both here at Hunterdon Central and at other sites." For more examples of how educators are using wiki, go

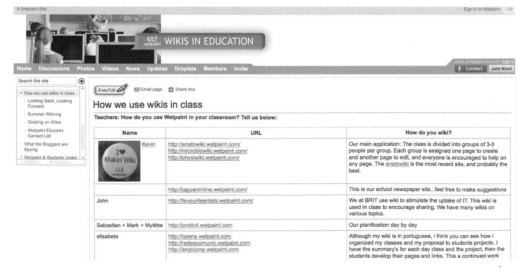

Figure 5.5.   Wikis in Education. Used with permission of Jeff Utecht, technology and learning coordinator, International School, Bangkok.

to a wiki hosting sites, such as Wikispaces or PBworks and enter a search topic such as science education. Also, Wetpaint Wiki offers a wikipage, "Wikis in the Classroom," (http://wikisineducation.wetpaint.com/page/Wikis+in+the+Classroom) that list examples of how wikis are being used in the classroom.

To help assess student created wikis, Vicki Davis proposes the following criteria: collaborative effort, visual appeal, organization, hyperlinks, original, intelligent wording, spelling, grammar and punctuation, and completion of the topic assignment (Davis, 2007). Using her suggestions, devise a rubric for assessment that could be given to the student groups before they create their wiki.

Figure 5.6.   TIP: Create a Rubric for Assessing Wikis.

Or visit Wikis in Education (http://wikisineducation.wetpaint.com/page/How+we+use+wikis+in+class?t=anon). Wikispaces holds monthly Webinars for educators to share and discuss the use of wikis in education. Users can check their blog for a schedule of Webinars (http://blog.wikispaces.com/) or listen to Jennifer Barnett presentation on school wikis (http://blog.wikispaces.com/2009/04/jennifer-barnett-presents-on-her-classroom-and-school-wikis.html).

Wikis support collaboration, critical thinking, and writing. They help to create learning communities and allow students to exchange ideas to broaden and deepen understanding, make decisions, and solve problems. Teamwork becomes essential: sharing and feedback can be provided from peers, teachers, and others, promoting respect for others' viewpoints and experiences. Student use critical thinking skills as they select, evaluate, and/or validate information to employ on their wiki. When student participate on a wiki, they employ their writing skills and hone their editing skills. They must continually add to the wiki and therefore go through many revisions (or versions) to meet success. Students analyze and critique what others have written as an aspect of peer review. Respecting the intellectual property of others becomes ingrained as students provide attribution to cited resources. In the process, students develop personal criteria to judge how effectively their own ideas are expressed for public (or at least semi-public, if it is a private wiki) consumption. What make them different from other collaborative online tools, according to Brian Lamb, is that they are unique, collaborative, have open editing, simple coding, and are evolving (B. Lamb 2004).

Ten Ways Wikis Support Learning

1. Supports planning, collaboration, and critical thinking skills
2. Facilitates inquiry
3. Encourages personal accountability
4. Provides practice in peer editing and reviewing
5. Empowers through shared authorship
6. Encourages responsible writing
7. Deters plagiarism by showing process
8. Engages and motivates students
9. Supports constructivist learning
10. Provides practice in validating information

Tips for Educators

1. Preselect a wiki service based on your project criteria.
2. Develop guidelines for student participation. Include requirements respecting the work of others, citing sources, fact checking, constructive criticism (when peer reviewing), using discussion space to provide rationale for editing another's work, language, spell checking, organization, and visual appeal.
3. Create a "Cheat Sheet" or a video tutorial using Jing (http://www.jingproject .com) to demonstrate how to edit, import files, insert widgets, use discussion space, create new pages, link (internal and external), and save.
4. Pose leading or essential questions for students.
5. Delineate student roles (author or editor), if applicable to the project.
6. Send a letter home to parents describing the purpose of the wiki, with the URL, and students' learning objectives so parents understand how this tool supports learning.
7. Develop an evaluation rubric, with students, for assessing the wiki design and content.

Focus on Wikispaces

There are over 108 wikis services to choose from; however, within education, three stand out: PBworks (http://www.PBworks.com), Wetpaint (http://www .wetpaint.com), and Wikispaces (http://www.wikispaces.com). To take a closer look at wikis, let's focus on Wikispaces. It currently has 3,400,000 members and 1,300,000 wikis, and over 230,000 of these are educational wikis. In 2006, Wikispaces decided to give away 100,000 free wikis to educators. To date they have given away 257,654 free wikis and they plan to continue to give another 250,000 ad-free, private K-12 Plus wikis. When creating an account, be sure to create a "Plus Space for K-12." This account is a step above basic and is equivalent to the pro account (which cost $50 annually for non-educators). This account is advertisement free. It allows unlimited users, pages, and messages. It also provides 2GB of file storage and per file size uploads cap at 20MB. The other two wiki services are also supportive of educators.

Creating a Wiki

When first creating a wiki, provide a wiki name that it will be incorporated into the wiki URL. Choose a name that relates to the class, subject, or perhaps a project—one that the students and educator will easily remember. Next, select the privacy level. Public means that everyone can view it and edit it. Protected means that everyone can view it, but only

Figure 5.7.   Wikispaces—Creating a Plus Space for K-12 Dialog Box.

members can edit it. Private means only members can view and edit pages. Whichever one that is chosen, there will be no advertisements if users check the box that certifies them as an educator.

A truly helpful feature in Wikispaces is that it will allow the educator to batch process the creation of student accounts, as long as he or she has a Wikispaces K-12 Plan.

Figure 5.8.   Wikispaces—New Blank Page with Tabs.

Up to 100 accounts can be created at one time. The steps to follow are:

- Go to the wiki and log in.
- Select "Manage Wiki."
- Under people, select "User Creator."
- Choose the wiki to add users to.

Enter student names as a comma delimited text file or comma-separated values (CSV) file, and then upload as an Excel CSV file, with usernames and passwords. It is highly recommended that users incorporate a school abbreviation as part of the student name. For example, if the school involved was Central Middle School, and the user can create accounts for Tom, Dick, and Harry (who do not have e-mail addresses):

cms-tom, password1
cms-dick, password2
cms-harry, password3

If the students do have e-mail addresses, the accounts would be set up as follows:

cms-tom, tom@email.com, password1
cms-dick, dick@email.com, password2
cms-harry, harry@email.com, password3

The user names must be at least three characters long and the passwords must be at least six characters long. If the teacher failed to set up a Wikispaces K-12 Plan, the teacher can then e-mail Wikispaces at help@wikispaces.com, and they will create the student accounts for him or her.

As with all wikis, there are three primary sections users need to be familiar with to get started: the tabs, the toolbar, and the area to manage the wiki. The tabs, usually on the top of the screen, provide access to the key wiki features: editing, discussion, history, and contacting the wiki owner.

Once clicking on the edit tab, the toolbar will appear showing the text formatting, hyperlinks, and image files buttons.

From the wiki home page, click on "Manage Space" to set permissions and features for the content, people, and tools in your wiki. In the content section, users can reach all the pages, files, templates, and tags. Set permissions, invite people, and review the

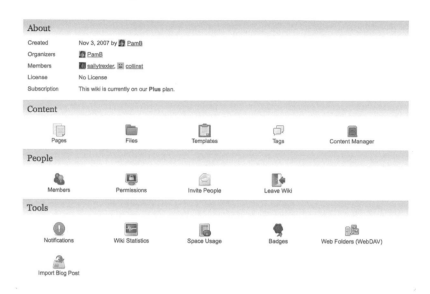

Figure 5.9.   Wikispaces—Managing Your Space.

members on the site from the people section. From the tools section, set up how to receive notification when changes are made to the space (if wanted), view wiki statistics, see how much file space has been used, and import blog posts (see Figure 5.9).

Top Features for Educators—Not to Miss!

1. **Unlimited pages**. This is a handy feature for teachers. They can contain and manage multiple classes' work in one site; makes it easier to manage permissions and notifications as site administrator of one site.

2. **Permissions**. The wiki site can be set up so only authorized users have editing or viewing rights and users can "lock" some pages within the wiki so they can no longer be edited (helpful when sections of work within a group project is completed). This feature is also helpful when trying to stop an "edit war," whereby one or more person persistently edits the same content to force his or her opinion. Page lock is also helpful when the educator posts material to the wiki which should not be edited. Set privacy levels for the wiki, so students stay in a "protected" area, if required by district policy.

3. **WYSIWYG editing**. There are no specialized programs or skills required; editing options are plentiful and are similar to Microsoft Word editing options.

4. **Really Simple Syndication (RSS) feeds**. Users can subscribe to the wiki so new content is delivered as it is published. The wiki administrator or creator can configure the "Notify Me" feature which will notify them when a change has been made to the wiki and by whom. It is very helpful for tracking student contributions and to quickly see if edits are appropriate. It will also allow users to enter a response and provide feedback to the student(s), letting them know if they are on task.

5. **Multimedia support**. Multimedia can be imbedded into the wiki and, in addition, third party tools such as VoiceThread, blogs, or widgets can be integrated.

6. **Revision history (chronological)**. This feature is helpful when there is a need to revert back to an earlier version of the content.

7. **Templates**. Teachers can create a common page layout and duplicate it as many times as necessary. This scaffolds and guides a student to include required content for projects.

Action Steps

1. Explore how other educators are using wikis to support learning. Start research with Wikis in Education (http://wikisineducation.wetpaint.com/page/How+we+use+wikis+in+class?t=anon). Choose a few and share them informally with colleagues.
2. Create a classroom wiki or library wiki (see Figure 5.10) to support a curriculum unit of study to investigate how a wiki might best support learning. Invite a teacher to join in to explore some of the features, such as importing, creating links, and editing text. When users feel comfortable, have students or student groups begin to add content to the wiki.
3. Introduce the faculty to wikis. Ask for time at the next faculty meeting or department meeting and demonstrate the some features and explain how wikis support collaboration and learning.
4. Develop a wiki users' guide that is sanctioned by the school. Align it with district policies regarding acceptable use and copyright.

Blogs in Education

A blog, simply put, is a Web space where a person shares his or her opinions or ideas and readers respond using a comment dialog box. Blogs started as personal diaries and have expanded over time to become far more than simple discussions in a text format. Today, blog postings contain personal thoughts as well as links, photos, videos, graphics, widgets, and podcasts, arranged in reverse chronicle order along with responses from outside viewers. They don't require any knowledge of coding, so anyone can start a blog and share their thoughts and interact with readers. As a long time technology educator and advocate puts it, "They democratize the Internet" (Ferdig 2004), giving everyone the opportunity to share their ideas and opinions.

The two technologies that blogs are most similar to are forum discussions and wikis; however, blogs have their own unique features and purpose. Blogs and discussion forums are similar in that they both share thoughts and opinions, have the ability to insert links, accept feedback, and archive content. However, their differences are more numerous. Blogs are open, serve a wider audience, can include others by invitation, have ability to imbed widgets and RSS, are free, have filters for better searching, employ tags to describe topic, allow for more flexibility in formatting, and have a shorter learning curve. Discussion forums, on the other hand, are usually private (requiring sign-in), intended for a smaller audience (such as a class), searchable only by thread, are fee-based, and have a higher learning curve (Wang 2008).

The same can be said when comparing a blog to a wiki—they are more dissimilar than alike. Blogs are focused more on the individual's perspective, one voice rather than a group's collaborative creation. It is the blog's feedback feature that is most important to the blogger; it is the gateway to the discussion that the blogger hopes to generate through his or her original posting. Feedback is given by posting comments on the blog, or between two bloggers responding on one's own blog with a link back, called a trackback, to the original posting (Educause, Blogs, 2005). Blogs have a structure that is more focused to a particular purpose (discussion), because postings are entered into a form, whereas wikis have all kinds of formatting features, from multiple pages to backgrounds and themes.

Create a Wiki

Wikis engage students in the learning process as they post and share their work and collaborate with their classmates. Librarians and teachers can use this template to plan a wiki with students.

Instructions:
1. Choose a Wiki provider (http://wikispaces.com; http://pbworks.com).
2. Determine the privacy level (open to world or only to members to view and edit).
3. Define the purpose of the wiki.
4. Decide on the content and create a site navigation scheme.
5. Choose from the suggested topic/pages below on the left and add to the work space on the right under Navigation Pane. Write a welcome message to students and decide on graphics.

Choose from the below suggestions to plan the content of the wiki.	Wiki Name:	
	Navigation Pane	**Wiki Purpose:**
Classroom Wiki: class syllabus homework help assignments curriculum standards language arts page group/team pages science page **Library Wiki:** pathfinders book reviews purchase suggestions Web 2.0 tools databases student work bookclubs search engines		**Welcome Message to Students:** **Graphics:**

Next Steps:

- Create an Acceptable Use Policy with students.
- Write a letter to parents explaining the purpose of the Wiki and the learning outcomes.
- Teach students/teachers to add text, links, and images; upload files, post a discussion and respond to others.

Figure 5.10.   Create a Wiki.

While blogs tend to reflect one voice, sometimes they are used as group blogs for families, communities, or corporations. The administrator of the blog can invite and give privileges to others to post to the blog and have the option of approving, disapproving, or editing comments before they appear on the blog. Editing the comments somewhat contradicts the end goal of soliciting uncensored expression, but in a school setting, the feature is very useful. Giving privileges to others is also helpful when the blog is large and has more of a thematic focus. Change.org is a perfect example of how a blog is used to create a community around various issues; it has 13 social issues such as immigration, climate change, homelessness, genocide, fair trade, and human rights. The various sections, each managed by a different person, contain the latest news on the topic as well tools for taking action on the topic (Braiker 2008).

Seven Ways That Blogs Support Student Learning

1. Supports critical thinking, encouraging students to think and reflect prior to writing.
2. Motivates and engages students.
3. Provides an opportunity to improve literacy skills.
4. Offers an authentic audience, encourages students to write responsibly.
5. Provides a forum for feedback, collaboration, and discussion.
6. Involves students in a community of learners.
7. Helps student develop their voice and provides equity.

There are many different types of blogs: artlogs, photoblogs, sketchblogs, vlogs, MP3blogs, as well as genre blogs (politics, travel, education, books and reading, technology, etc.) and new ones are always popping up. Educators are using blogs creatively to meet the learning needs of their students. A few examples include: to reflect on essential questions posted by their teachers, to continue to express opinions and reflect on class discussions, as an e-portfolio, classroom space for assignments, readings, media that enhances subject content, book trailers, reports and reviews, class newsletters or other publications, creative writing (stories, poems, essays, and letters), survey, archive of class activities and work, science lab results discussion space, and document field trips. Successful blogs contain content (which is still king) that is relevant, insightful and relatively brief postings; are updated frequently; don't contain too much personal information; and use humor (Bell, Blogging Redux 2008).

School Library Media Specialist and Blogging

School librarians blog primarily for two reasons: to express their personal perspectives on library issues or to share their expertise, experiences, or observations. Heyjude (http://heyjude.wordpress.com/), a blog created by Judy O'Connell of Australia, focuses on emerging technologies. She created her blog as a means to prompt herself to reflect on changes resulting from the emphasis on Library 2.0 and Web 2.0 topics. The Never Ending Search Blog (http://www.schoollibraryjournal.com/blog/1340000334.html), created by Joyce Valenza, a high school librarian in Springfield, Pennsylvania, and a leader in the field, offers her opinions on best practices relating to a wide variety of educational issues as they pertain to libraries, information fluency, and teaching in the twenty-first

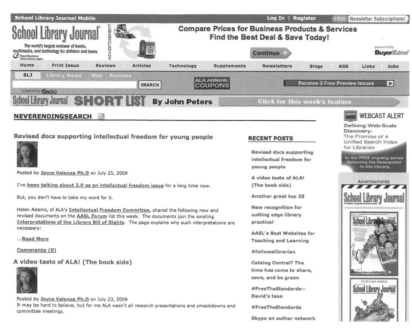

Figure 5.11.   Joyce Valenza's the Never Ending Search Blog.

century. A Library By Any Other Name blog (http://alibraryisa library.blogspot.com/), started by a public school librarian in Texas who goes by the initials VWB, discusses current events, conferences, and even promotes other librarians in her district for their achievements. VWB is also involved in 23Things, a blog that encourages users to learn 23 technical things as they play at the library.

David Warlick (2¢ Worth— http://davidwarlick.com/ 2cents/), Will Richardson (Weblogg-ed—http://weblogg -ed.com/), Vicki Davis (The Cool Cat Teacher—http://coolcat teacher.blogspot.com), Pam Berger (Infosearcher—http://www.infosearcher.com), and many other professionals contribute to the education community by calling our attention to articles, world events, and emerging tools, encouraging educators to keep on learning. Other librarians use their institution's blog to market library events, to post announcements, to publicize new materials, or other library news, relating perhaps relating to fund-raising endeavors or library renovations.

The topics covered in the above mentioned blogs run the gamut from professional learning, social wikis, classroom practice, constructivism, information literacy, collaboration, creativity, avoiding information overload to RSS, read/write Web, to communication tools, networks, mobile library apps, cloud computing, facilities planning, audio casting, virtual reference, eBooks, and the list goes on and on. Basically, professional educators use blogs to teach and learn. It's no surprise, because isn't that what we're all about?

Tips for Educators

1. Explore how other educators are implementing blogs *before* starting your own.
2. Give students a formal, hands-on training session on how to interact with your blog.
3. Provide an RSS feed on your blog.
4. Incorporate blog responses and ideas into class discussions.
5. Include trackbacks to the blogs of others that can be included on your blog.
6. Read feeds frequently to better manage the information flow.
7. If students have created blogs, subscribe to all of them on the aggregator so they will all be stored in one place and thus be easier to view and comment on.
8. Syndicate the feed of a Google News search result and place in the aggregator.
9. Use widgets to enhance your blog.
10. Have fun and enjoy blogging.

The Best Blogging Tools for Education

There are many hosted blogging tools available for use in education. Among them are Blogger, Class Blogmeister, Edublog, LiveJournal, Moveable Type, WordPress, and 21Classes. Regardless of the software, they share common characteristics that make them fairly easy to learn and implement. Blog software common features include:

- Entry or posting box—space into which thoughts are entered.
- Preview of new posting—area where users can see the new postings before saving.
- Feed creation (RSS or Atom)—method of allowing readers to subscribe to the blog.
- Comment box—area where readers respond to the posting.
- Themes—visually attractive layouts available to customize the look of the blog.
- Navigation area—pane that contains sections of the blog (acts as a table of contents, but not necessarily sequential).
- Links—hypertext to guide the reader to sites that support ideas presented or to enhance the content.
- Tags—descriptive word to indicate content focus.
- Mobile phone component—an additional mode to access blog.
- Auto save—eliminates the need to remember to save content.
- Widgets—mini-applications to place on blog (such as a calendar).
- Third-party integration applications—other tools to enhance the blog's content and appearance, such as a slideshow.
- Privacy settings—controls to keep content personal or available to a small group or to everyone (public).

Focus on Edublogs

Edublogs is one of the most popular blogging services. Currently it hosts over 404,021 blogs for teachers, students, researchers, professors, librarians, administrators, and anyone else involved in education. Set up blogs for students even if they don't have e-mail accounts. It is free and comes with 100MB of free space with 20MB in size for image uploads. It also has several different modes of support-video help, forums and FAQs, in addition to Edublogger, the how-to-use Edublogs blog.

Once deciding on the purpose of your blog and how it will support teaching and learning, the set up is not difficult. The first step is to register: enter user name, e-mail address, and check the terms of service box, blog domain (the blog's URL), blog title, privacy level, language, and blog type (teacher, student, or other).

When users receive e-mail verification, log on and go to the dashboard that contains the behind-the-scenes management tools for your blog (see Figure 5.12). Notice the tabs for write, manage, design, comments, and upgrades below your blog title on the left. To the far right are the settings, plug-ins, and users tabs.

Now users are ready to start adding content—to post entries. Click on "Write" to view the writing space toolbar that allows for text formatting and adding tags and categories that provide additional ways for readers to locate postings of interest to them.

Figure 5.12.   Edublogs—Dashboard and Toolbar.

There are buttons for adding media, such as images, video, audio, or other media—use the visual tab or the HTML tab. By using the "Publish Status" box, set your postings as unpublished, published, or pending review and indicate a date in the future that users want the posting to be published.

In the manage posts area, list all postings, and search in general, search by date, delete posts, filter posts, go back to add tags, and view the publishing status. Also view your media library, import posting from other blogging sites, export to other blogging sites users have written, and manage any forums created. There is also a links button that will list all links included in your blog that users can manage.

Click on "Design Tab" to select a theme other than the default theme for the blog; there are 100 or more very attractive themes from which to pick. Also use the widgets button to select from 14 widgets, such as calendar, tag cloud, links (blogroll), and RSS, to add to your blog. Descriptions of what they offer are provided.

Finding Blogs on the Web

Blog search tools help users to locate blogs on the Web. Besides using a dedicated blog search engine, it is also possible to use any general search engine and enter a search term with the term "blog." Rather than returning repeatedly to a particular blog to see what's new, a better idea is to subscribe to the blog using the RSS or Atom feed icon to get the feed and add it to a preferred aggregator.

Table 5.1.   Blog Search Engines.

Blog Search Engine Name	Blog Search Engine URL
Technorati	http://technorati.com/
Bloggernity	http://www.bloggernity.com
Google Blog Search	http://blogsearch.google.com
IceRocket	http://www.icerocket.com
Blogsphere	http://www.blogsphere.com/index.php
BlogSearch.com	http://blogsearch.com
BlogPulse	http://www.blogpulse.com
Blogscope	http://www.blogscope.net
Blog Search Engine	http://www.blogsearchengine.com

Aggregators

Blogs generate a background code commonly called a feed. The code is XML, somewhat like HTML. The feed is the item that permits the user to subscribe to the blog. When subscribing to a feed, it eliminates the need to repeatedly return to the blog to check for new content. To collect all feeds in one place, use an aggregator. Once a blog is included in the aggregator, the aggregator takes on the job of checking, usually frequently, for new content on that blog. Users decide when to read the chosen blogs; they will be left on the reader.

There are many different aggregators from which to choose, both desktop-based and Web-based. Titles included in the Web-based group are Bloglines, Google Reader, News-Gator, Pluck, FeedBucket, FeedShow, My Yahoo, and Rocket News.

Google Reader in Five Easy Steps

1. Go to Google Reader (http://reader.google.com) and sign up for a free account. *This account is for Google Reader.* Users are not signing up for a Google Gmail account. Use any e-mail account to sign up. If using Gmail, then just sign in. Begin by viewing the video or taking the tour of Google Reader, or jump right in and start to explore.
2. The Google Reader screen has a large viewing area on the right side, with options showing on the left side, such as add subscription box and your list of subscriptions.
3. Add a subscription by clicking on the "Add Subscription" box on the left. Enter the URL of the Web site, or manually find the RSS symbol and click to get the feed and copy and paste into the "Add Subscription" box, or use the automatic feed subscription box that is often offered and select Google Reader from the available options.
4. Subscriptions will be listed on the bottom of the left side pane. Create folders or add tags to organize the feeds by groups, such as news, movies, and education. Subscriptions in bold typeface are not yet read and the number in the parentheses indicates how many items the feed contains.
5. Click on any item and it will open in the viewing area on the right. Click the "List" button to scan the headlines only, or click "Expand" to see the whole article. Experiment to see how to e-mail, share, sort, and tag items. All are fairly intuitive processes.

Action Steps

1. Use a blog search engine to locate a blog on a topic of personal interest; read several postings and respond to one.
2. Create an account for a blog aggregator and begin to subscribe to several blogs.
3. Create a blog to use with students that supports the library program. Demonstrate to students how to post comments on your blog. Share it at a faculty meeting and ask for feedback from colleagues.
4. Ask students to help create user guidelines for blog participation.

Polls and Surveys

Powerful Tools

A survey, sometimes called a poll, is a study of what people think or believe about a particular topic. Most people associate polls with gathering political opinion to predict election results, while surveys are often associated with marketing and advertising research. In education, new Web 2.0 poll and survey tools can motivate and involve students in learning, in addition to gathering information for research. They can be used to access a variety of opinions quickly; for research purposes; to determine the attitudes of participants; to expose participants to the diversity of opinions; and to determine understanding of a subject. Online polls and surveys often permit the participant to retain their anonymity, a real plus for engaging the more reticent person.

Some common features of online survey tools include: custom-made start and end pages; conditional branching in questions; ability to insert HTML; various question types; ability to export data in a variety of ways, such as XML or CSV, by e-mail or RSS; multi-page surveys; and the ability to integrate with other tools (Web sites, blogs or wikis). A short list of such online tools includes:

SurveyMonkey—http://www.surveymonkey.com
Poll Everywhere—http://polleverywhere.com
SurveyGizmo—http://www.surveygizmo.com
PollDaddy—http://polldaddy.com
Free Online Surveys—http://www.freeonlinesurveys.com
Fo.reca.st—http://fo.reca.st/surveys/home
Quibblo—http://www.quibblo.com
Kwik Online Surveys—http://www.kwiksurveys.com
Pollograph—http://www.pollograph.com
Zoho Polls—http://zohopolls.com

Group Space

Group spaces are Web-based work spaces that students access to create, collaborate, and share information and documents with classmates. Previously in this chapter, blogs and wikis were reviewed, which are also collaborative in nature; however, group spaces differ from blogs in that content can be edited *synchronously*. It is the ability to invite others to view and collaborate *synchronously* that makes a group space so powerful for learning. The leading tools in this category are Google Docs and Zoho Suite. There are also several smaller tools that will be explored that do similar kinds of things, but on a smaller scale. Those tools include MyNoteIt, Evernote, Notefish, OurNotepad, Springnote, and UberNote.

Student Use of Group Space

Because of the many features, students use Google Docs for journaling, creative writing (stories, poems, and essays), reviews of books or artwork, collaborative research papers, and as a writing portfolio. With spreadsheets, they create stock portfolios with live data and create graphs, charts, and data for analysis. Presentations allow students to showcase their learning or understandings as individuals or in groups. Traditionally, teachers have had students use word processing and passed the document back and forth between authors. Each author would take a turn at improving the work, correcting, modifying, adding new content, and building on the work of the other author. The process was tedious, time consuming, and prone to error due to lack of version control, and formatting issues. Now with Google Docs, they can do it in a more convenient, effective, and collaborative manner. Students are able to co-author a digital document creating opportunities for real-time peer sharing, editing, and collaboration.

Google Docs

Google Docs is comprised of word processing, spreadsheets, and presentations. It provides space to create, edit, store as well as to collaborate online. Only ten people can view and collaborate at one time, although up to 200 people can be added as viewers or collaborators. An account is required and the user must be at least 13 years of age to use the resources. It is an example of "cloud computing," whereby the cloud is the Internet; the user no longer needs to purchase expensive office software and install on their hard drive because everything is done "in the cloud."

The user can choose to synchronize their Google Docs with their computer and doing so allows the user to edit offline (for Google Docs only, not yet available for spreadsheets or presentations). Export spreadsheets to work with them offline, then upload them to Google Docs again, when finished. The offline feature uses an open source browser extension called Google Gears. If working offline, edits are saved on your computer; once the user logs onto the Internet, changes are synched with the Google Docs servers and made available to collaborators. Google Docs frequently backs up data and touts their site's safety and security.

Creating accounts is easy. If students have e-mail accounts provided by the school, use the Google Apps Team Edition. As the teacher, sign up first, and then add your students' e-mail addresses to one account, quickly and easily. If your students have personal e-mail accounts, they would just sign up for an account on their own. If your students do not have e-mail accounts, probably check the district policy and seek permission from parents for the students to create an account using one of the many free e-mail services. The e-mail address that is used would also be used to access all the Google products, including Calendar, Sites, Groups, Maps, and Earth.

Once accounts are created, users can create, import, edit, search, organize, share (allow viewing), and collaborate (allow editing by others) on documents, spreadsheets, and presentations. Viewers can comment on shared documents, a nice feature to encourage feedback. If users publish their documents, they will be visible to anyone on the Internet. If users don't publish, they will only be visible to viewers and collaborators (those that have been invited). When publishing, a URL is generated and can be sent via e-mail to others (such as parents) or linked on a blog or wiki or Web site. If publishing a document, every time edits are made, users can opt to have the changes appear on the published version of the document too.

When using Google Docs, users can do all of the following:

- Create a document, spreadsheet, or presentation using a template.
- Upload a document, spreadsheet, or presentation from another source and continue working on it (file types include .html, .txt, .doc, .rtf, .xls, .ppt, and .pps,

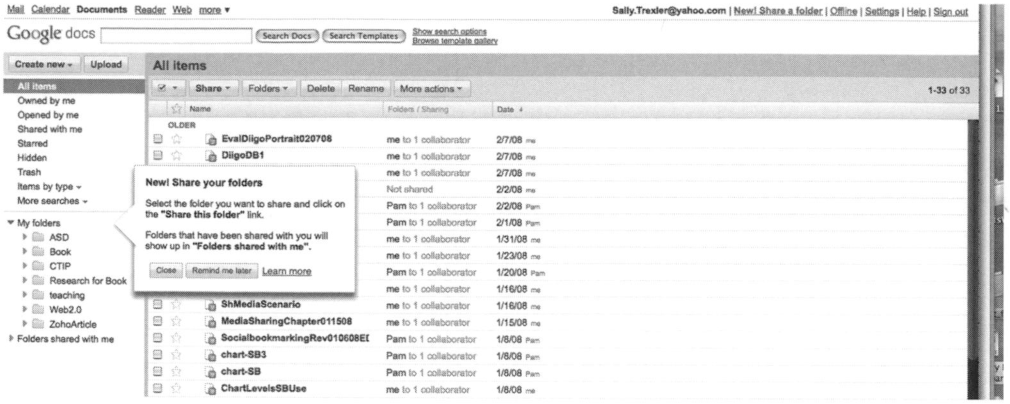

Figure 5.13.   Sharing Options for Google Docs.

among several OpenOffice [http://www.openoffice.org] versions of similar types of programs).

- Share, comment, collaborate, edit, export a documents, spreadsheet, or presentation, and allow either viewing or collaborating.
- Create forms, table of contents, and folders.
- Publish a document, spreadsheet, or presentation to the Internet for public viewing.
- Move, rename, and delete documents, spreadsheets or presentations to folders.
- Search for documents and previous versions of documents, spreadsheets, or presentations by various fields.
- Synchronize Google Docs with hard drive using Google Gears for offline access.

Zoho Suite

The Zoho Suite (http://www.zoho.com/) of products is another example of cloud computing. The suite includes over 19 applications, including Zoho Mail, Zoho Writer, Zoho Sheet, Zoho Show, Zoho Docs, Zoho Notebook, Zoho Wiki, Zoho Planner, Zoho Chat, Zoho Creator, and Zoho Meeting—and are all available on the Web. The tools are free to use for individuals and some have a subscription fee for organizations. They are all built on Ajax technology that creates interactive Web applications allowing Zoho to communicate with a server in the background, without interfering with the current state of the page—very important for synchronous communications.

The focus of the Zoho group is to integrate their applications; Zoho Mail and Zoho Chat are tools for communication, while the rest of the tools are for productivity and collaboration. And it is available in many languages: Zoho Writer supports 11 languages; Zoho Sheet supports 22 languages; Zoho Show supports 12 languages; and Zoho Wiki supports 4 languages. Import and export file formats include html, doc, docx, rtf, txt, odt, and sxw.

The Zoho applications operate differently from Google Docs. With Zoho, each application is a separate application that can integrate with the others. Google Docs contains three applications within itself—word processing, spreadsheets, and presentations.

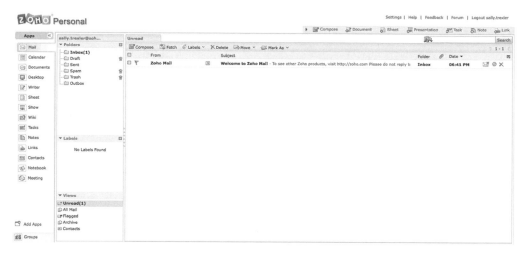

Figure 5.14.   Zoho Personal.

But like Google Docs, Zoho Personal is a starting area for working with all the applications (see Figure 5.14—Zoho Personal). Log on with ID and password and have access to all the other applications. Zoho Suite is far more robust than Google Docs, in both the number of applications and features available; however, Google Docs is more widely used because it has name recognition due to its hugely successful start in the Internet searching arena. The name Google has actually evolved from a noun into a verb; "we all Google." The pressing question is not which one to use, because both get the job done, but how will educators use it to support learning.

Airset

AirSet (http://www.airset.com) is a free, 24/7, Web-based computer desktop that allows the user to create multiple "cloud computers" for the collective management and sharing of information with various groups, such as family, friends, hobby enthusiasts, project teams, and sports teams. It contains a variety of applications—messaging, calendar, address book, lists, blog, photo albums, music playlists, forum, Web site, Web links, and file storage—and can be synchronized with many hand-held devices. The free version gives users up to 1 GB of free space across all their Web computers (not per Web computer) and the premium version allows up to 5GB of space for $20 a year across all Web computers, both of which are advertisement free.

AirSet has some great features:

- The layout is easy to navigate, consisting of the desktop, application toolbar, and a taskbar.
- Shortcuts can be added to the desktop or added to the shortcut menu on the taskbar.
- It has RSS capability to notify members when events have been added to the shared calendar, when new

Figure 5.15.   AirSet Applications.

items have been posted to the forum, when items have been added to a list or
when new Web links have been added.

- Calendar feeds are available for the day, week, month, or year.
- Document can be added to cloud computer in either HTML or txt format.
- Templates are provided in Web Publish.

The desktop has a simple clean design displaying the name of the Web computer
(in this case in the upper right hand corner), shortcuts to applications on the desktop,
an announcement box that can be edited, and a task bar along the bottom of the desktop. Overall, AirSet is an effective space for group collaboration. The only identifiable
weakness is the lack of a word processing application, although it does allow for content creation in the form of blogs, wikis, and Web sites. Documents and files created
elsewhere can be imported for storage and saving. It provides groups with effective
features to create content, communicate, collaborate, and handle complex scheduling.

Collaborative Note Taking Tools

Note taking is an important activity in the research process. The groups spaces
discussed in this section focus primarily on this task and include some unique features
to support collaboration.

- MyNoteIt (http://www.mynoteit.com) was designed for students and is a
  note taking/note searching tool. Since MyNoteIt could be set up to contain
  a calendar, message board, groups, and classes schedules, in addition to
  notes, it could be considered more of a group space than just a note taking
  space. Within a group, messages can be sent; assignment reminders can be
  sent; notes can be shared, and messages can be added to the message board.
  When taking notes, one can begin from scratch, or notes can be copied and
  pasted into the note taking area. Notes can be edited, printed, uploaded and
  downloaded, and can be searched by tags as well as by terms. And, due dates
  can be set for assignments. Files supported include txt, doc, sxw, odt, jpg,
  jpeg, gif, png, mp3, htm, and html. Subscriptions via RSS can be created,
  using My Yahoo!, Live Bookmarks, Bloglines, and Google.
- Evernote (http://www.evernote.com) is more of a personal note taking tool,
  but it does allow one to publish notes, thereby making them public using a
  direct URL. This site allows for notes, reminders, to-do lists, Web clips, tags,
  audio clips, and has a Web Clipper bookmarklet. Notes appear as notebooks
  and one can have as many notebooks as desired. Notes can be edited, deleted,
  printed, or e-mailed. A great feature is that files can be attached to notes. This
  would be an effective tool for a student to use and when working with a
  collaborative group, because they can share by making notebooks public or
  e-mailing notebooks to group members.
- UberNote (http://www.ubernote.com) has a unique feature—it allows users to
  add notes using the Web application, iPhone and other mobile phones, AIM, or
  e-mail. Notes are in a text format, but images can be inserted (or dragged and
  dropped), links can be added, and check boxes can be inserted to help track
  open tasks. Tags can be created and assigned to notes and all notes are

searchable by tags or terms. Notes can be made public (which is how to share them with non-UberNote members), can be printed, e-mailed, marked as important to make them stand out from other notes, and shared with other UberNote users.

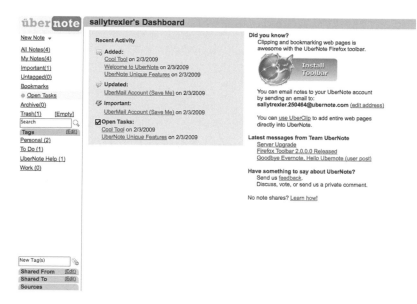

Figure 5.16.   UberNote.

- SpringNote (http://springnote.com) is a very robust note taking tool, allowing for personal notebooks and group notebooks. Address books for both the user and the group can be created. Notes can be viewed in XHTML, can be printed and can be subscribed to via RSS and files such as images, videos, tables, a line, and even a template can be added to them. The account contains a bookshelf (what users read, what users are currently reading, what users want to read in the future), a class timetable, a monthly calendar, a monthly quick list, a to-do list, a word of the day, and a profile. Notebooks can be shared via invitations to collaborate (read and write) or to view (read only). It offers plug-ins that will allow notes to be viewed as a slideshow, or that will create a list of sub-pages or a table of contents. Notes can be published, whereby anyone can view them or they can be exported to a blog and tags can be added to them. This tool has so much to offer a collaborative group, but there might be more of a learning curve because of all the available features.

- NoteFish (http://www.notefish.com) is a very focused note taking tool for gathering research from the Internet. It requires a browser extension, called Notefish:copy that comes into play as users search the Web. When coming across an item of interest, text, or image or both, highlight it, then click the "Notefish:copy" icon on the browser (that was previously dragged and dropped on the browser toolbar). It will copy the selected items into a Notefish note. Notes can be organized by positioning them where users want on the note page, by using colors on the note title bar to categorize or by creating sections on your note page for different groups of notes. They can also be tagged for easy searching and for sharing with particular people, perhaps in a project group, by creating a password and expiration date. Provide the group with the URL and password by sending them an e-mail (from regular e-mail system). To make note pages public for anyone to read, give the notes a tag or tags and do not set a password. This is an easy to use tool that does allow others to view notes, but does not allow for editing by others.

Table 5.2.   Top Features of Selected Collaborative Note Taking Tools.

Features	MyNoteIt	Evernote	SpringNote	UberNote
Privacy	X	X	X	X
Upload/Insert Files	X	X	X	X
To-Do List	X	X	X	X
Web Clips		X		X
Calendar	X		X	
Sharing	X	X	X	X
Collaboration	X	X	X	X
Tags	X	X	X	X
RSS	X		X	
Check Boxes				X
Groups	X		X	
Reminders	X	X		
Mobile Apps	X	X	X	X
Attachments		X	X	X

Six Ways Collaborative Note Taking Tools Support Student Learning

1. Encourages collaboration.
2. Provides practice in peer editing and reviewing.
3. Supports constructivist learning.
4. Provides a forum for feedback and discussion.
5. Engages students in a community of learners.
6. Develops team membership skills.

Skype

Can you hear me? Can you see me? Skype (http://www.skype.com/) is cross-platform software that enables users to make phone calls anywhere in the world, for free. It's Voice Over Internet Protocol (VOIP) technology that connects users with other users via audio and video. All users need is a computer with a high-speed Internet connection, a Webcam, and a microphone. The software for Skype is downloaded free, directly from their Web site. The free features include Skype to Skype calls, video calls, IM and group IMs, and conference calls. The appeal to educators is apparent. "For collaborators, Skype allows longer and more frequent interactions, eliminating cost constraints and creating opportunities to record conversations and engage in multiuser conversations" (Lomas, 2008). A short list of curricular uses for Skype includes:

- Author/expert interviews or "visits."
- Book discussions.

- Foreign language practice with native speakers.
- Cultural exchanges with students from other cities, states, and countries.
- Project planning with remote team members.
- Research discussions among team members.
- Student debates between local and remote sites.
- Live demonstrations or experiments, with the video feature engaged.
- Review of chats captured in Skype history feature.
- In the library environment, it can be used as a means to offer virtual reference service to students.

Skype in the Library and Classroom

Carolyn Foote presents a concise educational rationale for using Skype when she states, "Work environments in the 21st Century demand connectivity. I think our schools are no different. Our students must learn to communicate effectively in an ever more global environment and they need our help. You can start the conversation with Skype" (Foote 2008). In using Skype, students are taught important, real life skills that include how to speak publicly, operate a microphone, chat remotely with others to gain information and enhance understandings, present oneself to an audience, operate a Webcam, multitask, and plan and collaborate with local and remote groups of people (Mirtschin 2009).

Viki Davis, from the Coolcat Teacher blog, offers practical advice regarding Skype student profiles. She recommends that students never use their real name or share their location (leave the city blank in the profile box), don't have the software "sign me in" automatically or use the "SkypeMe" feature, and fix online setting to "invisible," so that strangers do not know when students are actually online using Skype. Demonstrate filling out the profile and check each of students' profiles and initiate a

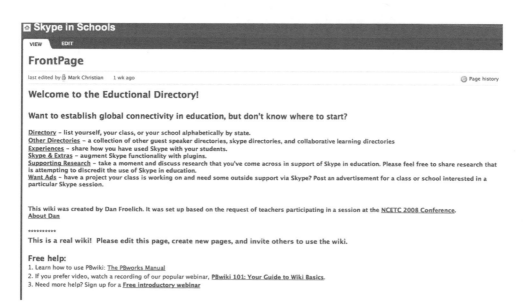

Figure 5.17.   Skype in Schools Web Site.

discussion about privacy and security. Have your students add their teachers and other educators involved along with classmates as Skype contacts. Davis monitors her student use of Skype and if any of her students fail to observe the rules, they lose the privilege of using Skype and are provided with alternate means to complete the assignment (Davis, http://video.google.com/videoplay?docid=-761086448175 7219171&q=genre%3Aeducational+coolcatteacher). For security and safety purposes, Wes Fryer suggests that teachers utilize ePals Classroom Exchange (http://www.epals .com/) as a source to locate other educators/classes with whom to work. Another good source is SkypeInSchools (http://www.skypeinschools.PBworks.com/). To assure an effective session, classroom management issues need to be addressed such as student seating during a Skype video conference; student roles and assignments; time management regarding "bell schedules" versus real-world schedule when communicating with others outside the building; practice time needed before going "live"; classroom discipline during a Skype session; backup plan in case of technical difficulties and planning, planning, planning.

Skype Overview

After downloading Skype and creating an account, configure a profile. Notice that there are dialog boxes for the user's name, gender, birthday, country, state, city, language, home, office and mobile phone numbers, homepage URL, about me, e-mail address, and an image (if desired). Be cautious when directing students to fill out the profile box. The student's real name should not be used, but their country and language would be safe items to include (see Figure 5.18).

Be sure to examine privacy settings, so Skype performs exactly as users want it to. The settings range from general to advanced, with privacy, notifications, audio, calls, short message service (SMS), video, chat, and file transfers falling between them. In the privacy settings, indicate to allow calls or chats from anyone or just from people in the contacts list. For students, be sure to select only people from the contact list, to keep the environment safe (see Figure 5.19).

The next step is to add people to your contact list. The simplest way to add a contact is to log into your account and click the "Add Contact" icon. When the dialog box appears, enter their Skype name, full name or e-mail address, and click the "Search" button. After the system searches, select the person from the list by checking the box in front of their name, then click on the "Add Contact"

Figure 5.18.   Skype Profile Dialog Box.

button. Also search your e-mail contacts to see who's on Skype; use the directory tab and click on "Find People" to locate and add friends already using Skype; or add a phone or cell phone number to your list of contacts (see Figure 5.20).

Then make a video call. Make sure that your Webcam is plugged in and the Webcam software has been installed and it is switched on. From your contact list, find the person to talk to and click on them. In the main window, click the green video call button. Start your conversation, while viewing your contact (see Figure 5.21).

To start a conference call, first log in. Then from the call menu, click on "Start Conference Call." Select the people from your contacts to add to the conference call. Users may have up to 24 conference participants, in addition to the call host. Click on the "Start" button.

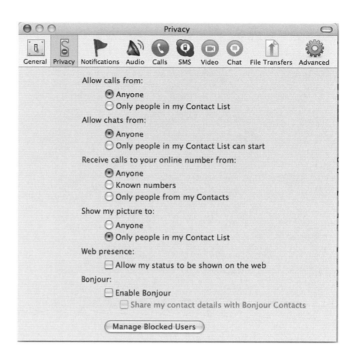

Figure 5.19.   Skype Privacy Settings.

Ten Top Features Not to Miss for Educators

1. Calls can be muted (handy if there is classroom disruption that needs to be addressed).
2. Calls can be put on hold.
3. Conference calls can include up to 24 participants, in addition to the host.
4. Video camera (when properly installed and configured) can be turned on while call is in progress.
5. Screen can be resized.
6. Chat can be initiated with an individual or with a group.
7. Files can be sent through the chat feature; no size limits on documents, video clips, or photos.
8. Supported image file types include jpeg, gif, png, pdf, and bmp.

Figure 5.20.   Skype Add Contacts.

Figure 5.21.   Skype Video Call.

Download Skype to a flash drive instead of installing it to a computer hard drive. The flash drive can be inserted into the computer when needed, and removed when not in use. Doing so should not require the help of the technology department, however, they will still have to allow the proper communications port on the school network to be opened in order for Skype to work.

Figure 5.22.   Helpful Tip.

9. Contacts can be imported from your address book.
10. Online help for Windows or Mac users, with detailed system specifications.

Action Steps

1. Collaborate with a classroom teacher to create a wiki pathfinder on a specific curriculum topic. Encourage students to explore and evaluate resources for the pathfinder.
2. Use Skype to help a teacher set up a debate with another class.
3. At the next school/district committee or task force meeting, suggest that members use Google Docs to collaboratively write the necessary documents.
4. Demonstrate Google Docs at a faculty meeting. Have two students on laptops collaboratively write while explaining the features they are using and how it supports the writing process.
5. Model use of the tool: Use Google Doc when collaboratively developing curriculum with teachers; show them how to access and edit documents.

Media Resources

Adding Feeds to Google Reader; May 24, 2007; 5:15 min.; http://www.youtube.com/watch?v=hm8rJuQlsGw.

Blogs in Plain English; November 29, 2007; 2:58 min.; http://www.youtube.com/watch?v=NN2I1pWXjXI.

Get Going with Wikispaces; April 29, 2008; 2:31 min.; http://www.youtube.com/watch?v=MNUsfMn-EFk.

Google Docs in Plain English; October 18, 2007; 2:50 min.; http://www.youtube.com/watch?v=muVUA-sKcc4.

Google Docs Tutorial for Teachers; February 1, 2008; 4:34 min.; http://www.youtube.com/watch?v=urrvY0YQWE4.

Google Reader in Plain English; August 20, 2008; 1:05 min.; http://www.youtube.com/watch?v=VSPZ2Uu_X3Y.

Making a Video Call with Skype; October 27, 2007; 2:08 min.; http://www.youtube.com/watch?v=zWq7n4w3cq4.

PBWiki Tutorial; July 15, 2008; 7:58 min.; http://www.youtube.com/watch?v=neHt9G3R7TE.

Video: RSS in Plain English; April 23, 2007; 3:44 min.; http://www.youtube.com/watch?v=0klgLsSxGsU.

Wetpaint Wiki in Plain English; October 2, 2007; 2:34 min.; http://www.youtube.com/watch?v=F7BAU2XX5Ws.

Why Let Our Students Blog? http://www.youtube.com/watch?v=OVK4dGNRdQY.

Wikis in Plain English; May 29, 2007; 3:52 min.; http://www.youtube.com/watch?v=-dnL00TdmLY.

References and Additional Resources

Achterman, Doug. 2007. The Wiki Way: Building Better Collaborative Library Projects. http://intergate.sbhsd.k12.ca.us/sbhslib/teacherhelp/wkiwaycsla2007ppt.pdf.

Bell, Mary Ann. 2008. Celebrating Communication: To Blog or Not to Blog. *MultiMedia & Internet @ Schools* 15:38–40.

Bell, Mary Ann and Tricia Kuon. 2008. Celebrating Communicating: Blogging Redux. *MultiMedia & Internet @ Schools* 15:36–38.

———. 2009. Home Alone! Still Collaborating. *Knowledge Quest* 37 (4): 52–55.

Bomar, Shannon. 2009. The Grammatically Correct Wiki. *Knowledge Quest* 37 (4): 51.

Braiker, Brian. 2008. Blogging Like the World Depended on It: Transforming Social Networking into Social Change. *Newsweek.* http://www.newsweek.com/id/163022.

Brescia, William F., Jr. and Michael T. Miller. 2006. What's It Worth? The Perceived Benefits of Instructional Blogging. *Electronic Journal for the Integration of Technology in Education.* 5:44–52. http://ejite.isu.edu/Volume5/Brescia.pdf.

Brisco, Shonda. 2007. Which Wiki Is Right for You? *School Library Journal* 53 (5): 78–79.

Byrne, Tony. 2009. Blogs Are Dead! Long Live Blogging! *EContent* 32 (1): 22.

Chu, Samuel Kai-Wah. 2009. Connecting with Wikis. *The School Librarian's Workshop* 29 (6): 22.

———. 2009. Using Wikis in Academic Libraries. *The Journal of Academic Librarianship* 35 (2): 170–76.

Cowan, Janie. 2008. Diary of a Blog: Listening to Kids in an Elementary School Library. *Teacher Librarian* 35 (5): 20–26.

Davis, Vicki. The Cool Cat Teacher Blog. "How to Set Up Skype and Use It in the Classroom." http://video.google.com/videoplay?docid=-7610864481757219171&q=genre%3Aeducational+coolcatteacher.

———. 2007. Wikis in the Classroom. http://www.slideshare.net/coolcatteacher/wikis-in-the-classroom/.

Diggs, Valerie. 2009. Ask-Think-Create: The Process of Inquiry. *Knowledge Quest* 37 (5): 30–33.

Duffy, Peter and Axel Bruns. 2006. The Use of Blogs, Wikis and RSS in Education: A Conversation of Possibilities. In *Proceedings Online Learning and Teaching Conference.* http://eprints.qut.edu.au/5398/.

———. 2009. Editorial: Computing in the Cloud. *Information Technology and Libraries* 28 (3): 107–8.

Educause. 2005. 7 Things You Should Know about Blogs. http://www.educause.edu/ELI/7ThingsYouShouldKnowAboutBlogs/156809.

———. 7 Things You Should Know about Wikis. http://connect.educause.edu/Library/ELI/7ThingsYouShouldKnowAboutWikis/156807.

Ekart, Donna F. 2009. So We're Publishers Now. *Computers in Libraries* 29 (4): 46–47.

Farkas, Meredith. 2009. From Desktop to Cloud Top. *American Libraries* 40 (4): 27.

———. 2009. My Office in the Cloud. *American Libraries* 40 (5): 37.

Ferdig, Richard E. and Kaye D. Trammell. 2004. Content Delivery in the "Blogoshpere." *THE Journal* 31:12–20.

Foote, Carolyn. 2008. See Me, Hear Me: Skype in the Classroom. *School Library Journal* 54 (1): 42.

Guth, Sarah. 2007. Wikis in Education: Is Public Better? In *WikiSym '07: Proceedings of the 2007 International Symposium on Wikis*, New York, NY: 61–68.

Hargadon, Steve. 2009. Microblogging: It's Not Just Twitter. *School Library Journal* 55 (1): 15.

Harris, Christopher. 2009. Go Higher with Cloud Computing. *School Library Journal* 55 (1): 14.

Lamb, Annette and Larry Johnson. 2007. An Information Skills Workout: Wikis and Collaborative Writing. *Teacher Librarian* 34 (5): 57–59, 71.

Lamb, Brian. 2004. Wide Open Spaces: Wikis, Ready or Not. *Educause Review* 39 (5): 36–48.

Langhorst, Eric. 2009. You Are There. *School Library Journal* 55 (6): 46–48.

Lomas, Cyprien, Michael Burke, and Carie L. Page. 2008. Collaboration Tools. *ELI Paper 2: 2008.* http://net.educause.edu/ir/library/pdf/ELI3020.pdf.

McPherson, Keith. 2006. Wikis and Literacy Development. *Teacher Librarian* 34 (1): 67–69.

Mirtschin, Anne. 2009. Using Skype in the Classroom. *On an E-Journey with Generation Y.* http://murcha.wordpress.com/2008/12/06/using-skype-in-education/.

Molen, Kendra. 2009. Wee Wikis: Implementing the Use of Wikis with Elementary Students. *Library Media Connection* 27 (4): 57–58.

Richardson, Will. 2008. The Hyperconnected Classroom. *Independent School* 67:40–45.

Smart Teaching. 2009. 50 Ways to Use Wikis for a More Collaborative and Interactive Classroom. http://www.smartteaching.org/blog/2008/08/50-ways-to-use-wikis-for-a-more-collaborative-and-interactive-classroom/.

Valenza, Joyce. 2008. Research Transparency: Shifting from Blogs to Wikis? *Neverending Search Blog.* http://www.schoollibraryjournal.com/blog/1340000334/post/340033434.html?q=research+transparency.

Wang, Shiang-Kwei and Hui-Yin Hsua. 2008. Reflections on Using Blogs to Expand In-Class Discussion. *Tech Trends* 52:81–85.

6

Media Sharing

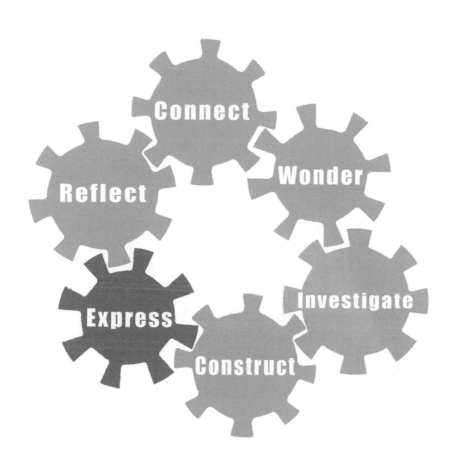

 ESSENTIAL QUESTIONS

What are media sharing tools?
Which media tools offer the best support to teaching and learning?
How are they used most effectively to support teaching and learning?

Figure 6.1.   http://www.wordle.net

Keisha quickly makes her way into the cafeteria to meet with Miguel, her science partner. Finding him, she breathlessly launches into her reason for interrupting his lunch. "You know," she says, "that only one team can work on the skeletal system for the year-end project, don't you? I want it to be us. Let's be first to sign up. Hurry up!" Keisha and Miguel both plan to study medicine when they graduate so they have a strong interest in their chosen topic, the skeleton system. They've already done some preliminary work on the topic in a previous assignment, and Ms. Todd, the school librarian, demonstrated a few media sharing tools to the class last week and posted a video tutorial exploring the features of each on the library Web site. Now, the only problem facing them is to determine which social media tool they'll use to demonstrate and share their learning. Miguel suggests a podcast but Keisha disagrees, they need to be able to show the sections of the skeleton. She explains they need to create an online presentation where they can use a variety of media—text, still images, audio, video clips, and perhaps even their own drawings. They look over the suggested social media tool list they downloaded from the library Web site and based on their criteria for an online presentation, they decide to check out VoiceThread. It will give them the flexibility of including graphics, video, text, and audio while also making it interactive, allowing their classmates to ask questions and comments on the individual "slides." Miguel agrees and quickly finishes his lunch; the two head off to class early to explore VoiceThread while they wait to be the first to sign up for their project topic.

What Is Media Sharing or Social Media?

Social media is collaborative, visual, and creative; a new kind of online media that encompasses text-based content and multimedia but also adds interactivity. In Chapter 5, the focus was on the text-based, content creation tools such as wikis, Google Docs, and Zoho Suite. This chapter will look at Web 2.0 tools that enable students to create, publish, and share multimedia. It's about creating or remixing content, audio, video, images or photographs, text, or their combinations, and posting the content on the World Wide Web for everyone to see and use.

Media has been around for a long time, but as much as hopeful enthusiasts keep predicting that it would change education, it has barely made a difference. Thomas Ludwig traces the history of media in the classroom from lectures using the chalkboard and demonstrations to slides, filmstrips, and 16-millimeter films, through the 1980s with overhead transparencies and videotapes and the 1990s with videodiscs, CD-ROMs, and DVDs (Ludwig 2004, 2). Individuals who owned production facilities, had an infrastructure to produce video and films and the ability to distribute it to teachers, produced the content. Students, for the most part, were passive receivers. Web 2.0 has changed this. The Pew Internet and American Life Project has found "that 64% of online teens ages 12–17 have participated in one or more among a wide range of content-creating activities on the internet, up from 57% of online teens in a similar survey at the end of 2004" (Teens and Social Media, 2007; http://www.pewinternet.org/Reports/2007/Teens-and-Social-Media.aspx).

Today, with the ever-lowering costs of computers, digital cameras, and video cams (such as the Flip video camera) along with the continuous development of social media Web sites means that students, starting at elementary school age, can create and publish content on the Internet.

Table 6.1.   Traditional Media versus Social Media.

Traditional Media	Social Media
One directional	Two directional
Individual	Community
Password protected or subscription based	Open (to feedback and ratings and access)
Passive	Active and participatory
Professionally-created content	User-created content
Content dictated by editor	Content dictated by need or interest
Require specialized skills, costly equipment	User-friendly, free, Web-based tools
Formats: audio, video, print, or audio/video	Formats: audio, video, images, text, mashups
Use of taxonomy through indexing	Use of tagging through search engines
Dates quickly	Immediate updating available

Media sharing tools and services share most or all of the following characteristics:

Creating—students can actively participate in and control the media

Conversation—traditional media is a one way; social media encourages a feedback and a two-way conversation

Remixing—mixing one media with another such as incorporating a VoiceThread on a wiki

Community—allows communities to form around common interests

How Does Social Media Support Learning?

Media sharing is incorporated into the inquiry process during the express phase when students share their new understandings. When student create their own media, they are active participants in their own learning; their interest and motivation increases because they are in control of their learning. When students are engaged, learning improves and products are created and made available to share, interact with, and learn from other students. The projects created through these tools are easily edited, encouraging students to get feedback from others and revise their work so that his or her final, posted work is the best it can be. In the past, the "audience" was usually only the teacher, or perhaps their parents or classmates. Sharing over the Internet has opened the audience to anyone in the world seeking the information contained in the created media (Sener 2007).

The use of the Web-based multimedia tools encourages student self-expression and creativity. When using storyboarding techniques, students learn to visualize their ideas and organize and sequence them so that they make sense. Students develop the ability, with practice, to discern key ideas and to learn to eliminate those that are non-essential. These Web 2.0 tools support the transition from one concept to another, providing memory cues. Remember the saying, "A picture is worth a 1,000 words?" Media sharing tools are effective learning tools because they incorporate audio and visual elements that enhance learning by stimulating comprehension and retention of information and incorporating a vast array of skills (research, writing, organization, technical, presentation, problem-solving, and speaking skills). American Association of School Librarians' "Standards for the 21st-Century Learner," encourage students to:

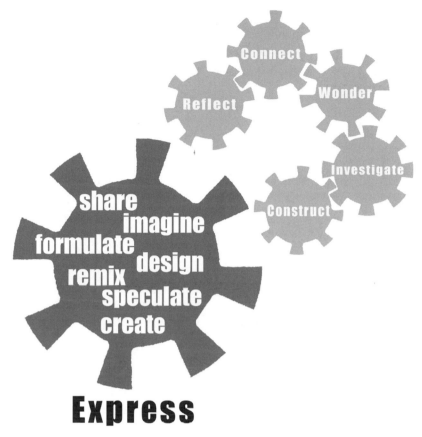

Figure 6.2.   Stripling Inquiry Model.

1.2.3 Demonstrate creativity by using multiple resources and formats.

2.1.6 Use the writing process, media and visual literacy, and technology skills to create products that express new understandings.

2.2.4 Demonstrate personal productivity by completing products to express learning.

3.1.4 Use technology and other information tools to organize and display knowledge and understanding in ways that others can view, use, and assess.

4.1.8 Use creative and artistic formats to express personal learning.

Excerpted from "Standards for the 21st-Century Learner" by the AASL, a division of the American Library Association. © 2007, American Library Association. Available for download at www.ala.org/aasl/standards. Used with permission.

Ten Reasons to Use Web-Based Media Tools in Education

1. Helps students to visualize ideas.
2. Creates an environment of active participants, often collaborative in nature.
3. Encourages self-expression and creativity.
4. Promotes differentiated instruction and addresses multiple intelligences and learning styles.
5. Incorporates various media for differentiation and multi-sensory experiences.
6. Facilitates editing content.

7. Enhances learning (comprehension and retention) by using audio and visual elements.
8. Raises student interest and motivation.
9. Allows students to address a larger audience than just the teacher or classmates.
10. Encourages students to use technology resources that many students are already familiar with and using for personal purposes.

Which Are the Best Media Sharing Tools for Education?

There is a large selection of media tools that incorporate text, narration, images, graphics, and audio and that can be saved and placed on blogs, Nings, wikis, or Web sites. The media sharing tools highlighted in this chapter—podcasts, VoiceThread, Animoto, Glogster, Jing, and TeacherTube—are among the best and the most popular in K-12 education. The literacies and skills students develop in using these tools make them valuable additions to your instructional toolbox. As students use them, create a library of student projects for others to view and learn from, "best practices" for students to analyze before they create their own presentation.

What Is a Podcast?

It its simplest form, a podcast is an audio file recorded on a computer and later shared with others over the Internet. It can also be a collection of digital media files that are distributed, often using syndication feeds for playback. Podcasts come in three types: audio, screen, and video. The audio podcast is similar to old radio shows; they use narration and sometimes use some music or sound effects. A screencast is a digital recording of computer screen output, also known as a video screen capture, often containing audio narration And a video cast, also known as a vidcast or vodcast, contains video, narration, and possibly music. The term podcast comes from combining the words "iPod" and "broadcast."

Most students already know about iTunes and how to use iPods, so creating podcasts extends these skills to make learning more interesting. "Well defined podcasting projects help students develop oral fluency, write with an audience in mind, develop a 'writers' voice,' and increase confidence. Podcasting projects such as radio plays and mock news broadcasts invite high level thinking and ask student to synthesize and

---

Creative Commons

What Is Creative Commons?

Creative Commons is a non-profit corporation, founded in 2001, for the purpose of expanding the creative use of the work of others in an easy and legal manner. The creative content can be educational, scientific, or cultural in nature and can apply to any type of media and text. Creative Commons offers six types of licenses that clearly spell out the limitations and freedoms allowed by the author(s) for the use of their material. Users of Creative Common licenses share their work so that others can build upon it. All Creative Common licenses require that attribution be given to the original author(s). For more information, please visit the Creative Common Web site at http://creativecommons.org.

showcase learning. Students are excited by this accessible technology and motivated to do great work for a real-world audience" (Fontichiaro 2007).

Discovering Podcasts

There are three ways to locate podcasts: use a podcast directory, a multimedia search engine, or a general search engine. Podcast directories are the fastest and most direct method to locate podcasts (see Table 6.2). They are especially useful because they list the podcasts by categories, such as education, science, or current events, which allows for easy browsing. iTunes, whether users have an iPod or not, makes locating and subscribing to podcasts very easy. Its user-friendly interface displays the most-often downloaded podcasts, featured content, and a search box. Type a topic in the search box and get a results screen that allows users to preview and subscribe to podcasts of your choice.

Although there are not many robust multimedia search engines available, those that exist include podcasts in their search results. Alta Vista (http://www.altavista.com), RAMP (http://www.ramp.com), and All The Web (http://multimedia.alltheweb.com) are examples of multimedia search engines. The third method to use to locate podcasts is to use a general search engine, such as Google. Enter the search term(s) and add the word podcast (i.e., "skeletal system" podcast).

Once a podcast has been found, manually download a podcast from a Web site or subscribe to a syndicated podcast that automatically downloads updated installments. The technology used to process the syndicated podcast is a Really Simple Syndication (RSS) feed. It "enables people to subscribe to various feeds of information-data that are continually streamed and collected into a file with the help of a tool called an aggregator. RSS aggregators check the information stream as regularly as every hour to see if there is anything new for RSS subscribers to read when they are ready; if there is, the aggregator copies and stores it" (Richardson 2006, 25). In other words, rather than having to visit a Web site to see if new content is available, files are automatically accessed and organized by an aggregator for immediate enjoyment.

Table 6.2. Podcast Directories.

Directory	URL
Education Podcast Network	http://www.epnweb.org
Fluctu8 Podcast Directory	http://www.fluctu8.com/
iTunes	http://www.itunes.com
Podcast Alley	http://www.podcastalley.com
Podcast Pickle	http://www.podcastpickle.com
Podcastdirectory	http://www.podcastdirectory.com
Podfeed.net	http://www.podfeed.net/
Podscope	http://www.podscope.com

formats including the MP3 format, and has effects and editing tools. If using a MAC, use GarageBand (http://www.apple.com/ilife/garageband/), which is built into the system by just looking for the guitar icon in the system tray. There is also a very detailed guide on using GarageBand online, and within the guide a great section on creating a podcast. Download Audacity (http://audacity.sourceforge.net/), a free sound editor, which is useful for creating audio podcasts. Also download LAME, which is an encoder for converting the file to MP3 format. (Audacity software is copyright © 1999–2009, Audacity Team. The name Audacity is a registered trademark of Dominic Mazzoni.) Two other good tools are WildVoice (http://www.wildvoice.com) and MyPodcast.com for Windows (http://www.mypodcast.com). There are some tools that defy platform, since they are Web-based: Odeo (http://www.odeo.com) and Podifier (http://podifier.en.softonic.com). These tools allow users to create an audio file right

Figure 6.5.   Our City Podcast.

on their Web site and download it to the desktop. From that point, continue to step two in the process.

Podcast Hosting Services

A hosting service is a place to store your podcast so others can find it and listen to it. The hosting service provides the Web address for the podcast; without it, users can't employ the feed aggregator. Some of the more well-known services include: Edublogs (http://edublogs.org), Blogger (https://www.blogger.com/start), WordPress (http://wordpress.org), PodPress (http://www.podpress.org), Pod-o-matic (http://www.podomatic.com), Podbean (http://www.podbean.com), Odeo (http://odeo.com), and OurMedia (http://ourmedia.org).

Users will also need an aggregator, such as iTunes, to collect podcasts in a single location for easy viewing.

Promoting Podcasts

Now that the podcast is created and posted, promote it by listing it with free podcast directories such as PodcastDirectory (http://www.podcastdirectory.com),

Education Podcast Network (http://www.epnweb.org), iTunes (http://itunes.com), or Podcast Alley (http://www.podcastalley.com). Next imbed the podcast address provided by your hosting service in your Web page, wiki, or blog. If building a series of podcasts on a topic, it is very important to provide the user with the capability of subscribing to your podcasts by creating a RSS feed. Tutorials on how to create a RSS feed can be found on YouTube (http://www.youtube.com) and TeacherTube (http://www.teachertube.com). It's a simple procedure, and when uploading a podcast to a host-

Figure 6.6.   Audacity: Free Sound Editor.

ing service, the service will provide the feed URL. Copy and paste the feed URL onto the Web page, blog, or wiki and it is done.

Evaluating Podcasts: What Makes a Good Podcast?

When evaluating podcasts, in addition to the standard criteria used for all media, such as authority, accuracy, and bias, and how it supports the learning process and is aligned with standards, consider the technical qualities, subscription availability, and availability of additional supporting materials, just to mention a few. Kathy Schrock's Guide for Educators (http://school.discoveryeducation.com/schrockguide/evalpodcast.html) (see Figure 6.7) is an excellent example of an evaluation tool for students, helping them to focus on key questions to consider when evaluating podcasts. As students begin to create their own podcasts, design a rubric with students using Schrock's tool as a guide. A free, Web-based rubric creator can be found at RubiStar (http://rubistar.4teachers.org/index.php).

What Is VoiceThread?

VoiceThread (http://voicethread.com) is a free online, asynchronous media tool, developed at the University of North Carolina that permits the user to import and display a variety of media for the purpose of group discussion. It's often described as a media album that is made of a series of different types of media, images, documents, and videos that others can comment on in multiple ways: using voice (with a microphone or telephone), text, audio file, or video (with a Webcam)—and share them with anyone they wish. A VoiceThread allows group conversations to be collected and shared in one place, from anywhere in the world. "By far the greatest potential of

What makes a good podcast?

When you listen to a podcast, or when you are making your own, consider these questions that target the qualities of a well-done podcast.

Your name: _____ **Date:** _____

Title of podcast: _____

Feed URL (or URL) of podcast: _____

Creator of podcast: _____

	YES	NO	N/A
1. Did the podcast include content that was useful / relevant for your purpose?			
2. Were the technical qualities (audio, slides, etc.) acceptable in the production?			
3. Was a written transcript of the podcast available?			
4. Was the podcast linked from a site which included subject tags?			
5. Was the podcast linked from a site which included links to other resources?			
6. Did the podcast adhere to the copyright guidelines in its use of music, pictures, etc.?			
7. Was the length of the podcast appropriate for its content? (20 min. or less)			
8. Was the podcast part of a regularly scheduled series?			
9. Did the subjects in the podcast have "personality" to keep you interested?			
10. Did the podcast flow smoothly (introduction, content, summary)?			
11. Was it obvious how to add the podcast feed to your aggregator? (RSS)			
12. If the item was an enhanced podcast, did the use of slides enhance the content?			
13. If the item was an enhanced podcast, was it available in various file formats to allow viewing on various hardware devices?			
In your own words, describe the podcast you listened to and its attributes.			
*N/A means *Not Applicable*—the question can't be answered or does not pertain to the podcast			

Figure 6.7. Kathy Schrock's Guide for Educators. Used with permission.

TIP: How to Add Value to Your Podcasts

Promote your Podcasts

Now that you have created and posted your podcast, promote it by listing it with free podcast directories such as PodcastDirectory (http://www.podcastdirectory.com), Education Podcast Network (http://www.epnweb.org), iTunes (http://itunes.com), or Podcast Alley (http://www.podcastalley.com). Also imbed the podcast address provided by your hosting service, in your Web page, wiki, or blog. If you are building a series of podcasts on a topic, it is very important to provide the user with the capability of subscribing to your podcasts by creating a RSS feed. Tutorials on how to create a RSS feed can be found on YouTube (http://www.youtube.com) and TeacherTube (http://www.teachertube.com). Basically, when you find a page that is interesting, it will often contain an RSS feed icon. Click on it and the feed URL will appear. Copy and paste the feed URL into your feed reader, such as Google Reader.

VoiceThread lies in the creative opportunity it provides for students to tell their own stories and to contribute to or directly critique the narratives of their peers" (Harris 2008, 22).

Bill Ferriter, a middle school teacher from North Carolina, believes that more students participate more actively in digital discussions than in the classroom and that they feel safe doing so. It levels the playing field for the shy or unsure student, who is often afraid to speak in front of classmates. He points out, "You don't have to be the loud one or the popular one" (Nichol 2008, 2). He offers a wide variety of VoiceThread resources that he created for his students on his wiki (http://digitallyspeaking.pbworks.com/Voicethread). His site contains such well developed guides and suggestions, that it is a perfect place to start an investigation of the tools. His site is could be renamed VoiceThread 101. Some of the resources available are:

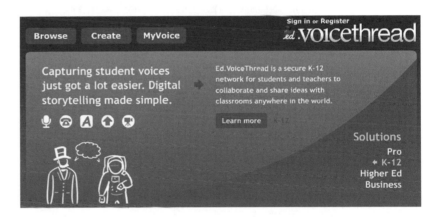

Figure 6.8.   Ed VoiceThread Is a Private Network for Educators.

- VoiceThread Overview
- VoiceThread Do's and Don'ts
- Tips for Teachers
- Planning a VoiceThread
- Commenting Tips for VoiceThreaders
  Rubric, VT Feedback
- Assessing VoiceThread Participation
  VT Scoring
- Teaching Students to Create and Moderate Threads
  VoiceThread Student Training Guide

- VoiceThread Handouts
- Sources for Images
- Citing Images
- Examples and Templates

Another good source is "VoiceThread in Teaching and Learning" section of the InfoTech4Lrng site (http://arllennium.wordpress.com/category/VoiceThread/), where the educational benefits of using VoiceThread is succinctly summarized:

Benefits of VoiceThread according to Joyce Valenza, Bill Ferriter, Wes Fryer, and Brenda Dyke (http://arllennium.wordpress.com/category/VoiceThread/):

- Simple and easy
- Focuses on the content instead of the tool; can serve as a form of free writing
- Requires simple hardware and minimal memory requirements; minimal tech-barrier
- Encourages collaborative storytelling
- Ability to use powerful images—one or many
- Users can zoom in to see detail and zoom out to see big picture
- Ability to add text
- Easy to capture voices
- Inspires ongoing conversation about each image
- Build fluency, precision, and voice in second language
- New dimension for creative analysis of historical photographs, maps, and artifacts
- Ability to give and receive feedback from peers, teachers (formative and summative assessment), parents, and other relatives, local and global community
- Effective tutorials
- Can be used "as a storytelling tool, a deep thinking tool, a research tool, an expository communication tool, and even an assessment tool"
- Allows for differentiation to accommodate different learning needs and styles, another option for struggling or reluctant writers
- Allows the teachers to seamlessly integrate digital collaboration into the curriculum
- Provides another opportunity to discuss copyright

Ned's Keeper (http://blog.discoveryeducation.com/ldaughrity/2008/10/04/38/), offers 40 ideas for using VoiceThread in the classroom. Below is a sampling of ideas listed:

- Kids define spelling words—or make sentences.
- Make a spoken menu for a foreign language or their home culture.
- How to video—step by step directions for a hobby/area of expertise for older kids.
- Make a visual tour of classroom/school/house/whatever.
- Make different slides for familiar words and have kids share their own words for that (names for grandmothers, grandfathers, times of day, or meals) to compare cultures.

- Make VoiceThreads for military holidays and send the links to troops overseas.
- Do the typical—take a picture of your class in front of a tree throughout the seasons and connect with classes around the world for each do the same and share in a common VoiceThread.
- Do an author study where the kids show what they are learning though a growing VoiceThread—different books could be illustrated by the kids or book covers could be the impetus for discussion.
- Have kids share the causes of conflict in important wars to make a timeline of causes/opponents/outcomes.
- Make an "I Spy" VoiceThread with primary source photos from American memory.
- Create a picture memory book throughout the year or of a field trip/special event.
- Kids do their book report on VoiceThread.
- Create optical illusions—have kids take pictures of something familiar REALLY close up and have others guess what it is.
- Have the scene from a story without the details in the picture. Read the story and have each student add-in one element that they think may be in the picture. This would be great for *The Hungry Caterpillar* all the way up to high school literature.
- Use common everyday pictures of scientific topics such as push or pull or the six simple machines and have the students tell what they are.

VoiceThreads can be used effectively in all curriculum areas:

- Students studying a language other than their native language could practice pronunciation of depicted objects by using the record button or practice sentence structure and vocabulary by using the text button.
- Teachers can guide students to effectively explore a primary document by preparing a short VoiceThread with voice and screen markings.
- The water cycle, photosynthesis, or other scientific processes can be broken down into smaller segments to incrementally build student understanding.
- Budding student artists, including photographers, can share their work and get feedback from invited friends or from the public.
- Students can view group projects and discuss them for further refinement.
- Mathematical charts, graphs, or multi-step problems can be shared and discussed; students explain the process so the teacher can assess if the student has mastered the mathematical concept.
- Original poems can be recorded, illustrated, and shared.
- Historical events and geographical places can be explained, discussed, and touted.
- Books can be discussed or promoted and literary concepts, such as symbolism, characterization, setting, and theme, can also be discussed.

Locate published VoiceThreads by clicking on the browse tab on the Voice-Thread home page. The browse tab contains the database of public VoiceThreads. Either scroll through the offerings, or search for VoiceThreads on specific topics by using the search box. Another way is to use a general search engine, enter desired term, and add the term VoiceThread to the search. Below is a list of some favorites.

Examples of VoiceThread

- The Tragedie of Hamlet for Children—http://voicethread.com/#q.b20471.i116493
- Water Cycle—http://VoiceThread.com/#q+water+cycle.b487524
- Fractions in Simplest Form—http://VoiceThread.com/#q+fractions.b95788
- Book Talk on The Looking Glass Wars (by Frank Beddor)—http://VoiceThread.com/#q+literature.b42080.i220608
- Symbols From The Glass Menagerie—http://VoiceThread.com/#q+literature.b477985
- Nineteenth Century British Poetry—http://VoiceThread.com/#q+literature.b273622.i1435877
- 8th Grade Literature, A-Z—http://VoiceThread.com/#q+literature.b416011
- 1st Grade Literature, Wangari's Tree of Peace—http://VoiceThread.com/#q.b357106

Create a VoiceThread Account

VoiceThread has two sections, one is open to the public (http://www.voicethread.com) and one is for the education section (http://www.ed.voicethread.com). The public, free version lets the general user create up to three VoiceThreads, containing up to 50 pages, with up to 50 invitations per day to be sent to friends, with 75MB of storage space. Of course, there is no fee for viewers to view public VoiceThreads. The education section permits educators to sign up for a *free* PRO account (a $29.95 value), by using their school e-mail address when registering. The PRO (or educator) account allows for up to 500 pages and 500 invitations per day, with unlimited storage space. It is highly recommended that teachers, librarians, and other educators create an educational account to use with their students, as registrants must be 13 years of age to create their own accounts. Potential users range in age from the very young to adults. The PRO account is such a gift for educators because of the generous number of pages, invitations, and space allowances. Educators can create one account and have all his or her students (in all their class sections, if secondary) utilize the particular educator's account. All the work of all the students in all of the teacher's classes will be contained within the one educator account, which is "protected." Educator accounts are not public, by default, but all users within the account can view and comment on VoiceThreads in the account. Student privacy and security is assured.

Creating a VoiceThread

The basic steps to create a VoiceThread:

1. Go to the VoiceThread Web site (http://www.VoiceThread.com) and register for an educator account. Users will be asked to provide their name, subject area, grade level, school name, school Web site, school address, school country, school zip code, and school e-mail address.

2. Then view public VoiceThreads by clicking on the browse tab on the home-page, just to get some ideas about how others are using it.

3. Then create your own VoiceThread by clicking on the create tab. Of course, as with any educational lesson, plan ahead. Choose a topic, and start to collect the images, documents, or videos to be included.

4. Upload the media. This can be done from your computer, from a URL, scanned images, Flickr, or Facebook. As users upload media, they will be prompted to add a title and brief description of the VoiceThread, as well as any tags that would describe the content for others to use when searching. After images are uploaded, a work area appears and it is in this area that you can arrange your images in a logical order for presentation. Also add titles and Web links to individual images in the work area. Media file types that are supported include ppt, pps, pdf, doc xls, jpeg, gif, bmp, and png, as well as several video file types.

5. Add comments by clicking on the comment button at the bottom of the upload window. Of course, scripting your narration before this point would be ideal. Next, upload an image to represent yourself (called an identity). Any time users comment on a VoiceThread, their identity will appear. It is not necessary to add a real photograph; use any appropriate image for this purpose. If no image is added, a default image of a chess piece appears. The identity feature is very helpful when developing accountability with students. Add comments five different ways—by telephone, camera (for Webcam), microphone, text (represented by the letter "A"), or by adding an audio comment. Another fun feature is to "doodle," meaning that users can use a pen tool and draw over the image, document, or video with circles, lines, or arrows to highlight an area to comment on. The doodles fade out after as the student's comment finishes.

6. Share VoiceThreads by clicking on "Add a Friend" to enter a friend's e-mail address. Add multiple friends and their names will appear in the "My Friends" drop-down list and then select from among the names available. Next, determine if your VoiceThread will be public or private and if others will or will not be allowed to comment on the VoiceThread. Another possibility is to imbed your VoiceThread on your Web site or wiki, by clicking on the embed button to locate the script needed to paste on your site. E-mail VoiceThread's links to others or get a script to put a smaller version of the VoiceThread on your Facebook page.

Animoto

Animoto (http://www.animoto.com) is a Web-based video creation tool that allows users to upload digital photos, add background music, and/or text on images, to create an animated video. This is a great tool to use for project-based activities. Animoto for Education permits teachers, grades K-12 unlimited access the full range of Animoto's services for free. The education account is a controlled, safe environment for students. Finished videos can be shared by e-mail, by posting to a blog or Web site,

Be Creative: Digital Storytelling

Bring the creative writing process alive by using the tools in this chapter for digital storytelling. "Digital storytelling is the practice of combining narrative with digital content, including images, sound, and video, to create a short movie, typically with a strong emotional component" (Educause Digital Storytelling). Students learn basic story elements, such as setting, character, plot, conflict, climax, and resolution and the various types of stories—instructional, historical, persuasive, and reflective. They experience the story writing process—generating an idea, conducting research, organizing, storyboarding, and writing. In *Digital Storytelling Changes the Way We Write Stories*, there are great tips for integrating digital stories into the classroom, pre- and post-production ideas, and examples of use (Crane).

Web 2.0 tools such as Flickr, VoiceThread, Slide, OurStory, Animoto, Picnik, Picasa, Slideroll, One True Media, PhotoShow, SlideShare, and Glogster can help in the creation of the digital stories. TeacherTube and SchoolTube can store and distribute the finished digital story. Additional sources of digital images are:

The Library of Congress's American Memory—http://memory.loc.gov/ammem/index.html
Digital History—http://www.digitalhistory.uh.edu/images.cfm
Pics4learning—http://www.pics4learning.com
The New York Public Library Picture Collection Online—http://digital.nypl.org/mmpco/
Picture History—http://www.picturehistory.com

by exporting to YouTube, or by downloading to your computer. It integrates with Facebook and both iPhone and the iTouch.

Animoto can be integrated into all curriculum areas and offer students an opportunity to express themselves graphically, and extend their video and storyboarding skills. Educators are using Animoto in innovative, exciting ways. Below are a few examples:

Grassland Biome—http://animoto.com/play/8PrjASJ85kksoAKf0ckcgQ
Teen Read Week at Lawrence High School, Lawrence, Kansas—http://library.lhs.usd497.org/2008TEENREADWEEK.html
Student Tech Teamx BTG 2009—http://animoto.com/play/OyPs2bOkJxgumDg0Aan50Q

Create an Animoto

Start by going to Animoto's education site (http://animoto.com/education) to apply for an educator's account. Provide name, e-mail address, school, class Web site/blog URL, and grade(s) level and subject(s) taught. Click the submit application button.

Once the account is activated, click on create video button to access the work area. Next, choose the video type. Animoto short is 30 seconds in length, with 12–15 images; a full length Animoto is an extended length with unlimited remixes. The Educator Account permits users to use the full-length feature.

Once the video type selection is made, an image upload area appears to add images, pulling them from your computer, Facebook account albums, Flickr, Photo-Bucket, SmugMug, Picasa, or from Animoto's own image collection. Hold the Ctrl or Shift key to select more than one image at a time. Image file types that are currently supported include jpg, jpeg, and gif. Image file size is maxed at 5120Kb per image (see Figure 6.10).

Go ahead and select images. They will appear in the image work area, where users can drag and drop them to reorder them. Add more images, add text, rotate images, spotlight images to make them stand out in the show, or delete unwanted images (see Figure 6.11).

At this point, the program presents information regarding your show. In the example in Figure 6.12, there are four images in the show, an estimated 0:08 seconds in length, without a soundtrack.

The second step is to select your music. Use music from Animoto's collection or upload music from your computer which must be in the MP3 file format. The example in Figure 6.13 displays Animoto's music collection, which is arranged into 11 genres, ranging from oldies, top 40/pop, hip hop, jazz, and classical, to name a few.

Preview soundtracks before selecting them and change the soundtrack, if desired. Once selected, review your selection, save and continue or change the soundtrack.

Next, customize your video, by selecting the video type, pacing and video screen selection. The video screen

Figure 6.9.   Animoto.

Figure 6.10.   Animoto Image Upload Area.

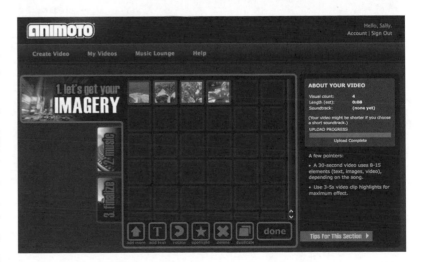

Figure 6.11.   Animoto Work Area.

Figure 6.12.   Animoto—About Your Video Info.

Figure 6.13.   Animoto Music Selection Dialog Box.

Figure 6.14.   Customize Your Animoto Video Dialog Box.

selection is only active with a full-length video. Press the continue option to finalize (see Figure 6.14).

At the next screen, name your video and add a description. Production credits will be associated with the user's name. If needed, click on the back arrow to return to the previous screen. If everything is a go, then click the create video button.

Animoto proceeds to create the video. The process includes processing, analyzing, and rendering.

When your video is fully rendered, the video will open in the same screen and be sent in an e-mail with the video link. The rendered video looks like the one shown in Figure 6.15. Notice the title, the date of creation, the length of the video (0:23 seconds), and the artist and song from the soundtrack. In the lower right hand corner, there are three integrated applications—Facebook, Twitter, and MySpace. Clicking on one of them will provide the steps to place your video on the partner site.

Clicking on the video toolbox (as seen in lower right hand corner of Figure 6.15) gives users several cool options.

- Click remix-saving the old video as well as the new one
- Edit the video
- Start a new video
- Delete the video
- Share
- Create a greeting card
- Embed (in Web site or blog script provided)

- Export to YouTube
- Order a high resolution DVD (for a fee)

Glogster

Glogster (http://www.edu
.glogster.com) is a free poster
creation tool (with a special section for educators) that contains
text, images, videos, links, and
audio (see Figure 6.16). It is fun,
imaginative, creative, and it is a
very motivating learning experience for students. It fosters independent creative self expression
and is being used in all curriculum areas various ways:

- To create historical
  timelines
- For book or textbook
  chapter summaries
- For annotated bibliog-
  raphies
- As a wiki homepage
- As a library homepage
- For book reviews
- As student portfolios
- For student artwork
- As a visual book
  report
- As alternative assess-
  ment tool
- For posters

Some graphic examples of
Glogster include:

"The Databases Glog" con-
tains library subscription database icons with descriptive text
about their contents, along with
an embedded link so that when
the viewer clicks on it, they are
taken to the log in page for the
library's account.

"The Oaklawn Elementary
Library Glog" contains highlights of the library, its program,
and resources: four paw prints
(their mascot is the panther),

Figure 6.15.   Rendered Animoto Video.

Figure 6.16.   Glogster for Educators.

representing student resources, databases, teacher resources, parent resources, and favorite authors. Links connect the user to the Accelerated Reader program, library catalog, destiny quest, kids click, Texas Book Awards, and more (see Figure 6.17).

The "Hot Dog Book Reviews" glog contains podcasts of book reviews written by elementary students, along with student artwork representing the book (see Figure 6.18).

There is a glog that promotes the Artemis Fowl series of books where characters are introduced and book jackets are displayed. It also contains a promo by the author, Eoin Colfer, and a video from YouTube on Artemis Fowl.

Additional examples are:

Science Life Cycles—http://suziq56.glogster.com/glog-340-655/
People of Science—http://emochild17.glogster.com/glog-7939-4563/
Quadratic Glogster Project—http://smmartin.glogster.com/Math-Project/
Of Mice and Men—http://dija.glogster.com/Of-Mice-And-Men/
Battle of Britain—http://xannus.glogster.com/glog-WW2battleofbritain/

Create a Glog

To start, register for an educational account (http://www.glogster.com/edu). The Terms of Service require that users be 13 years of age, so teachers with younger students will need to set up an account. When registering, indicate how many student accounts are wanted, up to 200. On your profile, it will indicate the number of "friends" listed—these are the students' accounts. By default, the students' glogs remain private. Although Glogster sets up the student accounts, teachers may change passwords that are generated by clicking on the password tab under the edit your account option.

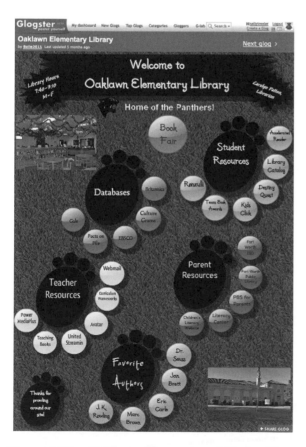

Figure 6.17.   Oaklawn Elementary Library Glog.

Glogster in Eight Easy Steps

- Register for a free account and upgrade to an educational account
- Create a glog
- Begin with the wall-select your glog background design
- Edit and change the layout if desired
- Add content, using links, video, audio, and images by using the edit tools and Glogster toolbar icons
- Save (as classic gold)
- Name the glog, assign a category, assign tags, and determine privacy settings
- Share with classmates, friends, family, or the world.

Some Key Concepts to Create a Glog

To create a glog, work with the basic toolbar to upload media, link to Web sites, grab a new video, audio or still image, preview, save, publish, and exit.

The magnet tool is used to add content to the glog. Click on any of the six buttons:

Graphics—a collection of offerings appear that can be placed in desired positions.

Text—a text box appears into which one types; font style, color, and size can be selected.

Image—browse to locate an image for placement on the page.

Video—import video from your computer.

Figure 6.18.   Hot Dog Book Reviews Glog.

Sound—browse for audio or to record sound in MP3 format.

Wall—offers a large library of wall backgrounds from which to select.

Sharing Glogs

Part of the fun of a glog is the ability to share it and this can be done in a few different ways.

1. Bookmark links, such as Google Bookmarks, Digg, Twitter, del.icio.us, Stumble-Upon, Technorati, Yahoo! Bookmarks, Ask.com, among others.
2. Import e-mail contacts from a mail account and then send out the glog link to selected recipients.
3. Click a "Share Glog" button and select from numerous profile services, such as MySpace, iGoogle, TypePad, Facebook, WordPress, Xanga, Live Spaces, Pageflakes, Blogger, Netvibes, plus over ten other tools.
4. Copy and paste an embed code that is created after saving and publishing the glog, onto a Web page, blog, or wiki (Glogs can be public or private).

Additional Media Sharing Tools

Jing

Jing (http://www.jingproject.com) is a free downloadable screen capture (screencasting) program that allows the user to capture and share an entire screen, a window, or a

Figure 6.19.   Jing.

specific area of the screen, making it a great tool to share video on TeacherTube (http://www.teachertube.com) and SchoolTube (http://www.school tube.com) (see Figure 6.19). Jing records up to five minute on-screen action in video, and annotates images with text, arrows and text comments, notes, or questions, and uses frames to call attention to noteworthy items on the image. Jing partners with Screencast (http://www .screencast.com) to offer 2GB of free storage with 2GB monthly bandwidth. User's content is private and only those invited can see it. It remains on Screencast until or when users delete it. Jing content can be shared by sending a link to others or by embedding code into a Web site, blog, or wiki, or by sending directly to a Flickr account. Anton Bollen's blog, "Welcome to Jing! A Guide for Taking Your First Capture" (http://blog.jingproject.com/2009/08/welcome-to-jing—a-guide -to-t.html) is a good place to start learning.

Jing is easy to use. When the program opens, the Jing Sun Launcher (see Figure 6.20) will appear. The launcher has three arms with buttons: capture, history, and more. Everything users need to do is contained in the launcher: capture images or video; access, manage, sort, and delete Jing content that's stored in your account; set preferences; and save and post content.

What Is TeacherTube?

TeacherTube (http://www.teachertube.com) is an online community for sharing educational videos, images, audio, and documents—very similar to You-Tube, but for educators (see Figure 6.21). Content posted on TeacherTube, which is reviewed before posted, is intended to meet one of the following three criteria:

1. Address a specific learning objective
2. Be intended for professional development for educators
3. Contain neither advertisements nor solicitations

Viewers can comment and rate the content; however, groups can be created and the content made only available to members. Currently, there is no limit as to the number of videos that can be posted, and there is

Figure 6.20.   Jing Sun Launcher.

no space limitations specified for users. Content posted on TeacherTube can be imbedded on a wiki, MySpace, Friendster, Edublogs, and WordPress; for personal or classroom educational use, and must provide a link back to TeacherTube as well as credit to the author. Content can also be tagged, so that searching is more efficient.

TeacherTube is being use in many different ways:

Figure 6.21.   TeacherTube. Used with permission of TeacherTube, LLC.

- Teachers create videos, images, documents, or audio, and use TeacherTube as a free hosting site, so that their students can access their products without software compatibility problems. Professional development trainers post materials for 24/7 learning.
- Teachers assign projects that require students to explore and create media to showcase their learning, often as an alternate form of assessment.
- Students create videos to benefit from their teacher's and their classmates' feedback.

Examples of media created by teachers and students:

In the "Video on a Legislative Hearing Committee" note the information to the right of the video screen (see Figure 6.22). It contains the date it was posted, the channel to which it belongs (high school), the playing time, support files (if any), the number of downloads by others, the video URL, and embed code (with player).

In the search results list for audio, an image of the book being discussed is provided. How long ago the audio file was uploaded is present, as is the creator's name, the number of playbacks, tags, and rating. One only has to click on the image to open the file to hear it.

There are a number of other sites similar to TeacherTube, such as SchoolTube (http://www2.school tube.com), Edublogs.tv (http://edublogs.tv/), and Teachers.tv (http://www.teachers.tv/). Besides those educational sites, there are general hosting sites for videos and other media, such as

Figure 6.22.   TeacherTube Video on a Legislative Hearing Committee.

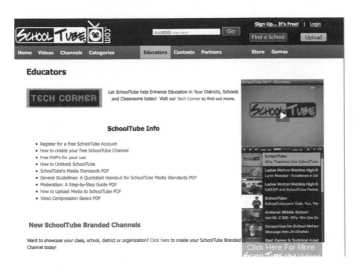

Figure 6.23. SchoolTube. Used with permission of SchoolTube, LLC.

YouTube (http://www.youtube.com), Google Videos (http://video.google.com), and Yahoo Videos (http://video.yahoo.com), but they do not focus on education. In fact, a teacher must be very careful when using the general sites because there may be inappropriate content, including advertisements on them (see Figure 6.23).

Flickr

Although there are a number of free online photo and video storage, sharing, and management tools, such as Picasa (http://www.picasa.com) and Photobucket (http://www.photobucket.com), Flickr (http://www.flickr.com) is the most popular among users, according to Alexa (http://www.alexa.com), the traffic monitoring site. Among the many features that enhance its popularity are:

- Tags
- Support for a wide range of image and video formats
- Variety of import methods
- Scripts to post to Web sites
- Phone application
- Searching options
- RSS
- Variety of sharing methods
- Privacy/safety levels
- Photostream (Slideshow)
- Geotagging
- Built-in photo editor (Picnik)

Teachers and students are using Flickr in many interesting and creative ways. Below are some suggestions compiled from three excellent sources—The Strength of Weak Ties (http://jakespeak.blogspot.com/2006/03/classroom-uses-of-flickr.html), Karen Montgomery's Think Photo Sharing With Flickr (http://thinkingmachine.pbworks.com/Think+Photo+Sharing+with+Flickr), and Suzie Vesper's Flickr page (http://educationalsoftware.wikispaces.com/Flickr).

- Advertise library programs (place photo set on library Web site)
- Photographical tour of the library
- Writing prompts
- Vocabulary/language skills practice, prompting with images

- Facilitate discussions around images using the notes feature
- Teach categories and classification for science class
- Capture school events and functions (open house, award ceremonies, science fair, sports banquets, homecoming, reunions, community service activities, etc.) for placement on school or district Web site
- Create color or number sets for primary students
- Create trading cards about famous people for biography unit
- Virtual field trip of "real" class field trip, city tour, architectural tour, places students are studying tour, or interesting place tour.
- Practice sequencing—showing step by step of a larger process
- Share and extend knowledge by adding notes to others' images
- Virtual storytelling
- Connect images to larger world using geotagging
- Illustrate a poem
- Art study, analysis, discussion through notes feature
- Virtual portfolio of student work (art work, mindmaps, posters, displays, etc.)
- Visual portfolio using the sets feature
- Label diagrams
- Storage site for class photos to use with third-party tools such as Bubblr, Big Huge Labs tool (features include Motivator, Mosaic, Magazine Cover, Warholizer, Movie Poster, Jigsaw, and Captioner), Foto Flexor, and Splashr to create new things with Flickr images. (Flickr images are reproduced with permission of Yahoo! Inc. © 2009, Yahoo! Inc. Flickr and Flickr logo are registered trademarks of Yahoo! Inc.)

How Does It Work?

After signing up for a free account, either search the public database for images to view or use (complying with licensing requirements) or import images to edit, organize, or share. Notice the options on the toolbar—you, organize, contacts, groups, explore, help, search, and sign out.

Some Basics . . .

- **To upload images**—Go to the you option, then click on upload photos and videos. When presented with the dialog box (see Figure 6.24), select the desired photos or videos, upload, then proceed to add titles, descriptions, tags, and add to existing sets or create a new set for the new upload.

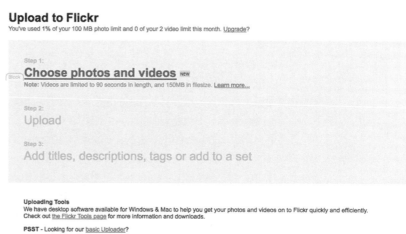

Figure 6.24.   Flickr Upload Dialog Box.

- **To create a set**—Click on organize on the toolbar. Click on create a new set under the sets tab. Name the set, provide a description of its content, and then drag images from the photostream into the sets work area, then save. Pull content for the new set from non-tagged items in your collection, from images not yet in sets, from geo-tagged images, from images uploaded on a selected date as well as from your other sets or groups (those that were created or those to which the users belong).
- **To create a group**—Select create a new group from the drop-down menu. Select from the three types of groups that you can create: public (anyone at all can join), public (people can join, but by invitation only), or private (this type of group can't be made public at a later date). Name your group and provide a description of its purpose. Select the safety level and click next. In the dialog box areas provided, indicate titles—what will the group administrator, moderator(s), and members be called.
- **To share**—There are a variety of ways to share your photos with others: invite others by e-mail, send photos as an attachment to an e-mail message, view a slideshow, embed them in Web site, blog, or wiki (see Figure 6.25), use contact list, or set up a Flickr Web address and share that with others (see Table 6.3).

Figure 6.25.   Flickr URL and HTML Code.

Strategies for Effective Student Use of Media Sharing Tools

1. For the first attempt, place students in small collaborative groups.
2. Remember, when they are first learning the technical aspects of the tool, no matter how easy it is, their focus will be on the tool, not the content. Choose topics that are fun and not too complex.
3. Create an evaluation rubric with the students, so that everyone is aware of all the elements that will be graded—content, technical aspects, creativity, spelling, and grammar.
4. Discuss intended audience with the students and how to use the tool's features to effectively target the content.
5. Teach student to respect copyright: to use their own images, ones from copyright free sites, or creative commons sites.
6. If narration is included in the presentation, encourage students to practice their speaking skills by reading their writing assignments aloud to the class—discuss pacing, pronunciation, and enunciation.

Table 6.3. Flickr Toolbar Options Explained.

Menu Items	Functions
You	Provides access to your photostream, sets, archives, tags, favorites, stats (only with Pro account), recent activity, upload photos and videos, account, profile, and FlickrMail.
Organize	Options under "Organize" include "All Your Content"; "Most Recent Upload"; "Your Sets"; and "Your Map." Under "All Your Content," you can batch organize. This includes: *Editing photos*—their titles, tags and descriptions, rotate, and delete. *Permissions*—where you can set the safety filter, set the content type, change settings to determine who can see, comment, and tag your photos. *Edit Dates*—all the photo dates can be changed to the same date. *Add Tags*—add tags to a new or an existing set. *Send to Group*—send photos to members of groups you belong to or to members of groups you have created. *Geoprivacy*—settings to indicate who can see where the items were taken. *Location*—add items to maps and remove items from maps. *Sets*—create a new set, open an existing set, or reorder sets by dragging them into the desired sequence. *Maps*—drag and drop photos or videos on the map.
Contacts	*Most Recent Uploads*—see new stuff from your friends. *Contact List*—has a variety of offerings, including "Who Calls You a Contact?" and a "Block List" (option for blocking someone who operates outside your comfort zone) *Find Your Friends*—using your address book for Yahoo!Mail, Hotmail, Windows Live, and Gmail account holders. *People Search*—locate people already using Flickr. *Invite Your Friends*—using their e-mail addresses. *Invite History*—view who has accepted your invitations, which ones are still pending. *Guest Pass History*—view whom you have sent a guest pass to and the expiration date that you set
Groups	*Your Groups*—allows you to view any groups you have created as well as groups you have joined. *Recent Changes*—shows new topics or replies posted in your groups (with a timeframe option). *Search*—from within all groups or from your own groups. *Create a New Group*—create new groups that are public, where anyone can join, public by invitation (helps to control membership), or private (useful when you want to share with selected individuals or family)
Explore	You will see the last 7 Days Interesting, Popular Tags, Most Recent Uploads, World Map, and Videos on Flickr, among other offerings.

Table 6.4.   Feature Comparisons among Selected Photo Sharing Sites.

Features	Photobucket	Picasa	Flickr
Cost	Free	Free	Free
Space	1 GB with up to 25 GB in monthly traffic	1 GB	2 Videos and 100 MB photos per month
Phone/Mobile App	X	X	X
Scripts to post to Web sites	X	X	X
Tags	X	X	X
Methods of Importing:			
Computer	No	No	X
E-mail	No	X	X
Phone	No	X	X
Upload Tool	X-up to 50 at a time	X	X
Camera	No	X	No
iPhoto Library	No	X	No
Webpages	No	X	No
Screen captures	No	X	No
Searchable by:			
Photographer or Name or Person	X	No	X
Tag	X	No	X
Text	X	X (Description)	X
Group or Group Album	X	No	X
Time	No	No	X
Place	No	No	X
Images	X	No	No
Video	X	No	No
Comments	X	X	X
RSS	X	X	X
Share by:			
Link	X	No	X
E-mail	X	X	X

continued

Features	Photobucket	Picasa	Flickr
Share Button	No	X	No
Scripts to Embed	X	X	X
Flickr Web Address	No	No	X
Groups/Group Albums	X	X	X
Sets/Sub-Albums	X	No	X
Export	No	X	No
Collage	X	X	No
Stamps	X	No	X
Privacy	X	X	X
Notes/Captions/ Descriptions	X	X	X
Slideshow	X-up to 50 images	X	X
Video	X-up to 5 min., up to 100 MB	X-1GB from Picasa; 100 MB from Mac Uploader	X
Geotag	No	X	X
Photo-editing built-in	X-Adobe Remix	X	X-Picnik
Statistics	X	No	No
"Toys"/Gifts	X	No	X

Action Steps

1. Look at the curriculum and identify topics or concepts that lend themselves to a multimedia presentation.
2. Explore the tools presented in this chapter and select one to use as a model for demonstration to the class, using one of the curriculum topics identified in step one.
3. Research and gather appropriate information to use in the presentation.
4. Storyboard the presentation, identifying needed images, graphics, or audio files.
5. Using search tools discussed in this chapter, locate and download multimedia files identified as needed. Be sure to observe copyright allowances, or use creative commons or copyright free sites for such files.

6. Script the vocal narration, or the informational text to accompany the images and graphics.
7. Create an introductory guide for your presentation, perhaps including key concepts and vocabulary associated with the topic, or a post-test quiz for students to take after viewing.
8. Integrate your product into the curriculum, demonstrating the various features included as instruction is provided on the topic.
9. Imbed the script into your blog, wiki, or Web site, or download the file to the school network so students can access your presentation whenever they need to.

Media Resources

An Introduction to VoiceThread; June 19, 2008; 4:35 min.; UPSITech; http://www.youtube.com/watch?v=nr0wod6JZIU.

Apple GarageBand Podcast Tutorial; April 22, 2008; 2:25 min.; http://www.youtube.com/watch?v=RimJ6BfQaTE.

Audacity Tutorial, Part 1; January 18, 2008; 5:32 min.; http://www.youtube.com/watch?v=lrPGMjZORCM.

Audacity Tutorial, Part 2; January 18, 2008; 5:40 min.; http://www.youtube.com/watch?v=6txQRfptawE.

Flickr; June 7, 2007; 4:02 min.; http://www.youtube.com/watch?v=YU1iO0HSkH8.

Flickr Tutorial Basic Tools; April 14, 2008; 7:20 min.; http://www.youtube.com/watch?v=Re05530ulS4.

Flickr Tutorial: How to Setup and Use Flickr; April 10, 2009; 9:55 min.; http://www.youtube.com/watch?v=SyXmR2PA6cM.

How to Create a Podcast (with Audacity); March 23, 2008; 3:57 min.; http://www.youtube.com/watch?v=-hrBbczS9I0.

How to Make a Podcast; April 19, 2009; 5:55 min.; http://www.youtube.com/watch?v=ps5rTJVysPE.

How to Upload a Video to YouTube; October 9, 2008; 1:58 min.; http://www.youtube.com/watch?v=9w-gQAwS2uc.

Introducing Picasa 3; August 21, 2008; 5:01 min.; http://www.youtube.com/watch?v=rskC6c_5L1M.

Introducing VoiceThread; October 27, 2007; 3:32 min.; http://www.youtube.com/watch?v=1XGpdy7c8DQ.

Online Photo Sharing in Plain English; January 8, 2008; 2:50 min.; http://www.youtube.com/watch?v=vPU4awtuTsk.

Picnik Tutorial; September 4, 2008; 8:13 min.; http://www.youtube.com/watch?v=ZpaFKFq49OI.

Podcasting in Plain English; April 21, 2008; 3:00 min.; http://www.youtube.com/watch?v=y-MSL42NV3c.

Using GarageBand to Build a Podcast; September 7, 2007; 8:49 min.; http://www.youtube.com/watch?v=3kXncJJNsNw.

Video Upload Tutorial: How to Upload Your Videos to YouTube; October 9, 2008; 1:58 min.; http://www.youtube.com/watch?v=9w-gQAwS2uc.

VoiceThread; May 6, 2008; 8:57 min.; http://www.youtube.com/watch?v=BULUq4LS10w.

What Is Podcasting? October 5, 2007; 8:11 min.; http://www.youtube.com/watch?v=eMIHgY8Q8C0.

References and Additional Resources

Adam, Anna and Helen Mowers. 2007. Listen Up! *School Library Journal* 53 (12): 44–46.

Braun, Linda W. 2007. *Listen Up! Podcasting for Schools and Libraries*. Medford, NJ: Information Today, Inc.

Campbell, Gardner. 2005. There's Something in the Air: Podcasting in Education. *Educause Review* 40 (6): 32.

Crane, Beverly. 2008. Digital Storytelling Changes the Way We Write Stories. *Information Searcher* 18 (1): 1+.

Dye, Jessica. 2007. Collaboration 2.0: Make the Web Your Workspace. *EContent* 30 (4): 8+.

———. Meet Generation C: Creatively Connecting through Content. *EContent* 30 (4): 38+.

Eash, E. K. 2006. Podcasting 101 for K-12 Librarians. *Computers in Libraries*. http://www .infotoday.com/cilmag/apr06/Eash.shtml.

Educause. VoiceThread. http://www.educause.edu/eli.

———. 7 Things to Know about Digital Storytelling. http://net.educause.edu/ir/library/pdf/ ELI7021.pdf.

Fontichiaro, Kristin. 2007. Podcasting 101. *School Library Media Activities Monthly* 23 (7): 22–23.

———. 2008. *Podcasting at School*. Westport, CT: Libraries Unlimited.

Garvin, Peggy. 2009. Photostreams to the People: The Commons on Flickr. *Searcher* 17 (8): 45–49.

Harris, Christopher. 2008. A Prescription for Transforming Libraries. *School Library Journal* 54 (10): 22.

InfoTech4Lrng. VoiceThread in Teaching and Learning. http://arllennium.wordpress.com/ category/voicethread/.

Jones, Nathan. 2009. YA 101: You're on the Air! Podcasting with Teens at the Library. *Voya* 32 (3): 200–203.

Lamb, Annette and Larry Johnson. 2007. Podcasting in the School Library, Part 1: Integrating Podcasts and Vodcasts into Teaching and Learning. *Teacher Librarian* 34 (3): 54–57.

———. Podcasting in the School Library, Part 2: Creating Powerful Podcasts with Your Students. *Teacher Librarian* 34 (4): 61–64.

———. Video and the Web, Part 1: More the Flickers on the Screen. *Teacher Librarian* 35 (1): 53–56.

Levine, Allen. 2007. Cogdogroo, 50+ Web 2.0 Ways to Tell a Story. http://cogdogroo.wiki spaces.com/50+Ways.

Ludwig, Thomas, et al. 2004. Using Multimedia in Classroom Presentations: Best Principles. http://teachpsych.org/resources/pedagogy/classroommultimedia.pdf.

Mardis, Marcia A. and Anne M. Perrault. 2008. A Whole New Library: Six "Senses" You Can Use to Make Sense of New Standards and Guidelines. *Teacher Librarian* 35:34–38.

McLellan, Hilary and Roger B. Wyatt. Tech Head Stories. http://www.tech-head.com/ dstory.htm.

Ned's Keeper. http://blog.discoveryeducation.com/ldaughrity/2008/10/04/38/.

Nichol, Mark. 2008. VoiceThread Extends the Classroom with Interactive Multimedia Albums. Edutopia. http://www.edutopia.org.

O'Leary, Mick. 2008. I Love YouTube. *Information Today* 25 (11): 33+.

———. 2009. Remarkable Outreach: Flickr Draws 10 Million Views. *Library of Congress Information Bulletin* 68 (1/2): 22–24.

Richardson, Will. 2006. *Blogs, Wikis, Podcasts, and Other Powerful Web Tools for Classrooms*. Thousand Oaks, CA: Corwin Press.

———. 2006. Making Waves. *School Library Journal* 54 (10): 54.

Robin, Bernard R. 2006. The Educational Uses of Digital Storytelling. http://digital
    storytelling.coe.uh.edu.
Sener, John. 2007. In Search of Student-Generated Content in Online Education. *e-mentor* 4 (21).
    http://www.e-mentor.edu.pl/_xml/wydania/21/467.pdf.
Troutner, Joanne. 2007. Best Sites for Educational Podcasts. *Teacher Librarian* 34 (3): 43–44.

7

Social Networking

 ESSENTIAL QUESTIONS

Why should educators bother with social networking?

How can social networking be used to engage students in effective communication and collaboration?

Which are the best social networking sites for education and how are educators using them with students?

Figure 7.1.   http://www.wordle.net

Ms. Cohen, a high school social studies teacher, is concerned about her students' ongoing lack of interest in American History. At a social studies conference, her interest is piqued as she is introduced to social networking and learns that the benefits include increased students motivation and engagement. She returns to school and immediately goes to the library to talk to Mrs. Suarez, the school librarian and resident guru on all things digital. Mrs. Suarez give her background information on social networking, directs her to some current articles on the library Web site along with educational examples of their use. She also suggests they collaborate to create a Ning for the American History classes' 1930s unit coming up in the next month.

Over the next weeks, the two educators collaborate during the school day and sometimes meet in the evening on Skype to create a private classroom Ning. They carefully choose the communication and collaboration features and content (video, graphics, links to relevant Web sites, podcasts, etc.) for the Ning to focus and support the students' research and thinking. The students, working in teams, construct a page on the classes' American History: 1930s Ning on one of 20 controversial debate topics, advocating a specific position. Their task is to research relevant information and facilitate a class discussion on the Ning forum. Rubrics (developed by teachers and students) and student journals (a blog on the Ning) are used as formative evaluation; a live classroom debate concludes the unit.

The outcome is successful: the students enthusiastically research and create a Ning page, interact with each other as they delve deeper into the content, analyze the content, and reflect on their own knowledge. It proves to Ms. Cohen that these kids can do quality work if they are connected and motivated. She decides to talk to Mrs. Suarez about some other Web 2.0 tools she heard about—maybe she'll integrate podcasting or wikis into her next project.

What Is Social Networking?

Social networking sites fall into the category of social technology, "computer-mediated communication environments that connect people for cooperation, collaboration and information sharing" (Lamb and Johnson 2006, 55). Social networks "focus on building online communities of people who share interests and/or activities or who are interested in exploring the interests and activities of others" (http://en.wikipedia .org/social_network_service). Steve Hargadon, in his blog on The Infinite Thinking Machine (http://www.infinitethinking.org/2008/01/social-networking-in-education .html), states that, "Social networks are really collections of Web 2.0 technologies combined in a way that help to build online communities." The focus is on building online communities that involve grouping specific individuals or organizations together. Social networking moved from "a niche activity into a phenomenon that engages tens of millions of Internet users" (Lenhart and Madden 2007). There are over 200 social network services worldwide, and they all have strong followings in different parts of the world. The general social networks in which membership is open to everyone includes Facebook, which is the most popular with 150 million users and MySpace, following with 76 million users (Web Strategy, http://www.web-strategist.com/ blog/2009/01/11/a-collection-of-soical-network-stats-for-2009/).

Figure 7.2.   Facebook.

Sometimes social networks specialize on one age or ethnic group, such as Bebo, best loved by young teenagers, Black Planet where African Americans spend time, Chinese people connect on QQ, and Brazilians hang out on Orkut. And there are more specialized networks such as LinkedIn for business, Match.com for dating, Goodreads for books, Flixster for movies, and Ravelry for knitting and crocheting.

Individuals and organization sometime start social network sites on specific topics such as art, technology, biology, or sites are created to strengthen communication and learning within a specific group such a teacher's individual classroom, a conference, school, or public library. These tend to be private, as opposed the general sites listed above. No matter which social network chosen, contrary to popular perception, most groups that form on social networks are not made up of strangers. Most people use social networking sites to support pre-existing real-life social groups (http://www.danah.org/papers/KnowledgeTree.pdf).

Overview

All of the social network sites have features that distinguish them from other Web sites:

Figure 7.3.   Goodreads.

The profile page: a page that allows users to describe themselves through text, video, and music.

A network of friends: a public or semipublic list of friends, usually displayed as small photographic icons.

A public commenting system: allows friends and strangers to write a short note or statement that will be displayed publicly on the profile page.

A private messaging system: enables friends to send private messages via the users' profile.

Table 7.1.   Social Network User Statistics (Pew/Internet Generations Online in 2009).

Social Network User Statistics by Age Groups	
12–17 yrs. = 65%	45–54 yrs = 20%
18–32 yrs. = 67%	55–63 yrs. = 9%
33–44 yrs. = 36%	64–73+ yrs. = 15%

Social networking is not just for kids. According the Pew Internet and American Life Project, social network sites are used across all age groups, with the 18- to 33-year-olds having the highest involvement (see Table 7.1). Some estimates indicate that upwards of 80–90 percent of U.S. college students have profiles on Facebook (http://www.educause.edu/ELI/7ThingsYouShouldKnowAboutFaceb/156828).

Why Should Educators Bother with Social Networking?

When the term "social networking" is mentioned, it's almost synonymous with Facebook or MySpace, the two most popular and well known social networking Web sites. "Online social networking is now so deeply embedded in the lifestyles of tweens and teens that it rivals television for their attention" (National School Board Association [NSBA] and Grunwald Associates, 2007, http://nsba.org/site/docs/41400/41340.pdf). This study found that nearly all (96%) of kids aged 9–17 are chatting, text messaging, blogging, and creating pages on social sites:

- Posting messages (41%)
- Blogging (17%)
- Creating and sharing virtual objects (16%)
- Participating in collaborative projects (10%)
- Submitting articles to Web sites (9%)
- Creating polls, quizzes, or surveys (9%)

"Further, students report that of the most common topics of conversation on the social networking scene is education. Almost 60 percent of students who use social networking talk about education topics online and, surprisingly, more than 50 percent talk specifically about homework" (NSBA 2007).

Research on Social Networking

In a first-of-its-kind study, researchers at the University of Minnesota discovered the educational benefits of social networking sites. The study found that "of the students observed, 94 percent used the Internet, 82 percent go online at home, and 77 percent had a profile on a

Social networkers use the noun "friend" as a verb, so in turn, the word "friending" evolved as the act of making friends on a social network. Some members collect as many friends as possible without regard to personal connection; however, people typically use social networks to interact with a small group of *known* friends. Check out this interesting article, "Primates on Facebook," on building networks of friends (http://www.economist.co/science/displaystory.cfm?story_id=13176775).

Figure 7.4.   Friending.

Figure 7.5.   Video Interview: MacArthur Foundation Research on Social Networking (http://www.macfound.org/site/c.lkLXJ 8MQKrH/b.4773383/k.8CB5/Mizuko_Ito_on_Why_Time_Spent _Online_Is_Important_for_Teen_Development.htm).

social networking site." One of the most significant findings was, "When asked what they learn from using social networking sites, the students listed technology skills as the top lesson, followed by creativity, open to new or diverse ways, and communication skills." The Mac Arthur Foundation, in the results from the most extensive U.S. study on teens and their use of digital media, found that America's youth are developing important social and technical skills online—often in ways adults do not understand or value. For over three years, researchers interviewed over 800 young people and their parents, both one-on-one and in focus groups spending over 5,000 hours observing teens on sites such as MySpace, Facebook, YouTube, and other networked communities. They conducted diary studies to document how, and to what end, young people engage with digital media.

The researchers identified two distinctive categories of teen engagement with digital media: friendship-driven and interest-driven. While friendship-driven participation centered on "hanging out" with existing friends, interest-driven participation involved accessing online information and communities that may not be present in the local peer group. Significant findings include:

- There is a generation gap in how youth and adults view the value of online activity.
  Adults tend to be in the dark about what youth are doing online, and often view online activity as risky or an unproductive distraction.
  Youth understand the social value of online activity and are generally highly motivated to participate.
- Youth are navigating complex social and technical worlds by participating online.
  Young people are learning basic social and technical skills that they need to fully participate in contemporary society.
  The social worlds that youth are negotiating have new kinds of dynamics, as online socializing is permanent, public, involves managing elaborate networks of friends and acquaintances, and is always on.
- Young people are motivated to learn from their peers online.

The Internet provides new kinds of public spaces for youth to interact and receive feedback from one another.

Young people respect each other's authority online and are more motivated to learn from each other than from adults.

- Most youth are not taking full advantage of the learning opportunities of the Internet.

Most youth use the Internet socially, but other learning opportunities exist.

Youth can connect with people in different locations and of different ages who share their interests, making it possible to pursue interests that might not be popular or valued with their local peer groups.

"Geeked-out" learning opportunities are abundant—subjects like astronomy, creative writing, and foreign languages (http://www.macfound.org).

Inquiry Learning

Social Networking supports all phases of inquiry as learners interact and collaborate. As mentioned earlier, social networks are really collections of Web 2.0 technologies combined in a way that helps to build online communities. When students are active members of a curriculum-based Ning they are sharing, questioning, organizing, managing, communicating, producing, and publishing. The American Association of School Librarians (AASL) in their new national standards, "Standards for the 21st-Century Learner," stress that students learn to collaborate, seeking diverse opinions, and participation in social networks:

2.1.5 Collaborate with others to exchange ideas, develop new understandings, make decisions, and solve problems.

2.3.2 Consider diverse and global perspectives in drawing conclusions.

3.1.2 Participate and collaborate as members of a social and intellectual network of learners.

4.1.7 Use social networks and information tools to gather and share information.

Figure 7.6.   Stripling Inquiry Model.

4.3.4 Practice safe and ethical behaviors in personal electronic communication and interaction.

Excerpted from "Standards for the 21st-Century Learner" by the AASL, a division of the American Library Association. © 2007, American Library Association. Available for download at www.ala.org/aasl/standards. Used with permission.

In addition, AASL identified nine common beliefs, one of which addresses the social aspect of learning. "Learning has a social context. Learning is enhanced by having opportunities to share and learn with others. Students need to develop skills in sharing knowledge and learning with others, both in face-to-face and using technology."

Twelve Reasons to Use Social Networking

1. Creates real-life friendships through similar interests or groups.
2. Enhances technology and communication skills.
3. Promotes creativity.
4. Presents new or diverse views.
5. Provides practice editing/customizing content.
6. Shares creative work.
7. Supports user's need to affiliate.
8. Offers opportunity to practice safe, ethical, and responsible use.
9. Creates an environment that fosters participation in online communities.
10. Expands/creates friendships.
11. Encourages user-generated content—videos and photos.
12. Allows educators to reach students through a medium they use every day.

NSBA recommends that schools:

- Consider using social networking for staff communications and professional development.
- Find ways to harness the educational value of social networking.
- Ensure equitable access.
- Pay attention to the nonconformist.
- Encourage social networking companies to increase educational value.

How Are Educators Using Social Networks to Facilitate Learning?

Librarians and classroom teachers are working to integrate positive uses of social networking into their classroom curriculum and library program and services. There are many examples of how students are being introduced to social networking in a meaningful, positive, and safe manner.

- An author sets up a MySpace page. Teen fans keep current on the author's reflections and new writings as well as biographical information and literacy events.
- A school library creates a Facebook page as a way to connect with students in the school who usually don't come into the school library but are comfortable with technology. They can find out about new books through easy access to the online catalog, use other research tools for class assignments, and answer surveys on what resources they want in the library.

continued

Table 7.2. Comparative Chart of Selected Social Networks.

Features	Facebook	MySpace	Ning
Age Requirement	13	13	13
Themes		X	X
Personalized URL		X	X
Photos	X	X	X
Blog		X	X
Friends	X	X	X
Block Users	X	X	X
Privacy Settings	X	X	X
Customize Code-HTML		X	X
Instant Messaging	X	X	
Tags	X	X	X
Groups/Create Groups	X	X	X
Mobile Component	X	X	iPhone, iTouch
Mail	X	X	
Videos(personal)	X	X	X
Music		X	X
Notes	X		X
Tabs	X	X	X
Badges	X		X
Events	X	X calendar	X
Forum	X	X	X
Support/FAQs	X	X	X
Profile Question			X
Import Address Book Application	X	X	X
Search By Name	X	X	X
Search By E-mail	X	X	X
Search By Zip Code/Location	X	X	X
Search By Keyword		X	
Search By School	X	X	X
Search By Interests	X	X	X
Search By Age		X	
Search By Work	X		
Search By College	X		
Search By Company	X		

- A high school student creates a Facebook page for English class on *Hamlet*. She researches his character, his culture, and his friends to be able to make it as true to Shakespeare's famous character as possible. Other members of the class post questions and the student responds "in character."

Young adult and college librarians have taken the lead in using social networks to reach out and interact with their patrons. Ask a Librarian's services allows libraries to provide personalized reference service. Facebook has applications such as a photo slideshow, a blog, and other third-party applications like World Cat and Flickr that can be imbedded on a library's social network, and groups can be created that allow for interaction with more than one person at a time while the Real Simple Syndication (RSS) feature on a social network enhances their flexibility even more.

Customized Social Networks: Ning

More often than not, however, because of the issues surrounding Facebook and MySpace, educators are favoring "white label" social networking sites that "enable their customers to build their own social networking (often from scratch) and to tailor these networks to a range of purposes. The idea of white labeling a network is to make the platform provider as invisible as possible to the social network's users and to brand the network with the builder's identity or intent" (Hendrickson 2007). These smaller, customized social networks provide more safety for students than the proprietary network, such as Facebook, MySpace, Hi5, Bebo, and Xanga, which is open to the world and whose features has already been set by the company. In a hosted do-it-yourself network, such as Ning, the user selects a theme as well as the features they'd like to incorporate from among those available and arranges them on the page according to their preference, invites and publicizes their Ning; the content, as with other social networking sites, is provided by the users. Ning appears to be favored by educators because it is free, fairly intuitive to setup, offers attractive themes for a polished look, and offers a variety of basic features for inclusion on the site (see Table 7.2 for comparison of three social networking sites: Facebook, MySpace, and Ning).

Hargadon has compiled a list of social networking sites being used in education (http://www.infinitethinking.org/2008/01/social-networking-in-education.html). Brief descriptions provide a glimpse of how educators are using Ning to:

- Organize research projects
- Support group projects
- Serve as an online classroom
- Showcase student work (involving parents)
- Provide an informative site based on curriculum content

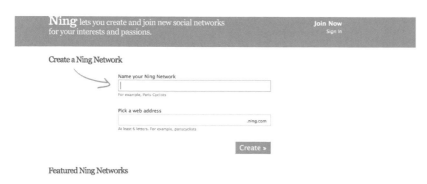

Figure 7.7. Ning.

Below is a selective list in the areas of professional

development, classroom, and libraries with descriptions of their intent. Access to these sites varies: some are open to the public to view but require membership to participate, such as commenting (MSP2, Teacher 2.0), others require membership to move past the home page (Projects by Jen); and others are closed for privacy and student safety. However, users can see the home page of all of the sites listed and that gives a glimpse of how Nings are being used in education.

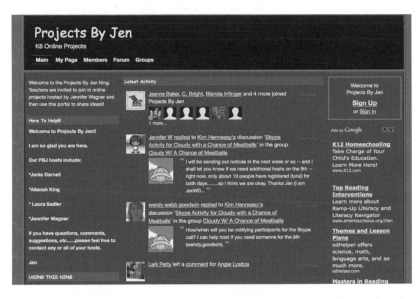

Figure 7.8.   Projects by Jen—For Teachers of Pre-K through 6th Grades (http://projectsbyjen.ning.com/).

For Teachers

MSP2 (http://msteacher2.org)—network for middle school math and science teachers

Flat Classroom Project (http://flatclassroomproject.ning.com)—the Flat Classroom Project partners high school students from different countries as they focus on globalization

Teachers 2.0 (http://teachers20.ning.com)—about teaching in the digital age

Pixels Please (http://pixels please.ning.com)—using digital images in the classroom

Vidsnacks (http://vidsnacks.ning.com/)—video training for teachers who want to incorporate video into their teaching

Classroom 2.0 (http://www.classroom20.com/)—created by Steve Hargadon as a community for educators interested in Web 2.0 and collaborative technologies (see Figure 7.9)

For Students

Mr. Bruns 360 (http://mr bruns.ning.com/)—network created for his high school social studies classes (see Figure 7.10)

Mr. Hedman's Math Class (http://hedmansmath.ning .com/)—created for his students

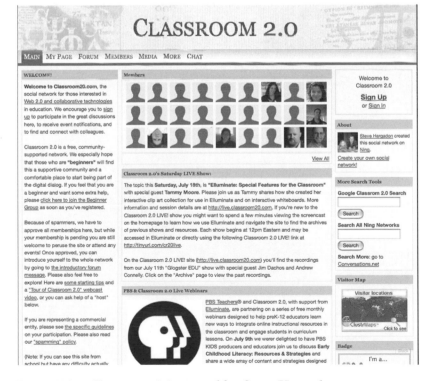

Figure 7.9.   Classroom 2.0, started by Steve Hargadon.

Figure 7.10.   Mr. Bruns 360 Network.

Museum Educational Social Network (http://mesn.museumpods.com/)—for students and museums to connect

For Librarians

Teacher Librarian Ning (http://teacherlibrarian.ning.com/)—a network for teacher librarians (see Figure 7.11)

Library 2.0 (http://library20.ning.com/)—network for librarians interested in Web 2.0 topics

American Library Association (http://alamembers.ning.com)—oldest American library organization for librarians

21st Century Teacher Librarians (http://21centurylibrarian.ning.com)—sponsored by the University of Colorado, Denver.

Savvy Librarian (http://savvylibrarians.ning.com/)—a place to connect and grow with other librarians

LIS Students (http://lisstudents.ning.com/)—for students in library and information studies, or recent graduates

Bready School Library (http://breadylibrary.ning.com/)—to review books in the Bready School library

KSC Librarians (http://kcslibrarians.ning.com/)—for librarians in Kanawha County, West Virginia

Focus on Ning

A Ning is quick and easy to create. An educator registers and constructs a social network in a few steps by pointing and clicking on features they want to include in their Ning. The main benefit of creating a social network is that it gives users control over content and membership. The features offered

Figure 7.11.   Teacher Librarian Ning Started by Joyce Valenza.

1930s Project for American History, Using Ning

Site Title

Tag Line

Tabs

Events

Forum

Notes

Important Course
Links

Photos from The
American Memory

Video on 1930s from
Teacher Tube

Text Box with Widget
Inserted

Text Box with Links
to Web 2.0 Tools
(Mindmeister,
Loosestitch, Google
Docs and SpringNote)

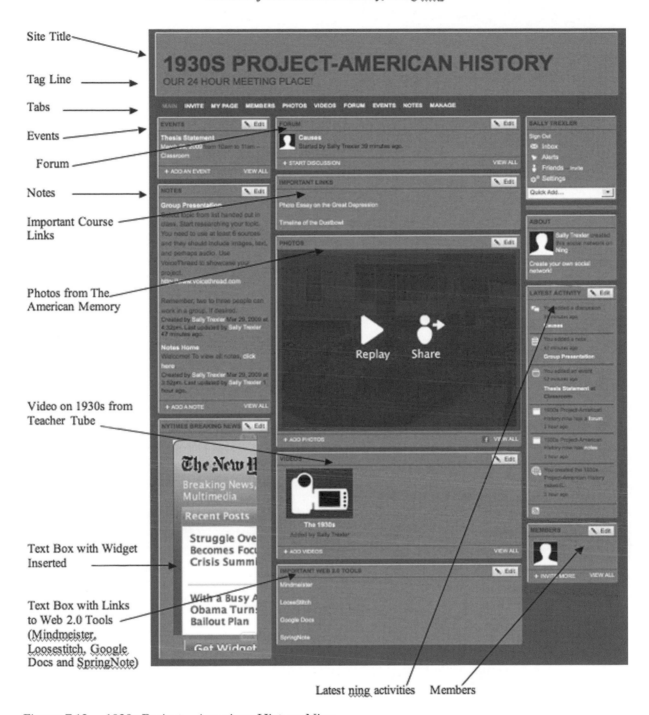

Latest ning activities   Members

Figure 7.12.   1930s Project—American History Ning.

by Ning allow for an effective social network, regardless of the social network's purpose;
choose which features to include in the Ning and where to place them on the screen. For
example, a social studies teacher creates a Ning for his twentieth-century American History class, targeting the 1930s unit; he has the option to add features such as groups,
forums, and notes, as well as podcasts, videos, and photographs (see Figure 7.12).

Create a Ning

Nings create community, encouraging students to collaborate, discuss and share resources. Educators can use this template to plan an instructional Ning with students.

Instructions:
1. Determine the purpose and topic of the Ning.
2. Go to http://ning.com to set up a Ning account.
3. Decide on the privacy settings: public or private.
4. Decide on the content and create a site navigation scheme. Choose from the available options below and add to the work space on the right.

Features:

Sketch the placements of your selected features in column 1, 2 and the bottom of column 3. They can be duplicated, (ex. two Videos, three Text Boxes,)

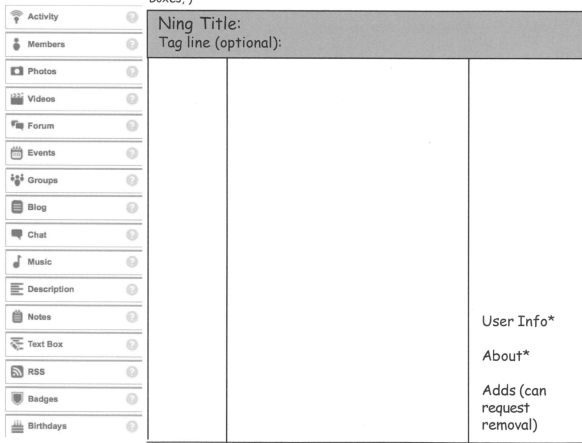

Features list:
- Activity
- Members
- Photos
- Videos
- Forum
- Events
- Groups
- Blog
- Chat
- Music
- Description
- Notes
- Text Box
- RSS
- Badges
- Birthdays

Ning Title:
Tag line (optional):

User Info*

About*

Adds (can request removal)

* set features

Next Step:
Explore the ManageTab: Spread the Word, Your Network, Your Members, and Resources to fine tune your Ning.

Figure 7.13.   Create a Ning.

Forums could be used to encourage discussion and investigation into historical events, offering students a means to express themselves. Links to videos and photographs can be inserted into discussions, as well as text. Interactivity is increased through the events or notes features that serve as a place to post upcoming assignments, readings, due dates, and test notices. Text boxes and links can be inserted to share relevant curriculum sites and RSS feeds could be included from sites dealing with subject matter presented in class.

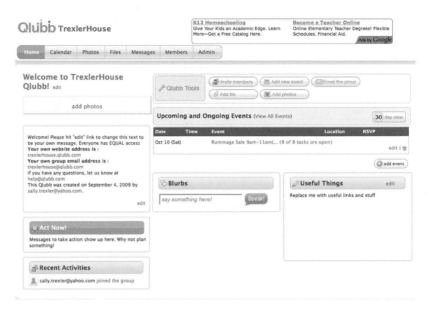

Figure 7.14.   Qlubb (http://www.qlubb.com). Used with permission of Qlubb, Inc.

In addition, each student can create their own "My Page" on the 1930s American History Ning selecting features that are relevant to them such as a blog, comment wall, and photographs, and choose their own theme. With a Ning, the content drives the design and choice of features; each Ning will be different. "Ning provides an avenue for instructors to take advantage of social networks in a neutral setting, offering functionality and experience that are familiar and comfortable to students. By creating social networks around academic topics, or even about specific projects for a course, an instructor can facilitate a strong sense of community among the students, encouraging personal interactions that can lead to the creation of new knowledge and collective intelligence" (http://www.educause.edu/ELI/7ThingsYouShouldKnowAboutNing/162903).

Take time to carefully plan the social network so it reaches its fullest potential. Some recommended steps (http://www.kickapps.com/download-our-whitepaper/index.php) include:

- Define your purpose and audience.
- If you are using it with students, analyze your curriculum, and decide which features are needed to support the learning outcomes.
- Engage members in the process; this will be their virtual learning space.
- Customize the social network's design and add rich content, so that the members will want to return.
- Make sure it is easy for members to contribute to the community; give members the opportunity to have their own page, contribute to a forum, and add photos.
- Promote the network (flyers, e-mail, newsletter announcement, parent involvement, etc.).
- Encourage active participation.

Table 7.3.   Additional Social Networks for Classroom Use.

Tool	URL
Webjam—social networking made easy	http://www.webjam.com
Qlubb—nice site for a book club	http://www.qlubb.com
Mixxt—contains a wiki	http://www.mixxit.com
Lefora—forums made easy	http://www.lefora.com
Soceeo—can opt out of advertisements	http://www.soceeo.com
Grou.ps—can host on own server or not	http://grou.ps/introduction.php

Twitter

"What Are You Doing?"

Twitter (http://www.twitter.com) is a free microblogging tool that can be utilized from a computer, a mobile phone, or a PDA. Postings, which are called "tweets," are limited to 140 characters, including spaces. It is very similar to text messaging, but tweets are published to the Web. People and institutions are using Twitter in a variety of ways.

- To start conversations
- To recommend books and online resources
- To track favorite authors
- To gain access to a greater pool of opinion
- To post helpful URLs
- To ask advice of experts
- To send reminders
- To share information from conferences
- To promote activities and events

One very unique way of using Twitter is exemplified by the profile, J. Q. Adams (http://www.twitter.com/jqadams_MHS). This site, sponsored by the Massachusetts Historical Society, offers a line-a-day diary entry of U.S. President John Quincy Adams, beginning with his journey to Russia on August 5, 1809. In addition, there are links from the diary entry to maps, showing his journey.

Another fun twitter to follow is written from the viewpoint of Charles Darwin from onboard the Beagle (http://twitter.com/cdarwin). It is associated with the Web site *The Voyage of the Beagle* (http://www.thebeaglevoyage.com/). Great examples of curriculum connections.

Twitter poses the question, "What are you doing?" to help start the "conversation." Most people usually "share" rather than just say what they are doing. The Twittersphere is large, 9.3 million people in the U.S, and growing; surprisingly, 65.4 percent of its users are 45 years or older (Kho 2009). Check out Twitter's site in the Help Resources area (http://help.twitter.com/portal) and try it; keep an eye on Twitter—we'll be seeing more instructional use in the near future!

Three Strategies to Use Social Networks

1. Create classroom guidelines for the Ning with students; be sure they comply with district policy.
2. Create a classroom or library social network. Invite students and encourage them to participate.
3. Discuss the privacy settings on popular social networking Web sites with students and teach them how to apply them.

How Can We Teach Kids to Be Safe Online

Any discussion of social networks is not complete without a thorough discussion of student preparedness. Even though the benefits of using social networks in education such as collaborating, data-sharing, cooperative problem solving, self-expression, and participating in a global conversation outweighed the risk factors, it is still necessary to prepare students to behave safely and ethically. Wesley Fryer, in his podcast entitled, "Safe Digital Social Networking" (http://www.speedof creativity.org), explains that adults have to do more than ban sites or pass laws to protect our children. Kids are not going to stop socializing and social networks are not going away, especially in view of their money-making ability. Educators need to prepare kids for the world in which they will live and that requires knowing how to be safe online. Fryer uses the metaphor of a teen learning to drive a car; adults wouldn't think of letting our child get behind the driving wheel without the training, the practice, or the skills to become a safe driver. In turn, adults need to provide safe opportunities online so that students can practice and learn how to navigate safely online. When students encounter the risks, they will know how to react properly, and how to report the offensive or inappropriate action to trusted adults.

Listed below are social network concepts that need to be addressed and discussed with students.

- **Profiles**. Although they play an important role in social media for identity formation, content ownership, and for the maintenance of online relationships, students should be aware of the type of information they should and should not include in their profiles. Students should never give out their name, age, e-mail, postal address, phone number, their photo, or school location without parental consent because interested outside parties can use the data provided to track them down.

  Try an eye-opening social experiment. Use one of these sites for students to observe: (http://www.411.com/reverse_phone, http://www.freeality .com/finde.htm, http://www.addresses.com, or http://www.best 411.com). Demonstrate how easy it is to look up a landline phone number, a cell phone number, an e-mail address, or a postal address. Students would also see that a map to the address is included with the search result. *Note: some of the sites require a membership or a small fee to see the full information, but it would be enough for students to realize how important it is to keep private information secure from strangers.*

- **Privacy settings**. Students need to understand the privacy settings features on blogs, wikis, and social networks and comprehend that using this feature gives them control over who views their information. There is a difference between public (anyone at all can see his or her information) and private (only those invited by the student can view his or her information).
- **Friending**. Students are social by nature but they need to understand that just because someone requests to be their friend, they are not obligated to honor the request. If students use the private setting and invite their real-world friends, they truly know with whom they will be interacting. Remind them that not every one online is who they say they are.
- **Cyberbullying**. This is the online environment version of bullying. Schools ban bullying and sponsor programs to teach students how to properly interact with one another. Schools include anti-bullying policies within their student code of conduct. Whether in person or online, students need to understand that what they say, what they do, and how they treat others can affect their own future as well as the victim's future.
- **Sexting**. Sending sexually explicit text messages or images via cell phones or computers is increasing. Unfortunately, some students do not understand that engaging in sexting could embarrass them in front of teachers, parents, coaches, future employers, and college admissions officers, now and in the future and place them in potentially dangerous situations. Such messages and images could be sent to a much larger audience than they had intended or be posted online for perpetuity.
- **Flaming**. The deliberate action of sending confrontational message to someone online breaks the rules of netiquette which encourage courtesy, honesty, and polite behavior in their online dealings.

Some common online acronyms used by students when they are trying to be secretive are listed below. Parents and teachers should become curious and/or concerned when they see children using them to a great degree.

- WTGP-Want to go private
- POS-Parent over shoulder
- PIR-Parent in room
- PAW-Parents are watching
- PAL-Parents are listening
- LMIRL-Let's meet in real life
- IRL-In real life
- F2F-Face to face
- ASL-Age, sex, location

Figure 7.15. Wired Safety (http://www.wiredsafety.org).

There are many online risks that educators, as well as students, must be aware of; however, with the proper education, students can be safe online. The Broadband Data Improvement Act (Public Law 110-385), passed into law in October 2008, now requires schools that receive federal e-rate discounts to educate students about online safety and online behavior (American Libraries 2008).

There are a number of organizations that promote online safety by offering tips, activities, lesson plans, and movies. Such organizations include:

- GetNetWise (http://www.getnetwise.org)
- Wired Safety (http://www.wiredsafety.org)
- NetSmartz (http://www.netsmartz.org)
- Internet Keep Safe Coalition (http://www.ikeepsafe.org)
- iSAFE (http://www.i-safe.org)
- Stay Safe (http://www.staysafe.org)
- National Center for Missing and Exploited Children (http://www.missingkids.com)
- National Crime Prevention Council (http://www.ncpc.org)
- National Cyber Security Alliance (http://staysafeonline.org)
- Safety Tips for Tweens and Teens (http://www.ftc.gov/bcp/edu/pubs/consumer/tech/tec14.htm)

Top tips compiled from the safety organizations are:

Teach children to:

- Never give out personal information such as name, school, address, phone number, email address, or photos of themselves. Once such information is placed online, it can never be taken back.
- Never make arrangements to meet in person someone that they've met online, without parental permission or without a trusted adult present at the meeting.
- Never post pictures of themselves or e-mail or send attachments of such photos to anyone without parental approval. Never should they be sent to strangers.
- Never include hints as to their real identity; use screen names that are nondescript.
- Never open attachments, Web sites, or URLs sent to them by strangers. They could contain viruses or inappropriate viewing material.
- Obey the age requirements posted by Web sites in their terms of service statement. Age restrictions are in place as a safety precaution.
- Know that they control who sees their information when they use the privacy settings offered by Web sites. They should use the setting that requires approval before accepting anyone as a friend.
- Never post anything about themselves or others that they wouldn't want their parents or teachers to see. That includes bad language or antagonistic remarks about other people or classmates. Neither should they respond to provoking remarks directed to them made by others. Such incidents should be reported to trusted adults.
- Never buy things online or enter online contests without parental approval. Personal information is usually required for such activities and should not ever be shared.
- Get parental approval before an account is created. Parents should keep a master log of all such accounts, as well as the user IDs and passwords.
- If students encounter offensive or dangerous material online, don't play the blame game. Use the opportunity to teach them to turn off the monitor and report the incident immediately to a trusted adult, so it can be reported to the authorities. Follow up with open discussion about safety concerns.

Figure 7.16.   Safety Tips for Tweens and Teens (http://www.ftc.gov/bcp/edu/pubs/consumer/tech/tec14.htm).

Action Steps

1. Identify a social network site that fits your interests (one on books, gardening, teaching, etc.) and sign up for a free account. Explore the site for a while but within a week, reply to a posting (add a comment) to move from a passive "lurking" role to active participation.
2. Create a Ning with a collaborative teacher to use with his or her class. Help the teacher to decide which features best meet the needs of the students.
3. Ask administrator to do a presentation at one of the faculty meeting on the latest research on social networking and the impact on student learning. Include some tips on how to keep kids safe in social networking Web sites.
4. Research and share a diverse selection of good social networking Web sites with the faculty to show the wide range that exists in addition to Facebook and MySpace.
5. Do an in-depth presentation for students on how to set up their social networking accounts to stay safe.

Media Resources

Adjusting Facebook Privacy Settings; August 11, 2008; 5:06 min.; http://www.youtube.com/watch?v=xUfisfI8qfE.

A Sample Ning Network; September 5, 2009; 3:12 min.; http://www.youtube.com/watch?v=gG9Bj8RA7vs.

Ning Ad Removal; February 29, 2008; 3:35 min.; http://www.youtube.com/watch?v=og8ATJ0NAws.

Ning Tutorial2 Creating Network; March 23, 2009; 6:45 min.; http://www.youtube.com/watch?v=phkcDYK6ypM&NR=1.

Social Networking in Plain English; June 27, 2007; 1:48 min.; http://www.youtube.com/watch?v=6a_KF7TYKVc&feature=related.

Webjam; November 1, 2007; 2:06 min.; http://www.youtube.com/watch?v=e8o7bOKLiYM.

What Is Facebook? August 14, 2008; 3:45 min.; http://www.youtube.com/watch?v=M5gtN16gOr8.

References and Additional Resources

Boule, Michell. 2006. Five Weeks to a Social Library. http://www.sociallibraries.com/course/prelimprogram.

Cooper, Jason. 2008. Facebook Applications for the Library Community. *The Alabama Librarian* 58:8–11.

Creating & Connecting: Research and Guidelines on Online Social—and Educational—Networking. 2007. National School Board Assoc., in association with Grunwald Associates LLC. http://www.nsba.org/site/docs/41400/41340.pdf.

Educational Benefits of Social Networking Sites. 2008. University of Minnesota. http://www1.umn.edu/umnnews/Feature_Stories2/Educational_benefits_of_social_networking_sites.html.

Educause. 2006. 7 Things You Should Know about Facebook II. http://www.educause.edu/ELI/7ThingsYouShouldKnowAboutFaceb/156828.

———. 7 Things You Should Know about Ning. http://www.educause.edu/ELI/7ThingsYouShouldKnowAboutNing/162903.

Fox, Vanessa. 2007. Searching for People in All the New Social Places. *Information Today* 24:25.

Hendrickson, Mark. 2007. Nine Ways to Build Your Own Social Network. http://www
.techcrunch.com/2007/07/24/9-ways_to_build_your_own_social_network.

KickApps Team. 2007. 9 Steps to a Successful Online Community: A Whitepaper. http://
www.kickapps.com/download-our-whitepaper/index.php.

Kno, Nancy Davis. 2009. Ten Things You Need to Know about Twitter. *Information Today*
26 (6): 1+.

Krivak, Thomas. 2008. Facebook 101: Ten Things You Need to Know about Facebook. *Information
Today* 25:1+.

Lamb, Annette and Larry Johnson. 2006. Want to Be My Friend? What You Need to Know
about Social Technologies. *Teacher Librarian* 34 (1): 55+.

Lenhart, Amanda and Mary Madden. 2007. Social Networking Websites and Teens: An Overview. Washington, D.C.: PEW/Internet. http://www.pewinternet.org/Reports/2007/
Social-Networking-Websites-and-Teens.aspx.

Owyang, Jeremiah. 2007. White Label Social Networking Platforms. http://www.techcrunch
.com/wp-content/wlsn_comparison_chart.html.

Roeder, Linda. 2007. Top 10 Social Networking Sites. http://personalweb.about.com/od/
easyblogsandwebpages/ss/2007topsnsites.htm.

Figure 8.1. http://www.wordle.net

8

Digital Mapping

 ESSENTIAL QUESTIONS

What is digital mapping and how does it motivate, involve, and support inquiry learning?

What are Google Earth's unique features and how do they relate to the curriculum?

What other mapping tools are available and how do they compare to each other?

As Mr. Nabinger, the school librarian, turns on the computer, the earth materializes and slowly rotates against the dark sky on the LCD screen. As he moves the mouse, the globe spins toward Africa and zooms in to the Jane Goodall Institute on Lake Tanganyika in Tanzania. The students watch in amazement as the terrain materializes and the rivers wind their way through the valleys below. Mountains approach and small yellow chimpanzees and binoculars shaped icons catch their attention. As they move in for a closer look, they can see the icons represent each of the wild chimpanzees the researchers are studying. The icons, scattered throughout the mountainous terrain, include the names of the chimps—Gaia, Gremlin, Fanni. Frodo, Patti, and so on.

The students are researching endangered species. They choose chimpanzees, hoping to show the plight of chimps across Africa. The students know that at the rate forests are being cut down and chimps are falling victim to the bush meat trade, it's possible that chimpanzees could be extinct in the wild in their lifetime. They click on the icons that show photos, journal observations, videos, and links to the Jane Goodall Institute Blog with chimp bios, landmarks, and park trails. They furiously gather information and find answers to their questions. Through satellite and aerial photography the students have a visceral experience of manipulating and navigating a three-dimensional world of chimpanzees. Teams of students explore the information, create custom tours, and lay the groundwork for their environmental advocacy presentations. They use the customized tours to show their classmates the specific park areas and chimps they are researching, zooming in and out to target specific data. The class is particularly interested in the young chimps' behavior, how they play among themselves, depend on their mothers for traveling through the forest, learn how to groom each other, and stay out of the way of the alpha male. Goggle Earth allows the young researchers to create a strong digital narrative embedded with current, authoritative information; they successfully advocate for an endangered species.

Figure 8.2.   Jane Goodall's Gombe Chimpanzee Blog from the Jane Goodall Institute.

What Is Digital Mapping?

Let's face it—everyone is intrigued with investigating our home—the planet Earth. What better way to teach students the power of maps and the limitless depth of geography than through digital mapping? Maps can help users see their position in the world but it's much more than simply being able to look at a map and identify localities by proper name. Geography can be a launching pad to learn about the world— politics, culture, climate, economics, and more. Programs such as Goggle Earth offer an interactive mapping experience that allows the user to navigate, or "fly," around the globe scanning digital imagery of locations with street views, borders, labels, mountains, 3D buildings, and more. Users can add their own points of interest with photos, text, videos by "geolocation (or geotagging), the name given to the practice of associating a digital resource with a physical location" (http://www.educause.edu/ELI/7Things YouShouldKnowAboutGoogl/156822). The kind of information associated is typically longitude and latitude, but altitude, and other descriptive information can be added. The benefit of using geotagging is that it provides another means of organizing digital resources and thereby provides better searching capabilities for such resources at a later date. Educators are starting to use these types of systems fairly regularly in their everyday lives. Geographic Positioning Systems (GPS) are often included in automobile purchases or in mobile phones that provide information relating to weather, traffic, eateries, and places to visit and are all based on the current location provided via wireless access points. Imaging tools such as Panoramio or Flickr both encourage geotagging of images and videos and even some digital cameras today have built-in GPS. Adding geographical metadata to images adds more depth and meaning to digital resources for the study of sociology, science, economics, ecology, and other fields of study.

What Is Google Earth?

Google Earth is the new face of geography and mapping. Simply put, Google Earth is free downloadable software and a geographic program that contains a wide array of features for the study of the earth, the sea, and the sky, but it's even more than that. Pedagogy in Action (http://serc.carleton.edu/sp/library/google_earth/UserGuide .html), a science portal for educators, describes Google Earth as "geobrowser" that offers satellite and aerial imagery, ocean bathymetry, and other geographic data over the internet to represent the Earth as a three-dimensional globe. Jan Segerstrom adds to that definition explaining that it is a "a database of images and geographical facts, a video game, and a search engine rolled into one, with a 3D graphics application" (Segerstrom 2009, 1).

Google Earth's features are amazing:

- Zoom in and out, scroll up and down, move from side to side, and rotate maps.
- Explore layers such as roads, 3D buildings, photographs, video, street view, borders and labels, traffic, and weather.
- Navigate the oceans by going below sea level to explore the underwater terrain, as well as view Cousteau Ocean World, shipwrecks, ocean expeditions, marine protected areas, census of marine life, underwater features, the National Geographic Ocean Atlas, plus several other ocean features.

- View the past with historical imagery that allows users to see how locations have changed over time.
- Explore planet Mars in 3D.
- Record actions and narrate them to create customized tours that can be shared with others.
- Share by e-mailing a Google Earth image, by saving a placemark as a file and then sharing by e-mail, or by sharing through the Google Earth community.

How Are Educators Using Google Earth to Facilitate Learning?

Google Earth can be integrated with almost any curriculum areas—geography, math, language arts, geology, history, art, social studies, or science. In high school language arts, students chart the geographic areas of a selected literacy themes or genres such as modern Irish literature (Séamus Heaney, W. B. Yeats, James Joyce, Seán O'Casey, etc.). They research and include locations associated with the authors' lives or settings in their works. For elementary culture, geography, and literature research units, teachers and students "fly" to locations around the world to investigate the country and create a placemark on the locations mentioned in the story and that the students learned about from their research. The class has a record of where they have virtually traveled and reflect on their adventure in their blogs. Art or technical drawing students research an architectural style of famous architects such as Frank Lloyd Wright, Antonio Gaudi, Leonardo da Vinci, Aldo Rossi, Albert Kahn, Frank Owen Gehry, or Carlo Scarpa and research five influential buildings of their careers. Students locate and visit each building via Google Earth, choose one identifying architectural element and use the ruler icon in the toolbar to measure distance and scale. Students demonstrate their learning by creating a short Google Earth Tour. Elementary social studies students are motivated and involved in researching and adding placemarks to denote major landmarks along the Oregon Trail from Missouri to Oregon, noting the terrain and landforms along the way. Students keep a blog diary to reflect and share their experience (curriculum ideas developed by Syracuse University iSchool students Karen Crawley, Grace Bacon, Megan Stasak, and Madeline Davis).

Students can also explore Google Earth Tours created by

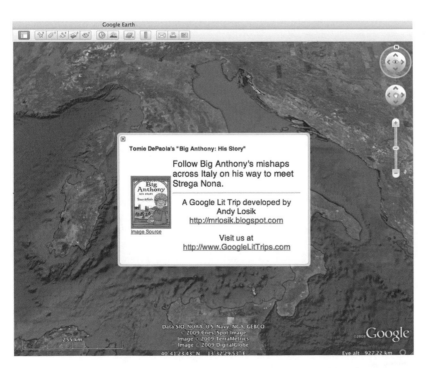

Figure 8.3.   Tomie dePaola's story, *Big Anthony: His Story*. Used with permission of Andy Losik.

others. Figure 8.4 shows a map of Italy, the setting of Tomie dePaola's story, *Big Anthony: His Story*. Big Anthony's home is represented by a yellow icon, shaped like a house. Scattered over the map, numbered blue placemarks represent locations mentioned in the story. If users click on the placemarks, a callout box appears, with text, photographs, and links to follow for more information about the story.

Figure 8.4.   Big Anthony Lit Trip.

Inquiry Learning

The interactive approach incorporated in Google Earth is especially helpful to engage students in inquiry learning. Google Earth amasses huge amount of data into an easy-to-use and visually striking interface. The tools' visual immediacy helps to connect and motivate students encouraging them to "fly" to different places and continue to investigate, to compare, and to document. "More than just a map, however, Google Earth lets users create and share personal resources. Browsing and exploring distant locales augmented with contributions from others users presents a compelling opportunity for discovery and learning. Contributing anecdotes, stories and histories will allow the users to communicate in a context of geography" (http://www.educause.edu/ELI/7ThingsYouShouldKnowAbout Googl/156822). The American Association of School Librarians' (AASL) "Standards for the

Figure 8.5.   Stripling Inquiry Model.

21st-Century Learner," encourages students to develop a global perspective and understanding within a real world connect:

> 1.1.8 Demonstrate mastery of technology tools for accessing information and pursuing inquiry.
> 2.3.1 Connect understanding to the real world.
> 2.3.2 Consider diverse and global perspectives in drawing conclusions.
> 3.1.2 Participate and collaborate as members of a social and intellectual network of learners.
> 3.3.4 Create products that apply to authentic, real-world contexts.

Excerpted from "Standards for the 21st-Century Learner" by the AASL, a division of the American Library Association. © 2007, American Library Association. Available for download at www.ala.org/aasl/standards. Used with permission.

Rather than targeting one phase of the inquiry process, Google Earth helps students to gain a more global perspective. It places imagery and other geographic information on a student's desktop while integrating with multiple curricular areas: it supports practically all the geography standards, several mathematics standards, many of the science standards and technology standards.

Nine Reasons to Use Google Earth

1. Provides a wide range of information in a geographic context.
2. Supports inquiry-based activities.
3. Applies to studies across the curriculum—history, literature, math, science, and current events.
4. Incorporates images, audio, video, and text in maps.
5. Enables users to create, display, and share their own data.
6. Helps students visualize patterns in their city, state, country, and the world.
7. Supports visual literacy.
8. Encourages collaboration.
9. Supports various learning modalities.

(Culled from http://serc.carleton.edu/sp/library/google_earth/why.html)

A few examples of tours that have already been developed in various subject areas are listed below; they are available in Google Earth by typing the full keyhole markup language (KML or KMZ) address/file in the Google search box.

- Trace the paths of the famous explorers Meriwether Lewis and William Clark took as they explored the United States (LewisandClark.kmz). The concepts of latitude, longitude, and altitude come alive for students.
- Items can be counted from an aerial view, such as in Maths in Las Vegas, where students are directed to count parking spaces in a parking lot (MathsinLasVegas.kmz).
- In history, students can study the growth of cities, tour a battlefield (Civil _War_by_Campaigns.kmz), record a tour of local interest, and investigate current issues.
- In art, students can take an architectural tour of 192 buildings worldwide (WeeklyDoses.kmz) or tour a city's museum.

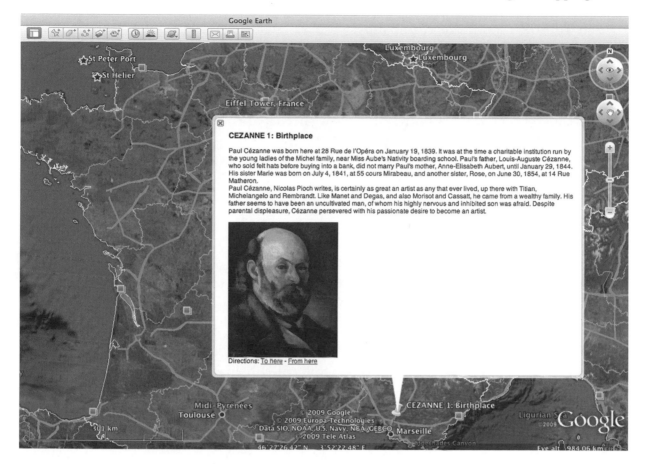

Figure 8.6.   Tour of Cézanne's Life (cezanneETITSept07.kmz).

- Take a biographical tour of an artist's life (with 48 placemarks and callouts), as in Cézanne (cezanneETITSept07.kmz) (see Figure 8.6).
- In language arts, students can create literature trips, like those found on GoogleLitTrips (http://www.GoogleLitTrips.com), or take a literature trip like the one created by Andy Losik, based on the book by dePaola, entitled "Big Anthony: His Story" (see Figure 8.3).

Focus On Google Earth

The Google Earth Interface includes a menu, a toolbar, a set of panes, navigation controls, a status bar, and a 3D viewer.

- **Menu**—contains file (save, e-mail, edit, and view), tools (ruler, GPS, and enter flight simulator), add (folder, placemark, path, polygon, model, tour, photo, image overlay, and network link) and help (user guide, keyboard shortcuts, start up tips, tutorials, and Google Earth Community).

Publishing is a wonderful way to collaborate with others; however, if users decide to publish something they have created, *be sure* to search through the community collections (probably the education category) to be sure it does not already exist; create and share original resources to expand available offerings.

Figure 8.7.   TIP: Publishing in Google Earth.

- **Toolbar**—contains hide/show sidebar, add placemark, add polygon, add path, add image overlay, show/hide ruler, show sunlight, switch between sky and earth, print, and view in Google Maps.
- **Panes**—contains an area for search, places, and layers.
- **Navigation controls**—includes a view rotator that permits users to look in all four directions, a point of view control, and a zoom slider to zoom in or out.
- **Status bar**—provides the image date, the latitude and longitude, elevation, and eye altitude.
- **3D Viewer**—allows users to look at the point of interest selected or searched.

Navigation

The second control button allows for scrolling up, down, left, and right. For more flexibility, users can place the cursor *between* two indicators on the second control, to smoothly scroll northeast or southeast or northwest or southwest.

SEARCH Pane

In the search pane, enter an address to locate businesses, institutions, and places of interest, and to get directions to a location. Searching can also be done by entering geographical coordinates (latitude and longitude), keywords, locale name, and community maps, noted with blue markers, which contains content that others have created. Figure 8.10 shows the search pane providing the locations of libraries near

Figure 8.8.   Google Earth Interface with the Places Layer (Manhattan), Road Layer, 3D Building Layer, Borders and Labels Layer, and Terrain Layer Engaged.

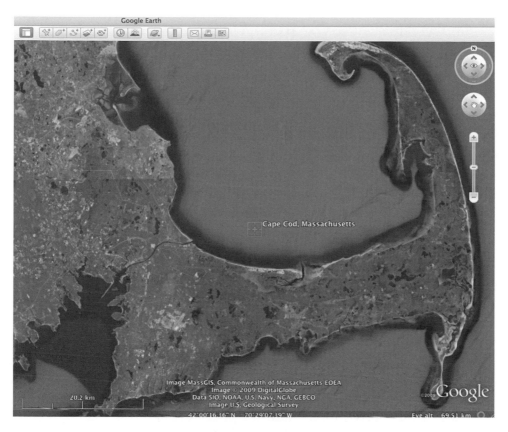

Figure 8.9. Navigation Controls Shown at Far Right of Map.

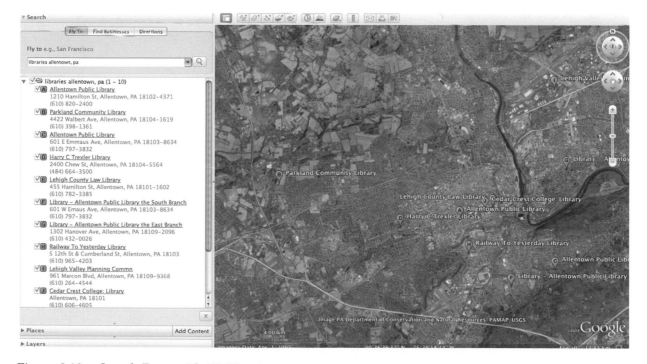

Figure 8.10. Search Pane with 3D Viewer.

Macungie, Pennsylvania. The red markers, which are alphabetized, align with libraries, and their addresses. Click on the "Printable View" to print out the directions with a travel map.

PLACES Pane

In the places pane, users select from 22 pre-selected choices (located in the sightseeing folder), including Disney World, Grand Canyon, Eiffel Tower, and the Imperial Palace in Japan, among others (see Figure 8.11). My places, also found in the places pane, includes sites users have searched and saved which are usually KML or KMZ (KML files that are compressed) files. Both KML and KMZ files are based on an XML language scheme that expresses geographic information such as latitude, longitude, altitude, placemarks, images, polygons, 3D models, and text for display in Google Earth, Maps, and Mobile or any other 3D Earth browser implementing the KML encoding (http://wikipedia.com/KML). KML is the equivalent of HTML for Web pages. Clicking a link to a KMZ file from a Web page will launch Google Earth with the contents of the KMZ file turned on. Some other familiar tools that use KML files include Google Maps, Earth Browser (fee-based), Yahoo! Pipes, and Microsoft Virtual Earth. View fascinating content from the KML Gallery such as 3D models of space satellites, real-time earthquakes, major league baseball stadiums 3D tour, a grand prix racing tour, Jane Austen's life and works, and much more.

To view these and many more tours:

1. In the places panel, click "Add Content." A browser window opens and displays the KML gallery.
2. Click "Open in Google Earth" beside any content that might interest the users.

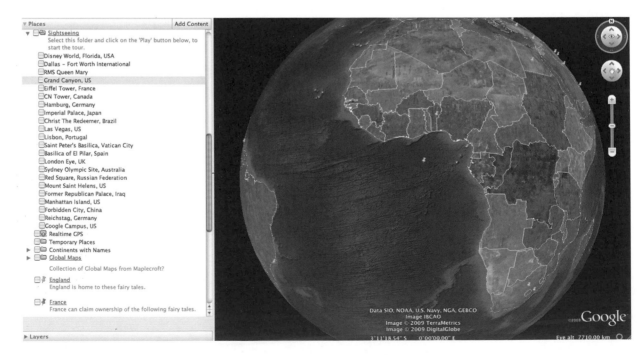

Figure 8.11.   Places Pane with Pre-Selected Sightseeing Locations.

LAYERS Pane

The layers pane offers 13 options, including roads, street view, traffic, weather, ocean, places of interest, and gallery with sub-layers available under those layers along with other headings. For example, under the gallery layer, users will find 22 sub-layers, including ancient Rome 3D, earthquakes, gigapixel photos, the Google Earth Community, volcanoes, YouTube, and 360 Cities. Under ancient Rome 3D, users will find 3D renderings of architectural features from A.D. 320 (such as bridges, temples, theatres, or geographic features, such as hills), that when clicking them, open a pop-up a window with a photograph, descriptive text, links, and downloadable files. Take time to explore the content in the layers; it was created by Google or its content partners such as Wikipedia (collaborative articles), Panoramio (photographs), YouTube (original videos), *National Geographic* magazine (images and stories of the world), Discovery Networks, European Space Agency, NASA, and *The New York Times*.

The Google Earth Toolbars

Google Earth toolbar offers users an opportunity to actively participate in adding valuable information and more depth and meaning to the maps presented for viewing. The toolbar options allow the user to:

- Turn the sidebar on or off.
- Denote a particular location by using a placemark—indicated by a pushpin.
- Select an area on a map by using the polygon, a freeform creation tool.
- Create a line, sometimes even a sequential itinerary by using the path icon tool.

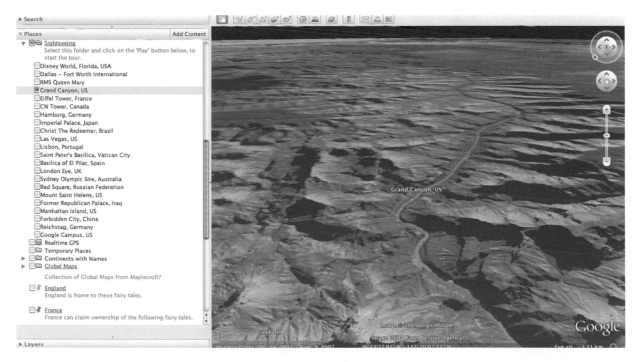

Figure 8.12.   Places Pane with 3D Viewer of the Grand Canyon.

Figure 8.13.   Layers Pane Showing Ancient Rome 3D in the 3D Viewer.

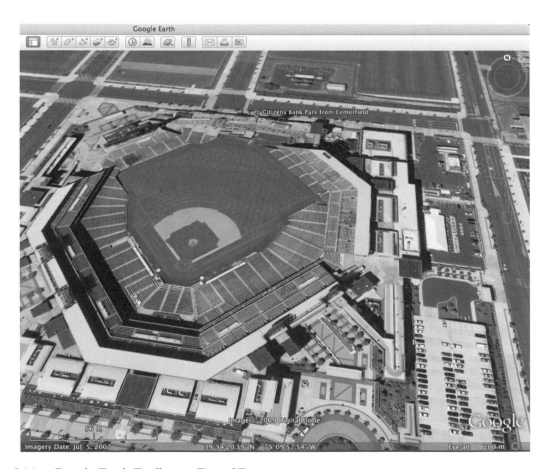

Figure 8.14.   Google Earth Toolbar at Top of Frame.

- Add overlays of historical maps to the current Google Earth imagery to allow for comparison and contrast (e.g., overlay of the California coastline from 1950 on top of the current coastline to visually see the erosion that has occurred over time).
- Use the ruler tool to check distance and altitude.
- View a location over time, using the clock icon, which represents Google Earth's archive of historical images.
- See the effect of sunlight on a location throughout the day.
- Toggle between Google Earth and Google Sky.
- Print out maps.
- Toggle to Google Maps.

How to Add a Placemark

1. Search for the point of interest.
2. Select the "Pushpin" icon from the toolbar.
3. Enter site name and any descriptive information users want included (notice that the latitude and longitude is provided).

How to Add a Polygon

1. Search for location.
2. Select "Create Polygon" icon from toolbar.
3. In the dialog box, select preferences (line thickness or color), enter descriptive text, and name the location.

How to Record a Tour

1. Select "Record a Tour" from the toolbar.
2. Push the red button (record/stop button).
3. Select the audio button (looks like a microphone) and narrate.
4. Save recording.
5. To locate the tour, look in the places pane.

Historical Imagery

The historical imagery feature of Google Earth adds the richness of historical context to the image. Now one can view the historical past of a location by using the timeslider, represented by the clock icon on the toolbar, to scroll through the image archives by date for that particular location. Not all locations have historical images collected and saved in the archives; however, Google Earth is in the process of gathering more images and dates to add to the collection. The United States has the greatest number of historical images, especially from the late 1980s through the 1990s. Tick marks on the timeslider indicate that the images are available for viewing. For example, when looking at San Francisco, there is wonderful imagery going back to the 1940s. There are tick marks on the timeslider, each representing an image for the date indicated. Figures 8.15 and 8.16 provide a comparison of images taken of San Francisco in 1946 and 2009.

Figure 8.15.   San Francisco in 1946.

Figure 8.16.   San Francisco in 2009.

How to Use Historical Imagery

1. Search for desired location.
2. Select the "Historical Imagery" icon from the toolbar (it looks like a clock face).
3. Operate the slider to move backwards and forwards through time (the date will be shown).

Google Oceans

Although 70 percent of the biosphere is water, less than 5 percent has been explored according to Sylvia Earle, a recognized marine explorer (http://google-latlong.blogspot.com/2009/02/deep-dive-into-ocean-in-google-earth.html). Version 5.0 of Google Earth now brings focused attention to the oceans, where users can dive below the water's surface to explore with top marine experts, learn about ocean observations, climate change, endangered species, and discover shipwrecks. Many different authoritative agencies worked together to develop the ocean feature, such as the U.S. Navy, National Oceanic and Atmospheric Administration, NASA, National Geographic Society, BBC, and many other institutions and organizations. Before diving into the ocean, click on "View" in Google Earth, to make sure "Water Surface" is checked. Also click "Ocean" in the layer panel, which contains over 20 content layers from over 100 partners. They include:

- **Explore the Ocean**—provides an oceans overview in a 7:36 minute video, sponsored by National Geographic Society and narrated by Sylvia Earle.
- **National Geographic**—contains magazine quiz (bubble with image and ocean facts with a question and answer options to be submitted) and ocean atlas.
- **BBC Earth**—offers the viewer a tour of ocean places with beautiful images, videos, and additional links.
- **Cousteau Ocean World**—provides selected videos in pop-up bubbles, with text and links.
- **Ocean Sports**—features surf, dive, and kite surfing spots, with links to additional photographs and comments by surfers, deep sea divers, and kite surfers.
- **Shipwrecks**—pinpoints shipwrecks worldwide, providing brief text information in a bubble, with a link leading to more information, including ship name, weight, nationality, place launched, service history, and cause of sinking.
- **Ocean Expeditions**—takes the viewer on a tour of expeditions, with links to sources of more detailed information.
- **Marine Protected Areas**—shows protected areas worldwide with stories, facts, links, videos, images, and allows for information to be added by the user. Two such examples are the Great Barrier Reef Park and the Marine Mammal Sanctuary of the Dominican Republic. Areas included are protected for various reasons.
- **ARKive: Endangered Ocean Species**—contains images or videos of endangered sea life with its status, information about the creature, threats against it, placemark details, and links to more information. This resource can be located under the global awareness layer pane (see Figure 8.17).
- **State of the Ocean**—features ocean observations, sea surface temperature, Arctic Sea ice, human impacts, dead zones (marine zones without enough oxygen to sustain life), **MBA: Seafood Watch**, and **MCS: Fish to Eat**

Figure 8.17.   ARKive Northern Fur Seals.

- **Animal Tracking**—indicates tagging information such as tag number, gender, length, weight, animal facts, photo, and swim with me video for Global Tagging of Pelagic Predators program.
- **Census of Marine Life**—provides statistics and influences on marine life.
- **Marie Tharp Historical Map**—gives a map of the ocean floor charted by famed oceanographer Marie Tharp; downloadable and viewable; can zoom and pan.
- **Underwater Features**—pinpoints reefs, troughs, shoals, seamounts, banks, ledges, basins, canyons, holes, and ridges worldwide.

Google Sky

Google Sky allows users to view planets, constellations, galaxies, the Earth's moon, and much more. Download the latest version of Google Earth, then users are on their way to checking out planets in motion and supernova explosions. The navigation feature in Sky works the same as it does in Google Earth. Users can rotate, pan and zoom, search by object name or in this case, search by right ascension, and declination (figures similar to the more familiar longitude and latitude, but for the sky). When first viewing Google Sky, either by using the icon in the Google Earth toolbar or by clicking on view then "Sky" (PC users need to click on "Explore" and then "Sky"), users will be presented with the default "Welcome to Sky" screen (see Figure 8.18). If users wish to view the sky above the last location viewed in Google Earth, just deselect the checkbox for "Welcome to Sky option" in the sky layer pane. If user is a novice astronomer, it is recommended to use the "Welcome to Sky" feature and take either the "Getting to Know Sky" tour or the "Touring Sky Tutorial." When in Google Sky, Google Earth is hidden and a view of the sky is seen in the 3D viewer.

Another way to explore Google Sky is to launch into the options available in the sky layers panel. Layer options can be engaged or disengaged and can be collapsed, if desired. Below are the options:

- Welcome to Sky—click on the bubble to read available information or take a tour or learn more about Google Sky.
- Current Sky Event—highlights upcoming events in the sky.
- Our Solar System—contains time-based solar objects and their positions in the sky.

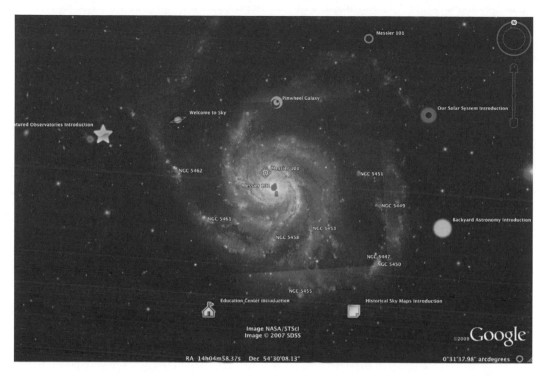

Figure 8.18.   Welcome to Sky.

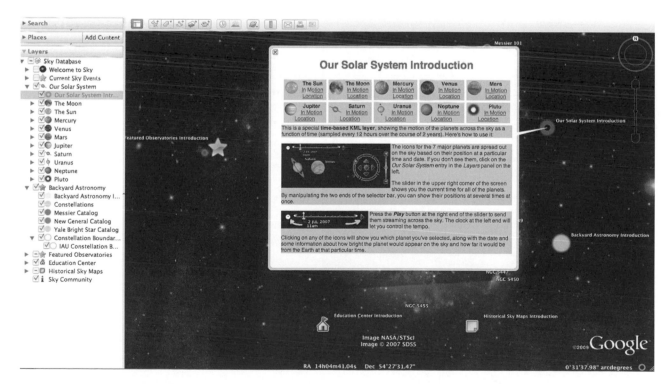

Figure 8.19.   Sky Layers Pane.

To locate kmz or kml files in Google:

Type the following into the Google search box: filetype:kmz term or phrase.

To locate kmz files about biomes, type filetype:kmz biomes.

Notice that there is a space between the kmz filetype and the term biomes.

Figure 8.20.   TIP—How to Locate KMZ Files.

- Backyard Astronomy—showcases sky objects visible to the naked eye or with a simple telescope.
- Featured Observatories—contains information from six of the world's leading observatories.
- Education Center—introduces astronomy and astrophysics.
- Historical Sky Maps—includes celestial artwork as well as older sky maps.
- Sky Community—offers user-generated content.

Google Earth Help

Google Earth provides a user's guide, startup tips, keyboard shortcuts, tutorials, and the Google Earth Community, however, additional help and support for Google Earth is abundant on the Internet. A search in a general engine search will generate a large number of documents, tip sheets, how-to guides, lesson plans, and KML and KMZ files created by others for use in Google Earth. YouTube also contains a number of videos on how to perform various tasks in Google Earth.

Table 8.1.   Selected Resources That Support Google Earth Implementation.

Site	URL
Google Earth Blog	http://www.gearthblog.com/index.html
Google Earth EDU Geo Education Site, K-12	http://www.google.com/educators/geo.html
Google Earth Education Community	http://edweb.tusd.k12.az.us/dherring/ge/googleearth.htm
Google Earth Lessons	http://gelessons.com/lessons/
Google Earth Lessons	http://www.shambles.net/pages/learning/GeogP/gearthplan/
Google Earth Gallery	http://earth.google.com/gallery
Google Earth Hacks	http://www.gearthhacks.com/
Maplecroft Maps	http://maps.maplecroft.com
Noel Jenkin's Juicy Geography	http://www.juicygeography.co.uk/
Google Earth in the Classroom	http://joewoodonline.pbworks.com/Google+Earth+in+the+Classroom

Table 8.2. Comparison of Mapping Tools.

Features	Google Maps	Yahoo! Maps	Live Search Maps	Mapquest
Directions for:				
Walking	X			
Car	X	X	X	X
Public transit	X			
Roundtrip		X	X	
Reverse	X	X		X
Search by:				
Address	X	X	X	X
Business	X	X	X	X
Roads/intersections	X		X	
POI (places of interest)	X	X	X	
Coordinates	X	X	X	
Airport codes		X		
Postal code		X		
Geographical Features	X		X Landmarks	
Multipoint directions	X	X	X	X
Has layers:	X			
Photos	X			
Weather	X			
Public transit	X			
Maps	X			
Create custom maps	X			
Save custom aps	X			
Send/Share maps	X			
Create email w/link	X	X	X	
Provide link for email	X			X
Provide link for IM	X		X	X-MSN Msgr.
Provide HTML to imbed	X		X Blog	
Send map to phone	X	X	X	X
Send map to car*	X	X	X	X
Send map to GPS			X	X

continued

Table 8.2. (continued)

Features	Google Maps	Yahoo! Maps	Live Search Maps	Mapquest
Different views:	X			
Map	X	X	X	X
Terrain	X			
Satellite	X	X	X	X
Street view	X-GoogleEarth		X-Virt.Earth	
Hybrid		X		
Traffic	X	X	X	X
Bird's eye			X	
Neighborhood footprint	X	X	X	
Invite collaboration	X			
Embed photos	X		X	
Embed videos	X			
Navigation controls	X	X	X	X
Zoom in/out	X			X
Overview map	X	X	X	
Save locations	X	X	X	X
Mobile component	X	X		X
Print maps	X	X	X	X
Wikipedia articles	X			
Photos for larger cities	X-GoogleEarth		X-Virt.Earth	
Add content from others	X	X	X	
Other service integration	X	X	X	

What Are Other Good Mapping Tools to Use with Students?

Google Maps (http://maps.google.com), Yahoo! Maps (http://maps.yahoo.com), Bing Maps (http://www.bing.com/maps), and Mapquest (http://www.map quest.com) are online mapping sites that offer similar feature such as satellite photos, maps, and driving directions. They allow users to plan a trip, sightsee, find businesses, create personalized maps, and check traffic in real time. They are not as robust as Google Earth, nor do they have the interactive features, but they do have many

Educator's Pre-Planning Guide: Google Earth Trip

Topic:_____

Curriculum/Discipline: _____ Grade Level:_____

Standards Supported (numbers): _____

Does this topic have enough of a geographical component   Yes   No
to warrant a trip?

How many locations will be on the trip? _____

Will you have sufficient supportive details for each placemark   Yes   No
on the trip?

Are there definitive starting and ending points for the   Yes   No
trip?

Will trip placemarks be numerically sequenced to follow
a natural progression?   Yes   No

Can the trip be sub-divided into multiple smaller units?
If so, what are some sub-topics?

_____

_____

Should the trip be annotated (text) or narrated (audio) ?   Yes   No

What elements will be incorporated into the trip?
(circle)   Text   Links   Images   Video

Will images and/or videos be student-created?   Yes   No

Will the trip be created by individual students or collaborative   Yes   No
teams?

Will students be involved in the development of a trip   Yes   No
assessment rubric?

Figure 8.21.   Educator's Pre-Planning Guide: Google Earth Trip.

From *Choosing Web 2.0 Tools for Learning and Teaching in a Digital World*
by Pam Berger and Sally Trexler. Santa Barbara, CA: Libraries Unlimited. Copyright © 2010.

desirable features that students can use with ease and users do not need to download software as with Google Earth. Bing offers a bird's eye view, adding a 3D dimension to the map image. Google Maps, used more widely than Google Earth, has traditional maps that are viewable from within a Web page. Of this group, Mapquest has the greater market share of the online mapping business, with 39.4 percent. Google Maps follows closely with 35.67 percent, Yahoo! Maps has 10.24 percent, and Bing trails with a 3.57 percent of the market (Lardinois 2009). What is interesting is that Mapquest is the most popular tools used, but doesn't come close to the features of the other three tools. It just provides directions to specific locations and it does it well.

Action Steps

1. Download Google Earth to your computer and experiment with the features. Get a feel for the interface by using the search, places, and layers panes, using familiar places for practice. Try entering the school address and turn the various layers on and off to see how they affect the map.
2. Demonstrate a KMZ tour to the faculty. Share a list of interesting tours that would be appropriate to the curriculum for them to continue exploring.
3. Use the Educator's Pre-Planning Guide: Google Earth Trip (see Figure 8.21) to help plan a trip or tour.
4. Create a simple tour, aligned with a desired standard, using Placemarks with text in callouts. Share the tour and briefly how to use Google Earth tours with the faculty.
5. Introduce Google Earth to students. Create a scavenger hunt of local or state points of interest or one that relates to an instructional standard that students can use to familiarize themselves with the basic operation of Google Earth.
6. Encourage students to create tours based on their favorite book. Organize a contest and have the winner share his or her winning tour with the board of education.

Media Resources

Finding Your Way with Yahoo Maps; April 15, 2009; 1:41 min.; http://www.youtube.com/watch?v=CJQx2yiz_gQ.

Google Earth Creating Paths; February 14, 2009; 8:48 min.; http://www.youtube.com/watch?v=6Pqu-i3SW2w.

Google Earth5—New 3D Ocean; February 2, 2009; 3:27 min.; http://www.youtube.com/watch?v=KOG-iAiDiko.

Google Maps Introduction; November 4, 2008; 2:39 min.; http://www.youtube.com/watch?v=pq7UA_Y5bsI.

How to Create a "My Map" in Google Maps; December 8, 2008; 3:27 min.; http://www.youtube.com/watch?v=TftFnot5uXw.

Submerge Yourself in Google Earth; February 2, 2009; 6:02 min.; http://www.youtube.com/watch?v=lx0Od83J4sk.

Yahoo Maps Power Tips; April 16, 2009; 2:01 min.; http://www.youtube.com/watch?v=Y_dy39OHMPs.

References and Additional Resources

Adam, Anna and Helen Mowers. 2007. Got the World on a Screen: Google Earth Serves Up More Than a Geography Lesson. *School Library Journal* 53 (4): 40–42.

Bates, Mary Ellen. 2008. Mapped Out. *EContent* 31:42. http://www.econtentmag.com/Articles/Column/Info-Pro/Mapped-Out-51003.htm.

Bomar, Shannon. 2009. The Genocide Project. *Knowledge Quest* 37 (4): 11.

Buchanan-Dunlop, Jamie. 2009. The Digital Explorer. *Geographical* 81 (1): 67–69.

Byerly, Greg. 2008. Where Can We Go and What Will We Find? Geography Websites. *School Library Media Monthly* 24:36–38.

Educause. 2006. 7 Things to Know about Google Earth. http://www.educause.edu/ELI/7ThingsYouShouldKnowAboutGoogl/156822.

Elliot, Robert. 2009. Using Google Maps for Classroom Projects. *TESL-EJ* 12 (4): 1–13.

Jacobsen, Mikael. 2008. Google Maps: You Are Here. *Library Journal* 133 (17): 25–28.

Lardinois, Frederic. 2009. Old Habits Die Hard: Mapquest Still #1 Mapping Service. *Read Write Web*. http://www.readwriteweb.com/archives/old_habits_die_slowly_mapquest_still_number_one.php.

Segerstrom, Jan. 2009. Google Earth and Beyond, Part I. *Information Searcher* 18 (2): 1, 3–8.

Glossary

Aggregator: A tool to collect all your feeds in one place. It constantly checks for updates to your subscriptions so you don't need to.

Blogroll: A collection of blogs that the blogger recommends for his viewer to read. It is usually placed in a sidebar on a blog.

Comment: A response to a posting.

Cyberbullying: Online version of bullying.

Flaming: The deliberate act of sending a confrontational message to someone online.

Folksonomy: An informal taxonomy created by the common "folk" using tags rather than a controlled vocabulary.

Friending: The process of adding someone as a friend on a social networking site, thus giving them the permission to view, read, comment, etc., on your content and activities.

GPS: Geographic positioning systems.

Geotagging: The process of adding metadata, in the form of coordinates, altitude, or place name to media, such as images, videos, or Web sites.

KML/KMZ: Keyhole Markup Language file which is zipped or compressed.

Layers: Data points displayed on a map.

Metadata: Information about data.

Nodes: Associated with graphic organizers, a node is the place on a graphic organizer structure where one concept connects to another concept.

Placemark: A location mark using latitude and longitude.

POIs: Points of interest on a map.

Post: An entry published on a blog.

Privacy settings: Features on many Web 2.0 tools allowing the owner/user to determine who can view, read, comment, etc., on his or her content. Settings usually include private (invitation only) and public (to any registered user or any Internet user in general).

Profile: Feature of many Web 2.0 tools where the registered user creates an identity, including such things as screen name, e-mail, blog URL, wiki URL, and favorite music.

RSS (Really Simple Syndication): A syndication system for delivery of your bookmarks, by tags or by your user name, to interested like-minded people who want to be aware of updates as you add them.

Satellite image: Also known as an aerial image, meaning it was taken from above ground level.

Sexting: The act of sending sexually explicit text messages or images via cell phones or computers.

Skype: Software that permits telephone calls over the Internet to other Skype subscribers for free. Calls can also be made using Skype to landlines or to cell phones for a fee.

SMS (Short Message Service): Text messaging format for cell phones.

Start pages: World Wide Web pages customized by the user to contain images, text, photos, links, video, audio, feeds, or widgets, based on his or her preferences.

Tag: A label or descriptive word that describes the page/video/image content.

Tag cloud: A visual representation of a collection of tags, with the more frequently used tags appearing in a larger font than the others.

Taxonomy: A formal, structured classification system using controlled vocabulary created by professionals.

Trackback: The means by which a blogger references the content of another's blog on his own site. A signal called a ping is sent to the owner of the original content alerting him to the fact that he has been cited.

Twitter: Free social networking software that can be used on the computer or on a cell phone that allows short messages (up to 140 characters) to be sent to individual Twitter subscribers or to members of Twitter groups. A post is called a "tweet" and is equivalent to mini-blogging.

Web feeds: Allow software programs to check for updates published on a Web page. A feed can contain headlines, summaries, or full-text articles. Formats that support Web feeds are RSS, ATOM, and XML.

White Label: A product or service produced by one company for use by another company or institution without the appearance of the producer's brand, but with all the features enabled.

Widget: A micro-application for a Web page. Examples include calendars, clocks, weather conditions, news feeds, and to-do lists in an attractive graphical interface.

Appendix

Tool Chart

Tool	URL	Chapter
21Classes	http://www.21classes.com	5
30 Boxes	http://30boxes.com	4
Airset	http://www.airset.com	5
AllTheWeb	http://www.alltheweb.com/	2
AltaVista	http://www.altavista.com/	2
Animoto	http://animoto.com	6
Answers.com	http://www.answers.com/	2
Ask.com	http://www.ask.com	2
Ask Kids	http://www.askkids.com/	2
Ask Maps	http://maps.ask.com/maps	8
Audacity	http://audacity.sourceforge.net/	6
Bebo	http://www.bebo.com	7
Bing	http://www.bing.com	2
Bing Maps	http://bing.com/maps	8
Bla Bla List	http://blablalist.com	4
Bling	http://www.bing.com/	2
Black Planet	http://www.blackplanet.com/	7
Blinkx	http://www.blinkx.com/	2
Blog Pulse	http://www.blogpulse.com	5

Tool	URL	Chapter
Blog Search	http://blogsearch.com	5
Blog Search Engine	http://www.blogsearchengine.com	5
Blogger	http://www.blogger.com/start	5
Bloggernity	http://www.bloggernity.com/	5
Bloglines	http://www.bloglines.com	5
Blogsphere	http://www.blogsphere.com	5
box.net (Lite)	http://www.box.net	5
Browys	http://browsys.com/finder/	2
Bubbl.us	http://www.bubbl.us	4
Cambridge Rindge	http://www.crlsresearchguide.org/ NewOutlineMaker/ NewOutlineMakerInput.aspx	4
carbonmade-portfolio make	http://www.carbonmade.com/	4
Checkvist	http://checkvist.com	4
Class Blogmeister	http://classblogmeister.com/	5
Clickcaster	http://www.clickcaster.com/	6
Clusty	http://clusty.com/	2
Cozi	http://www.cozi.com	4
Creative Commons Search	http://search.creativecommons.org/	2
Crowdvine	http://www.crowdvine.com	7
Delicious	http://delicious.com/	3
Diigo	http://www.diigo.com	3
Direct Search	http://www.freepint.com/gary/direct.htm	2
Ditto.com	http://www.ditto.com	2
Dogpile	http://www.dogpile.com	2
Drupal	http://drupal.org/	5
Education Podcast Network	http://epnweb.org/	6
Edublogs	http://edublogs.org/	5
Edublogs.tv	http://edublogs.tv/	6

Tool	URL	Chapter
Evernote	http://evernote.com	4
Exalead	http://www.exalead.com/search/	2
Facebook	http://www.facebook.com	7
FeedBucket	http://www.feedbucket.com/	5
FeedForAll	http://www.feedforall.com/	6
Feed Show	http://www.feedshow.com	5
Feed Validation Services	http://feedvalidator.org/about.html#opensource	6
Findsounds	http://www.findsounds.com/	6
Flickr	http://www.flickr.com/	6
Flixster	http://www.flixster.com/	7
Fluctu8	http://www.fluctu8.com/	6
Gcast	http://www.gcast.com/	6
Glogster	http://www.glogster.com	6
Goodreads	http://www.goodreads.com/	7
Google	http://www.google.com	2
Google Alerts	http://www.google.com/alerts?hl=en	2
Google Blog Search	http://blogsearch.google.com	5
Google Coop	http://www.google.com/cse/tools/create_onthefly	2
Google Docs	http://docs.google.com	5
Google Earth	http://earth.google.com/download-earth.html	8
Google Calendar	http://google.com/calendar	4
Google Maps	http://maps.google.com/	8
Google Reader	http://reader.google.com	5
Google Scholar	http://scholar.google.com/	2
Google Videos	http://video.google.com/	6
Groups	http://grou.ps/introduction/php	5
Gubb	http://www.gubb.net	4

Tool	URL	Chapter
Hi5	http://hi5.com	7
iGoogle	http://www.google.com/ig	4
Internet Archive	http://archive.org	2
IPL	http://www.ipl.org	2
Ice Rocket	http://www.icerocket.com/	5
Infomine	http://www.infomine.com	2
Intute	http://www.intute.ac.uk/	2
iTunes	http://www.apple.com/itunes/download/	6
Jimdo	http://www.jimdo.com/	5
Jing	http://www.jingproject.com/	5
Juice	http://juicereceiver.sourceforge.net/	6
Jux2	http://jux2.com/	2
Kartoo	http://www.kartoo.com/	2
Lefora	http://www.lefora.com/	7
Library 2.0	http://library20.ning.com	7
LiveJournal	http://www.livejournal.com	5
LooseStitch	http://loosestitch.com	4
ma.gnolia.com	http://ma.gnolia.com/	3
Mahalo	http://www.mahalo.com/	2
Mapquest	http://www.mapquest.com	8
Mind42	http://www.mind42.com	4
MindMeister	http://www.mindmeister.com	4
mixxt	http://www.mixxt.net/	7
MovableType	http://www.movabletype.com	5
My Note It	http://www.mynoteit.com	4
My Podcast	http://www.mypodcast.com	6
MySpace	http://www.myspace.com	7
My Yahoo	http://my.yahoo.com	4

Tool	URL	Chapter
Netvibes	http://www.netvibes.com	4
Netvue.com	http://www.netvue.com	2
NewsGator	http://www.NewsGator.com	5
Nexo	http://www.nexo.com	5
Ning	http://www.ning.com	7
Notefish	http://www.notefish.com	4
NoteTaker	http://www.readwritethink.org	4
Odeo	http://odeo.com/	6
One True Media	http://www.onetruemedia.com/	6
Online Outliner	http://www.2learn.ca/senior/compass/senoutline.html	4
Orkut	http://www.orkut.com	7
Our Notepad	http://www.ournotepad.com	4
Our Story	http://www.ourstory.com/	6
Ozline Thesis Builder	http://tommarch.com/electraguide/thesis.php	4
PageFlakes	http://www.pageflakes.com	4
PB Works	http://pbworks.com/	5
Photobucket	http://photobucket.com/	6
Picassa	http://picasa.google.com/	6
Picnik	http://www.picnik.com/	6
Pics4learning	http://www.pics4learning.com	2
Picsearch	http://www.picsearch.com	2
Pluggd	http://www.pluggd.tv/	6
Podbean	http://www.podbean.com	6
Podcast Alley	http://www.podcastalley.com/	6
Podcast Blaster	http://www.podcastblaster.com/	6
Podcast Bunker	http://www.podcastbunker.com/	6
Podcast Directory	http://www.podcastdirectory.com/	6

Tool	URL	Chapter
Podcast Feed Validator	http://www.smoothouse.com/podcast/validator.php	6
Podcast.com	http://podcast.com/login.php	6
Podcast Pickle	http://www.podcastpickle.com/	6
Podfeed.net	http://www.podfeed.net/	6
Podifier	http://podifier.en.softonic.com/—downloadable	6
Pod-o-matic	http://www.podomatic.com/featured	6
Podscope	http://podscope.com/	6
Protopage	http://www.protopage.com	4
Qlubb	http://www.qlubb.com	7
Quintura	http://www.quintura.com/	2
Quintura Kids	http://quinturakids.com/	2
RSS Validator	http://validator.w3.org/feed/	6
Remember the Milk	http://www.rememberthemilk.com	4
Rollyo	http://rollyo.com/	2
RubiStar	http://rubistar.4teachers.org/index.php	6
SchoolTube	http://www.schooltube.com/	6
Scrapblog	http://www.scrapblog.com/	6
Scribblar	http://www.scribblar.com	5
Scriblink	http://www.scriblink.com	5
Scirus	http://www.scirus.com/	2
Shelfari	http://www.shelfari.com	7
Simplybox	http://simplybox.com	4
SkreemR	http://skreemr.com/	2
Skype	http://www.skype.com	5
Slide	http://www.slide.com	6
Slideroll	http://www.slideroll.com/	6
Slideshare	http://www.slideshare.net	6

Tool	URL	Chapter
Slidestory	http://www.slidestory.com	6
SmugMug	http://www.smugmug.com	6
Solodox	http://www.solodox.com	5
Springnote	http://www.springnote.com	4
Sproutliner	http://sproutliner.com/	4
Stumpedia	http://www.stumpedia.com/	2
TaDa	http://www.tadalist.com	4
Taskbin	http://www.taskbin.com	4
Task THIS	http://taskthis.elucidata-apps.com/	4
TaskToy	http://tasktoy.com	4
Teacher Tube	http://www.teachertube.com	6
Technorati	http://technorati.com	5
Ten by Ten	http://www.tenbyten.org/	2
ThinkFold	http://www.thinkfold.com	5
ToDoist	http://todoist.com	4
Track This Now	http://www.trackthisnow.com	8
Twitter	http://twitter.com	7
Ubernote	http://ubernote.com	4
VoiceThread	http://voicethread.com	6
Voki	http://www.voki.com	6
Webjam	http://www.webjam.com	7
Wetpaint	http://www.wetpaint.com	5
Wikispaces	http://www.wikispaces.com	5
Wildvoice	http://wildvoice.com	6
Wisemapping	http://www.wisemapping.com	4
WordPress	http://wordpress.org	5
Wridea	http://wridea.com	5
Write Design Online	http://www.writedesignonline.com/organizers/	4

Tool	URL	Chapter
writeboard	http://www.writedesignonline.com/organizers/	5
Xanga	http://www.xanga.com	7
Yahoo!	http://www.yahoo.com	2
Yahoo! Calendar	http://calendar.yahoo.com	4
Yahoo! Kids	http://help.yahoo.com/l/us/yahoo/kids/	2
Yahoo! Maps	http://maps.yahoo.com/	8
Yahoo! Pipes	http://pipes.yahoo.com/pipes/	8
Yahoo! Videos	http://video.search.com	6
YouTube	http://www.youtube.com/	6
YourDraft	http://www.yourdraft.com	4
Ziepod	http://www.ziepod.com/	6
Zoho	http://www.zoho.com	5
Zoho Planner	http://planner.zoho.com	4

Index

Italicized page numbers reference figures and tables.

About the Authors

Photo by Carol Morton

PAM BERGER, Director of Information and the Southern Westchester BOCES School Library System, is editor of *Information Searcher*, a newsletter focusing on technology in schools. Ms. Berger is an adjunct instructor at Syracuse University iSchool and has presented workshops and seminars in over 45 states in addition to Australia, Canada, Switzerland, United Kingdom, Belgium, Thailand, South Africa, and Singapore. Berger's blog, Infosearcher at http://www.infosearcher .com, offers updates on new resources and strategies for building capacity in libraries and on using technology effectively in the teaching and learning process.

Photo by Ron Trexler

SALLY TREXLER, a recently retired school library media specialist with 34 years of experience in Allentown School District, PA, is a library consultant and columnist for the *Information Searcher*. During her tenure in Allentown SD she served as Lead Librarian, Technology Program Coordinator, and district Webmaster. Sally also has experience in academic library work: reference, special projects, and circulation. She teaches graduate courses in library science and is also a national training consultant for library automation. Her writing focuses on the instruction and integration of Web 2.0 in the classroom.